HE REALLY HAD SOMETHING TO SAY

The Ideas of Rabbi Samuel Wohl
A Biographical Presentation and World
Perspective of Scope and Compassion

HE REALLY HAD SOMETHING TO SAY

The Ideas of Rabbi Samuel Wohl
A Biographical Presentation and World
Perspective of Scope and Compassion

by

Theodore H. Wohl
Amiel Wohl

KTAV PUBLISHING HOUSE, INC.

Library of Congress Cataloging-in-Publication Data

Wohl, Theodore H.
  He really had something to say : the ideas of Rabbi Samuel Wohl : a biographical
presentation and world perspective of scope and compassion / by Theodore H. Wohl,
Amiel Wohl.
     p. cm.
  Includes bibliographical references and index.
  ISBN 0-88125-877-6
  1. Wohl, Samuel, 1895-1972. 2. Rabbis—Ohio—Cincinnati—Biography. 3. Isaac M.
Wise Temple (Cincinnati, Ohio) 4. Reform Judaism—Ohio—Cincinnati. 5. Cincinnati
(Ohio)—Biography. I. Wohl, Amiel. II. Title.
BM755.W56W55 2005
296.8'341'092—dc22

2005008563

Manufactured in the United States of America
Distributed by
KTAV Publishing House, Inc.
930 Newark Avenue
Jersey City, NJ 07306
(201) 963-9524
FAX (201) 963-0102
www.ktav.com
Email: bernie@ktav.com

This book is sincerely dedicated to the Isaac M. Wise Temple congregation, Samuel Wohl's rabbinic teachers and colleagues, and the Wohl family children and grandchildren.

Table of Contents

Acknowledgments

I n the earlier stages of conceptualizing our book, we were aware
that a person could be perceived as truly unique only through
his interactions with life's changeable contexts. Samuel Wohl
shared his humanity with his congregation, the Jewish people, his
alma maters (the University of Cincinnati and Hebrew Union
College), various local, state, and national organizations, and, of
course, his wife and two sons. By the same token, the above enti-
ties all molded him in their own images, lending wisdom and inspiration to his ideas and leadership.

Valuable assistance was provided by the Temple Library (of
Cleveland), the Cleveland and Cincinnati public libraries, and the
libraries of the Isaac M. Wise Temple, Hebrew Union
College–Jewish Institute of Religion (Klau Library), the Jacob
Rader Marcus Center of the American Jewish Archives, and the
Western Reserve Historical Society. Sincere gratitude to several
administrators who advised and guided us regarding the utilization
of sources and such arcane literary areas as publication and biblio-
graphic construction. These very helpful and informed individuals
were Jacob R. Marcus, late director and founder of the American
Jewish Archives; Abraham J. Peck, former administrative director
of the Archives; Herbert Zafren, former chief librarian, Klau
Library, HUC-JIR; and Judah Rubenstien, Cleveland guide and
Jewish literary mentor. We acknowledge the ubiquitous support of
Alfred Gottschalk during his presidency of HUC-JIR.

The boards and presidents of the Isaac M. Wise Temple
admired Samuel as a person and regarded him as vital to the world-
wide evolution of Judaism. In addition to their congregational

impact, they were enthusiastic in supporting this book and contributing to its contents. Joseph Stern, Jr., Milton Bloom, and Sidney Meyers freely shared Temple history, their opinions and personal observations. Rabbi Alan Fuchs, Edward Saeks, M.D., and Jacob Stein provided leadership and practical judgment to facilitate our beginning efforts.

Emeritus Rabbi Albert Goldman is himself an important figure in the book and offered positive criticism. Senior Rabbi Lewis Kamrass provided ongoing organization to our efforts. He was able to impart the imprimatur of a congregational project and was unfailingly cooperative and permissive.

Sharon Kohn shattered several precedents when she accepted the position of cantor of the Isaac M. Wise Congregation. We were elated that she consented to read critically our sections on liturgical developments within the Reform movement.

Several individuals provided sensitive and scholarly background to major areas of the book:

Professor Irwin Weil: Distinguished Slavic and Russian expert. A student and later an adviser of Samuel Wohl through many years. Their frequent correspondence was illuminating and inspiring. We were honored when Professor Weil agreed to provide the foreword to the book.

Ezra Spicehandler: Distinguished Service Professor Emeritus of Hebrew Literature, and former dean of HUC-JIR. Offered comprehensive criticism regarding general religious trends and Zionistic issues.

Michael Meyer: Prominent Jewish historian and chronicler of HUC in the years 1875–1975. Basic source for descriptions and perspectives of professors and general educational issues.

Jonathan D. Sarna and Nancy H. Klein: Effective, significant presentation of Cincinnati's Jewish community. *The Jews of Cincinnati* was published by the Center for Study of the American Jewish Experience, Campus of Hebrew Union College–Jewish Institute of Religion.

Lloyd P. Gartner: Finely detailed and well-researched *History of the Jews of Cleveland*. A publication of the Western Reserve Historical Society, Dr. Gartner's work reveals the editorial imprint of Sidney Z. Vincent and Judah Rubenstien of the Jewish Community Federation of Cleveland.

Thomas F. Campbell and Edward M. Miggins: This edited project, *The Birth of Modern Cleveland*, developed from Cleveland's expansion and the attendant social, economic, cultural, and political changes that occurred during the span of 1865–1930.

Rabbi James G. Heller: Among his international, national, and congregational achievements, produced a handsomely bound volume, *As Yesterday When It Is Past: History of the Isaac M. Wise Temple. . . . 1842–1942*. This book was utilized by the authors as a major resource.

Walter Laqueur: Does not claim objectivity in his *A History of Zionism*. However, he dealt with a huge source literature with rare dispassion. His work served as a backdrop for the unfolding drama of Zionism until 1948.

Sham and Nachum Eden: Genial but intense Zionists. Maintained a long-standing friendship with Samuel Wohl and graciously conveyed their perspectives regarding the history of Labor Zionism in Cincinnati to the authors.

Simon Dubnow: Provided a cross-sectional and richly interpretive history of East European Jewish existence from the latter part of the nineteenth to the early twentieth century.

The Wohl Memorial Committee helped to defray the publication costs of a book presenting the ideas and life of Rabbi Samuel Wohl. They were interested in focusing on the development of the dynamic Isaac M. Wise Temple Congregation. The honorary chairperson was centenarian Florence L. Weil, who, together with Abraham Braude, Jack Benjamin, Betty Benjamin, Louis Ullman, Joseph Stern, Jr., Edward Saeks, and Sidney Meyers, successfully established a Temple fund supported by many congregational families and individuals.

Several hundred letters were sent to Rabbi Samuel Wohl on the occasion of his retirement and sixty-fifth birthday. Many contained analyses of his life and career. Information provided by the following people served as a further resource: Abba Hillel Silver, W. Gunther Plaut, Harry J. Stern, David Polish, Max Nussbaum, Joseph Stern Jr., Justin Friedman, Max Neuman, Victor E. Reichert, Boris Smolar, Abraham Shusterman, Jacob Weinstein, Jacob Shankman, Joseph Schwartz, Samuel Schmidt, Sidney Weil, Eliahu Elath, Harry Essrig, Jerome Folkman, Samuel Cook, Pinchas Cruso, Sally Brown, Stanley Brav, Brady Black, Jacob Barmore, Abraham Braude, Betty Benjamin, Jacob Agus, David Ben-Gurion, Levi Eshkol, Zalman Shazar, Maurice Eisendrath, Irwin Weil, Golda Meir, James Magrish, Julian Marks, Harriet Lazarus, Abba Housie, James Levy, Jeffery Lazarus, Eugene Lipman, Jacob Katzman, Isaac Hamlin, Roland Gittelsohn, Israel Goldstein, Suggs Garber, Solomon Freehof, Eric Friedland, Julian Feibelman, Maurice Eisendrath, Carl W. Rich, Stanley R. Shrotel, Alfred Segal, Murray Seasongood, Benjamin Schwartz, Charles Taft, Dan Tehan, Guy Thompson, Dorothy Dolbey, Walter Bachrach, Roger Blanchard, Edward Bloch, Marshall Bragdon, Samuel Beck, Morris Berick, Karl Alter, Sam Levenson, Frank Lausche, John Gilligan, Edward McCarthy, Henry Hopson, Robert Goldman, Roger Ferger, Jakob Petuchowski, A. L. Sachar, Abraham Franzblau, Abraham Cronbach, and Jacob Marcus.

Toiling in obscurity and providing necessary secretarial and clerical support were Nancy Stubbeman, Melissa Simmons, Jody Shelden, and Rachel Wohl.

Preface

Despite his many achievements, Samuel Wohl was modest and self-effacing. He extended himself with enormous warmth and care, be it in scholarship, public relations, or international affairs. He was acknowledged for this, with gratitude, in his lifetime and on his death. Little of Samuel's writing appears in books or articles. He once speculated, wryly, that he lacked self-discipline. However, he left a treasure trove of correspondence, newspaper reports, photographs, transcribed speeches, and dictated memoirs.

From the Ukraine of his youth, dominated by tsarist Russia, Samuel drew upon and later utilized experiences and ideas that would shape Jewish existence. He eagerly applied this knowledge to his new American-Jewish milieu. Cleveland was his first home in the United States, and it was there that his ideas, blossoming in a newfound freedom, coalesced and were translated into action. Here he established his remarkable ability to cherish and educate others. He was actively and exquisitely sensitive to national and international events. Palestine and the ideals of Zionism were always in the forefront of his commitments.

In Cleveland, Samuel met and married Belle Myers, who, in the first years of a life-long companionship, helped to convince him that he should depart for Cincinnati and study for the Reform rabbinate. In Cincinnati, his personal and public life came together as he became at once a father and the rabbi of a large, historic congregation. He quickly embarked upon a variety of efforts to remedy what he perceived to be American Jewry's major problems: Jewish illiteracy, a pervasive sense of apathy, and a lack of pride. He developed and inspired formal Jewish learning, conscientiously counseled his flock, and promoted public events that would enhance an appreciation of Jewish culture. In addition, he established firm lines of communication with the city's movers and shakers, Jewish leaders and Christian clergy. He created innovations in Reform liturgical practices, always striving, however, not to discard meaningful traditions. His attempts to sustain the beauty of observance included devising new ceremonies, revising traditional practices, and surrounding his congregation with visual and liturgical beauty.

Samuel directed his wisdom and energy toward the miraculous rebirth of the State of Israel. His actions were inspired by his Labor Zionist ideology. Later he counted most of the leaders and great thinkers of the new state as personal friends and confidants, and brought them the gift of his ideas. He represented a shining example of a Jewish leader and his need to know and understand.

We wish to emphasize that the space allocated to various persons, ideas, and events in the following narrative is roughly proportional to their role in Rabbi Wohl's life or their enhancing effect on the reader's interest. Omission of many important names and events is not meant to denigrate their memory or subtract from their achievements. Finally, to better validate our data, we not only searched our memories but also consulted with surviving family members and friends who knew him.

The task of the writers is difficult indeed, and we are sure only of our desire for responsibly chronicling and analyzing the events and ideas that will be set forth in this book. We knew Samuel Wohl well. He really had something to say to all of us.

Foreword

A s a young child in the 1930s, I first became part of a large and active Cincinnati Reform Jewish congregation, the Isaac M. Wise Temple. One of its leaders was a dynamic, passionate lover of all things Jewish—his name was Rabbi Samuel Wohl. Even as a five-year-old child, I soon recognized the sincerity and deep feeling behind all the wonderful stories and instruction he put before our eyes, and even more important, before our ears. His voice, with its slight Russian accent and its musical Hebrew intonations, was one that broadened our imaginations to a world that went far beyond—in time and in space—our small world in the Jewish part of Cincinnati. To this very day, some seventy years later, that voice still reverberates in my ears and makes connections with my deepest feelings.

I learned something more about Rabbi Wohl in my home, where my father and mother, Sidney and Florence Weil, often talked about their work and activities with him, always on behalf of important and vibrant Jewish causes. Whether it was the building and strengthening of a congregation, or the amelioration of Jewish experience throughout the world, Rabbi Wohl's name was always on their lips—and not only on theirs.

As I grew older, the Jewish world experience become much more bitter, in the terrible years of the Second World War. That time was a crucible for the relationship between my father, who worked demonically to raise funds to help our fellow Jews, and for Rabbi Wohl, who spoke soul-searing words on behalf of his beloved fellow Jews who were suffering the hell that was Nazism. I shall never forget his words when victory finally came in Europe in

1945. He spoke modestly of how he and others had tried to help the victims of Hitler's vicious crimes, always wishing that we had done more. He spoke triumphantly of our dreams for the future, when Jews and all people would live better lives, liberated from the nightmare of the would-be *Herrenvolk*—the Supermen of destruction.

Such moments are not forgotten over a lifetime of subsequent experience.

Later came my days of higher education at the University of Chicago and at Harvard. Rabbi Wohl did not forget about the education of the young people whom he had tended, if I may utilize the biblical metaphor, as a shepherd tends his flock. He always made sure that I had the latest publications, especially when he learned that my specialization concerned the land where he was born, the land of the former Russian Empire and the contemporary Soviet Union. He understood my growing love for the Russian language, and he nourished it with the best publications and phonograph records he could find.

As the years went by, he regularly visited me, later together with my growing family, and tried to make sure my mind and heart were growing. At the same time, he also opened up somewhat about his own precious ideas and his experience with the congregation, whose members he truly loved as a father loves his family. I began to understand the depth and breadth of his concern for the welfare of literally hundreds of people and scores of families whom he knew and nurtured. Seldom, in my lifetime, have I met a man with such a deep and heartfelt concern for the humanity around him.

This extended to all kinds of people: young and old, foreign and domestic, people of all creeds and races, both men and women. He was an early advocate of an excellent education and strong intellectual development for women. My wife, Professor Vivian Max Weil, often remembers vividly his determination that young women should get the same education which the Jewish tradition has produced at its highest and finest moments.

His concern for both the education and welfare of his congregation was expressed not only in his activities in the United States. He traveled widely throughout the world, and met many of its most active politicians and thinkers. He brought back the knowledge and wisdom that this inspired and continually tried to broaden the perspectives of those around him. Once again, his passion and engagement served him and his congregants well.

His two sons, my old and cherished friends, have done a remarkable job in preserving his memory and his archives. Rabbi Amiel Wohl continued the rabbinical tradition of care and wide activity; Dr. Theodore H. Wohl continued the tradition of psychological help and sustenance. They have combined their efforts to produce a sustained and lively account of Rabbi Wohl's remarkable life. From a small town in the Ukrainian part of the Russian Empire, to an education in the American Midwest, to a major congregation in the Reform Jewish movement, to a man with wide political and intellectual connections with a large part of the world—they have put together a fascinating mosaic. I am deeply grateful to them for their extensive work and care.

Above all, I am grateful for the chance to introduce readers to the sacred memory of an extraordinary human being and a totally committed Jew. May the kingdom of heaven be his! And, in the oft-repeated words, *zekher l'v'rokhoh tsaddik*—ever blessed be the memory of an upright human being.

Irwin Weil
Emeritus Professor
Slavic Department
Northwestern University

Introduction

Samuel Wohl was born in Eastern Europe in 1895, and was an unusual eyewitness to contemporary Jewish history from 1913 to 1972.

He became rabbi of a major Classical Reform Jewish congregation in Cincinnati, was a pioneer innovator in Reform Judaism, and is acknowledged as the originator of consecration and other accepted ceremonies in contemporary Reform Judaism.

He was an originator of institutes for Christian clergy and was a significant bridge between local and national Jewish communities as well as between Jewry and the immediate and more extended non-Jewish environments.

He gave freely of his counsel and advice, which was eagerly sought by national and international leaders. Indeed, he was a recognized expert on international affairs and their impact on world Jewry.

He was an outstanding American Labor Zionist, who participated in World Zionist Congresses and promoted the cause of Zion as both a refuge for beleaguered Jews around the world and a means for enrichment of American Jews.

He experienced climactic events in the Soviet Union and observed the Five-Year Plans.

He was in Munich, at a Hitler rally, as Streicher spewed his anti-Semitic venom.

He surveyed the plight of French Jewish war orphans.

He stood on the reviewing stand with Premier David Ben-Gurion, in 1948, when Israel's independence was declared.

He toured thirteen South American countries for consultation with that continent's Jewish leaders.

Jew and non-Jew alike gave testament to this rabbi's exceptional scholarship and personal warmth.

Part I
Wellspring: Russian Roots

Chapter 1
Life in the Pale and Beyond

The earlier land of Samuel Wohl deserves study and earnest consideration—far more than we will grant it. Nonetheless, knowing a man's origins usually clarifies and deepens our understanding of his life and works.

Most of the Jewish communities in Ukraine, which later constituted the southwestern part of the Russian Empire, were founded when the kingdom of Poland/Lithuania penetrated the region at the end of the fourteenth century. Emigration from Poland soon established viable Jewish communities in Ukraine and the area that is now Belarus. Torn by national strife and internal revolt over a long period, the Jews were decimated by sporadic massacres and pogroms systematically planned and coordinated by the secular and religious authorities. Indeed, one may well conclude that neither the rulers (lay and religious) nor the peasant masses ever really came to terms with the Jewish presence, generally considering them aliens, "enemies of Christ," and a convenient scapegoat for economic failures and international misfortunes.

The majority of the Jews in the western regions annexed to Russia during the three partitions of Poland in the eighteenth century were more or less forced into the occupations of trade, crafts, brokerage, leasing, and inn-keeping. These pursuits placed them squarely between the aristocratic landowners and the enslaved peasants. They were needed but cynically manipulated by the former and fiercely hated by the latter. Historians, more dispassionately, deem the Russian government and even the people to have been highly ambivalent regarding the Jews. During the "high points" of anti-Jewish hostility, the government apparently took steps to maintain Jewish (target) visibility—that is, enabling them to maintain a certain autonomy in practicing their religion while systematically pauperizing them by discriminatory laws and severely limiting their freedom of movement within the country.

This was crystallized in a series of "Jewish statutes" under Tsar Alexander I and the establishment of the Pale of Settlement, a region of 286,000 square miles and twenty-five provinces which encompassed the western flank of European Russia: north-south from the Baltic to the Black Sea, and eastward from Austria-Hungary in the west toward, but not including, the cities of Rostov, Kharkov, Smolensk, and Jakobstadt (Jekabpils). During the reigns of subsequent tsars, the Pale became a significant means of dealing with the "Jewish problem," a term which has reverberated with chilling significance to the present day. However, it should be noted that tsars, church, and aristocracy attempted to solve this so-called problem by the triune method of progressive assimilation of the Jews into Russian culture, expulsion, and blaming them for almost every conceivable problem, national, international, and economic. Although government and police actively participated in pogroms, there was never a plan, the means, or even the motivation to systematically exterminate the entire people. Despite the emancipation of the serfs under Alexander II, Jewish freedom of movement became even more restricted and was strictly limited to the Pale, although there was a slight relaxation of these laws toward the end of the nineteenth century under Nicholas II.

The Russian census of 1897 was completed just around the time that Samuel Wohl entered his second year of life. The results shows that there were almost 5,000,000 Jews living in the Pale, comprising approximately 94 percent of the total Jewish population of the Russian Empire and 11.6 percent of the local population. Ukrainians and Byelorussians were the most numerous national groups in the region where Samuel was born. By the machinations of history and government, Jews were greatly restricted in occupational choice. Almost 40 percent were in commerce and 36 percent in crafts. Some 72 percent of those engaged in commercial pursuits in the Pale were Jews.

Life in the Pale was harsh and the economic competition was fierce. Jews were denied permission and opportunity to engage in agriculture. Western Europe and the Americas received outpourings of Jewish refugees as pogroms inundated their poor communities, especially during the years 1881–84 and 1903–6. A very small but zealously idealistic number made their way to Palestine. Education of most Jewish children was in the cheder and yeshiva. Access to secular forms of education was strictly limited, but the Jews had their own religiously based schools and seldom sent their children to Russian schools. Jewish thinkers, literature, and newspapers flourished. More contemporary movements, such as Zionism, the Bund, and socialist parties added to the ferment until World War I and the disintegration of the Russian Empire finally destroyed the Jewish world of the Pale.

In 1895, the year of Samuel's birth, his hometown, Novaya Ushitsa, was a county seat in the district of Kamenets-Poldolski in the province of Podolia. The census of 1897 records 2,213 Jews in the town and its environs, comprising 35.5 percent of the population. Located on a minor tributary of the Dniester River, amidst rolling treeless steppes of short grass crisscrossed with meandering streams, Novaya Ushitsa was a relatively busy town, with Jews heavily involved in commerce and skilled crafts. Small farms, greatly helped by the dark humus soil, temperate summers, and variably cold-dry winters provided a constant flow of goods for barter and distribution to the Russian provinces of the north and east and to the Crimea. Considerable quantities of materials were conveyed on the Dniester to the Black Sea. The people of the area benefited only slightly from their location in the "bread basket" of Russia, because by virtue of timeless tradition and social structure, most of the commercial gain was contributed to the interrelated coffers of the landowning aristocracy, the church, and, of course, the reigning monarchy.

Samuel was the eldest of the six children born to Mordecai and Rachel Wohl; his siblings were named Maurice, Sophia, Jack,

Alexander (Zolya), and Theodor (Zioni). Despite the distracting and sometimes opposing forces mentioned above, the parents maintained a successful dry goods business. Mordecai was a respected communal leader. Slight and frail, his piercing gaze and deep voice riveted attention. He possessed the requisite scholarly credentials and made sure his children attended cheder (Jewish parochial school) in their early years. Nevertheless, he was always seeking new ideas and was, in fact, attuned to the world around him. During and following the Russian Revolution, he became an honest broker and mediator between the Reds and the Whites, the Bolshevik revolutionaries and the various Ukrainian and other counter-revolutionary factions, whose ongoing conflict always implicated the Jews. His intellectual dynamism and achievements were complemented by a warm and genuine concern for his family and community.

In the patriarchal society of the Jewish Pale, Rachel probably was *not* considered an exemplary wife and mother. Her aptitudes were not centered around hearth and home. Household chores and other kinds of maternal housewifery were left to servants. She was a competent business person who was organized, direct, and aggressive. If there really is such an attribute as cold, steely blue eyes, she surely possessed it. Mordecai participated with her, side by side, in a successful commercial venture. He developed a leather wholesaling business on one side of the store, while Rachel sold dry goods in her section. Rachel's competence left Mordecai with ample time for study, communal good works, and relating with his children. There is no question that Samuel closely identified with his father, but he and the rest of the family greatly benefited from their mother's strength and determination.

Samuel was a slender, pale, clear-complected lad. During adolescence he attained his permanent height of five feet, five inches. His face was sensitive and quietly reflective. A very high forehead was crowned by luxuriant, well-groomed russet hair, which, when combed, formed a natural pompadour. As a boy he wore the loose-fitting trousers and finely embroidered linen shirts of the Ukrainian private school, which merged into the more finely cut and well tailored suits affected by young men of the era. Startlingly, he frequently wore a hat that resembled a British boater, giving him an uncharacteristically rakish appearance.

While aware of the harsh realities surrounding him, Samuel found, nonetheless, that he could enjoy life. He was adept at social and folk-dancing and sang frequently from Ukrainian folksongs, arguably the most copious and varied collection of any country in the world. His early postcards and letters, written in Russian script and dispatched from various Ukrainian locales, contain more than a sprinkling of clever rejoinders and mildly satirical comments. These cards seem unique by today's standards. On the outside facing, a card might contain a portrait of a great man, a poem, a photograph of the sender, or perhaps a photo with the sender's head superimposed in a carnival scene or on a different body. The inside facing was devoted to the written message and the address.

From these sources one may note Samuel's interest in and devotion to his immediate and extended family, as well as corroborative evidence of an active social life including several long-term female relationships. A theme entitled "The Trials of Youth," submitted to meet a 1925 course requirement of the University of Cincinnati's English department, is an unlikely source for insight into his youthful preoccupations and wry consternation as an author. The theme reflected the summer of 1913, months before Samuel's departure for America.

> Sonia and Poupa! What a dilemma! Watch your step. . . .
> The night was mute and cool, filling my lungs with odors of acacias, and every step seemed to murmur "Sonia-Poupa-Sonia-Poupa." . . . Youth, it's your time of song and joy; you need not wait for it; it rushes upon you like gushing cascades.

Samuel quickly came to acknowledge Sonia's infinite superiority.

> Sonia and America! How could I reconcile the two. I had determined to leave darkest Russia, but here was a sea of

sunshine: —Sonia; . . . my brother handed me the "governor's passport" [permission to emigrate] which had been received that afternoon by mail . . . and I pleaded with her to let me love her, remain here with her, —I would tear up the passport, I would not leave for America. Yes, she loved me, she admitted, but I must never think of staying here in Uschitza, in Czarist Russia. . . . Your love will give me hope and courage here until we shall be reunited, appealed Sonia. . . . I hoped she would weaken and permit me to remain but she was immovable; and on a September evening I clasped her hand to my breast and [then] rushed into the waiting carriage which carried me to the railway station toward the Land of the Future.

We, the authors, groaned collectively as we read this Victorian prose.

The drama of our future existence was being played out in the angst and emotional conflicts of two idealistic teenagers. Samuel's prose was soon to stabilize, and his thinking became more rational and parsimonious. However, he *always* retained the capacity to respond from the heart rather than from metaphysical abstractions (the clergyman's disease). His emotions and remarkable capacity for empathy were powered by his perceptions and reactions.

The early prototype of Samuel's personality and his propensity for posing challenging questions to people "of substance" occurred during his fourteenth year. We have mentioned that he was reflective, with a particular gift for grasping the total pattern. Even as a youth he understood the essential immorality of Russia's existence: a centuries-long oligarchy and theocracy, little removed from the Middle Ages, cynically manipulating the suffering masses. The position of the Jew in this maelstrom was always precarious—the object of malice and persecution, a "marginal man" in an indeterminate position between nobility and peasants, despised by both.

Samuel wondered, especially, at the implicit role of Christianity in the suffering of his people, as manifested in the established Ukrainian Orthodox Church. He admired the services and liturgy, which conveyed a sense of awe and wonder in the face of God's presence, and, in fact, he never lost his love for the solemn majestic male choirs whose soaring tenors and deep growling basses could create a sense of sublime transport. Yet the priests and others of the church hierarchy frequently utilized the Easter season (the climax of the liturgical year rather than Christmas) as a forum for inciting the populace against the Jews, resulting in looting and pogroms. The Ukrainians were Marianists; that is to say, Mary, the virgin mother of Jesus, had been elevated to a very lofty position in their faith and in their worship service. The gentleness and love thus symbolized the sense of resurrection; the aura of Easter finery and greenery were stark contrasts to the bestial savagery and blood accompanying the slaughter of innocent people.

Although he had never actually witnessed a pogrom, Samuel wrote a letter to Count Leo Tolstoy, a giant of literature regarded by many authorities as the modern world's most outstanding novelist. By way of background, Tolstoy's view of the Jews was inconsistent but certainly much more liberal than the views espoused by his two chief Russian rivals for literary prominence, Turgenev and Dostoevski. Tolstoy had undergone a religious conversion around 1870. Samuel's letter centered on the question of how Christ's teaching of love and compassion could give rise to such violent behavior. Tolstoy's answer seems both profound and evasive:

> The words spoken by Christ are not so important or need to be believed because they were spoken by Christ.
>
> But they were spoken by him because they are true and inscribed in the heart of every man.

Chapter 2
Thinkers, Activists, and a Fateful Departure

We have noted already that Samuel was afforded a traditional Jewish education at which he excelled, but his father countered the prevailing Jewish suspicion and distrust of secular schools. He determined that the children would benefit from a Russian secular education as well as traditional Jewish indoctrination. There were formidable obstacles; legalistic quota systems, cultural exclusion, and fusion with Eastern Orthodox religious precepts were only a few of them. However, by luck, ability, and sheer determination Samuel prevailed, finally completing the gymnasium (high school) before emigrating to the United States in 1913 after attaining his seventeenth birthday. He thus joined a narrow stratum of the Pale, and, at a very youthful stage of his development, could be aptly described as a member of the cultural intelligentsia. His face, as it were, was pressed against the window looking outward, perplexedly viewing the more encompassing and dynamic events of Western Europe and North America.

Indeed, this was a period of accelerated significant change. The Industrial Revolution was finally having an impact on Eastern Europe, Jews continued to be gravely persecuted, and the proverbial winds of change were blowing strongly. At the same time, seminal Jewish thinkers and activists were attempting to conceptualize a way to bring Jews into greater congruence with the modern world. A flood of arguments poured forth as eloquent proponents attempted to reassess the past and the present. The disparate viewpoints swirled around Samuel, influencing him strongly, and formed the substantial basis for his later convictions and actions. Even more remarkably, by the age of seventeen, his ideas, dreams, and convictions were well formed, pressing for release. Let us examine briefly the more pertinent aspects of this blend.

The great Polish-Russian historian Simon Dubnow considered the year 1881 as the point of departure. The assassination of Tsar Alexander II was regarded as the date of the beginnings of Jewish nationalism and of the mass migrations to the West, and, perhaps, of an accelerated spiritual awakening. The outbreak of pogroms in Ukraine and southern Russia (1881–84) proved a traumatic shock to the Jews in those regions, who were numerically fewer and more modernized than their brethren in Poland and in the northern provinces. Ideological shock waves rocked the *maskilim*, or Jewish intelligentsia, working to achieve a Western (European) lifestyle— that is, the emancipation of East European Jewry. The formal reactions of the Russian government, the established church, and educated society, all of which failed to condemn the reactive slaughter of Jews, contributed to what rapidly became an agonizing, protracted reappraisal of Jewish goals and identity. At the same time, Western Europe, including the Hapsburg empire, Germany, and France, were experiencing a resurgence of anti-Semitism.

Dubnow skillfully described how Alexander II's "Russification" program caused Jews to stream from all reaches of the Pale to avail themselves of Russian studies. Proponents of Russification and West European–style assimilation probably intended no threat to the body of the Jewish people but rather, as Dubnow observed, "the removal of the obnoxious excrescences . . . obsolete forms of Jewish life which obstructed healthy development; . . . the fierce superstition of the Hasidic environment, the charlatanism of degenerating Tzaddicism . . . the impenetrable religious fanaticism which was throttling the noblest striving of the Jewish mind."

Russian-Jewish newspapers flourished and some young Jews became secular revolutionaries, espousing an idealistic populist-socialist philosophy and prominently participating in the political trials and public manifestations of the seventies. When these youths were imprisoned and languished in Siberian camps, their sacrifices had little significance for the development and destiny of their people. Many of these activists saw little to admire in Jewish peoplehood and instead embraced and spread new secular ideals among the peasantry. A far more positive approach emerged from the founding of the Bund, the General Jewish Workers' League, established in Vilna in 1897. A prominent historian and author, Salo W. Baron, explains that the Bund was a general coalition of Jewish socialist groups and labor unions aimed at increasing the welfare of Jewish workers, obtaining civil rights, and "above all, combating the discriminatory anti-Jewish laws." By 1906 it had 40,000 members who manifested their strength and forcefully espoused their ideas at local and international socialist gatherings.

Effectively parting the ideological mist, Zionism soon became a dominant force and permeated the major social strata of East European Jewry. Leon Pinsker of Odessa (near Novaya Ushitsa) proclaimed the intent to establish a Jewish national home in Palestine. He stressed the hopelessness of Jewish adjustment everywhere in the world "as an alien splinter within the national bodies of sovereign nations." He forcefully defined Jews as a nation and stated that only a territory of their own, either Palestine or in America, could provide safeguards against anti-Semitism and second-class citizenship. He argued that only international cooperation between Jewish groups could bring this about. Pinsker's message fell on the deaf ears of the relatively assimilated Jews of Western Europe but stirred Russia's Jews as few events previously.

Concurrent with Zionistic developments were the stirrings of what has been termed the "neo-Hebraic Renaissance." A few writers began a continuing attempt to restore the Hebrew language through the media of literature, drama, and poetry. Dubnow remarks that the poet or novelist often turned into a fighter "who attacked the old order of things and defended the new." Abraham Mapu powerfully moved Russian Jewry with his historical novel *The Love of Zion*, and Judah Leib Gordon became a critic and analyst of Jewish life with his poems and moralistic fables heralding a period of Jewish self-criticism. Perez Smolenskin, the editor of a widely circulated Hebrew magazine, fought against the fanaticism of Orthodoxy. His novels bring out the conception of a "spiritual nation" that was utilized by many a Zionist orator in later years. Chaim Nachman Bialik predictably achieved eminence as a poet in Odessa. After the First World War, thanks to the intervention of the Russian writer Maxim Gorky, he was permitted to emigrate to Palestine, where he brilliantly and unsurpassingly raised the level of Hebrew poetry and, at the same time, expressed the inner yearnings of his generation. Unlike many other writers and poets of the day, he greatly respected rabbinic learning. He expressed revulsion and horror over the dead of the Russian pogroms.

When one analyzes the later opinions of Samuel Wohl, both as a rabbi and as a Zionist, one is strongly impressed by the pervasive influence of Ahad Ha-am, né Asher Ginsberg, the great essayist, thinker, and leader. Born in Ukraine's Kiev province in 1856, Ahad Ha-am soon gravitated to Odessa, which, as we have observed, was the dynamic center of Jewish culture in the Pale. From his first controversial essay, wherein he incisively questioned the methods of political Zionism, to his later repeated emphases on Jewish historical and national continuity, he seemed to return always to the concept of Judaism as a nexus of creative energy and to the urgent necessity for Jews everywhere to identify with a reinvigorated heritage. He viewed the Jewish religion as a developmental process, not subject to deliberate reform, but, by the same token, never the same. Any system of religious laws (Halakah) must change with the passage of time. Samuel naturally identified with the fact that Ahad Ha-am, like a sizable number of his compatriots, had a traditional Jewish education during his early years but later discarded many aspects of this upbringing because he could not perceive himself or the world in such terms.

Ahad Ha-am wrote essays developing many Jewish and Zionistic concepts. How does one reconcile the educated Jew with such concepts as the "will to live" and a "national ego"? Samuel eagerly seized the common thread of pragmatism penetrating through all of Ahad Ha-am's writings. His later speeches, sermons, and letters reflect Ahad Ha-am's "practical Zionism," that is, his distrust of impetuosity and prematurity in tackling very complex issues, and the nourishing of "unfettered" Jewish spiritual creativity so as to enable identification with a strengthened heritage. On the other hand, unlike Ahad Ha-am, Samuel strongly believed in the Zionist movement as a *potential* answer to world-wide Jewish woes. Later, he was to digest the great man's thinking more thoroughly at the Hebrew Union College in Cincinnati.

Ahad Ha-am's writings constituted a necessary bridge between Pinsker's earlier tracts and the spasmodic awakening of political Zionism. It was *political* Zionism, represented by the towering, portentous figure of Theodor Herzl, that thrilled Samuel to the core, catalyzing his thinking and preparing him for the additional spark that would provide more than the requisite motive power for the rest of his life.

The charismatic and handsome Herzl, whose life tragically expired while he was in his early forties, was sensitized to anti-Semitic occurrences in his native Austria and was horrified by the events of the famous Dreyfus trial in France. Very soon he became aware of the total subjugation of Eastern Europe's Jews. He became convinced, even obsessed, by the necessity of providing, somewhere in the world, a place of refuge, a center that would inspire and spiritually rally these people who were suffering or vulnerable in most of the civilized countries of the world. Pierre Van Paassen, in his preface to an edition of *Excerpts from Herzl's Diary*, describes Herzl as the first "Jewish statesman" in eighteen hundred years (conceiving world-wide Jewry as a nation).

Herzl strove to overcome "the inertia of centuries." Max Nordau, one of his principal followers, described him as a "genius for action." Herzl's collected writings show deep reflection, literary skill and sensitivity, and alas, considerable frustration with unpleasant reality. Herzl joined common cause with the Zionist visionaries of Eastern Europe, convened the first Zionist Congress, which in turn created the World Zionist Organization in Basle in 1899, and demanded of individuals and governments that the wilderness of Palestine be turned over to the Jews as a national homeland.

He negotiated with the mighty of the gentile world, and had endless conferences with Jewish philanthropists and the leaders of other groups. He sacrificed his career and fortune in the fight for revived Jewish nationhood. Yes, Samuel was deeply impressed, and it is also true that most of Russian Jewry looked to Herzl as the savior who would lead them to the Promised Land. We shall examine Zion and Zionism in greater detail later in this book.

Around 1912, meanwhile, Samuel took stock of himself and his situation. He reasoned that he could not remain in Russia. Waves of political and spiritual reality were cresting and breaking over him, leaving him awash in emotion. We have noted that there were nationalistic stirrings, dramatic inroads of technology, and new ideas of liberty and justice. Samuel knew that this did not bode well for the Jewish presence, because periods of nationalistic unrest were almost certain to result in blame and persecution. At the same time, he was vulnerable to the infamous Russian military conscription laws, which traditionally were utilized to force assimilation and religious conversion, and to punish and exploit Jewish boys and young men.

Samuel, like most Jewish youths, did not share the downtrodden peasants' love for "Mother Russia." She was, at best, an intensely rejecting mother, who, like the monster witch of the Beowulf legend, would devour him. Nor did he then or ever romanticize or reminisce in maudlin fashion about his village or even about shtetl life in general. Despite his relatively privileged position, he clearly saw the ugliness and poverty around him. He perceived the sterility of the Jewish people produced by centuries of defensively turning inward. He experienced "the compulsive scholarship leading to a highly complex and frequently superstitious theocracy with little appreciation of actual human need."

Unlike many of his peers, he also appreciated that life in the Pale was not totally negative. Even then he saw what current scholars and historians now acknowledge, given the perspective of time: the Pale of Settlement was modern-day proof that a Jewish nation could exist and perpetuate its own culture. They now recognize what he could not possibly have known: "that the massive outflow of penniless Jews from eastern Europe would establish flourishing cultural centers in many countries located in North and South America, South Africa, and, of course, Israel."

Samuel began to evolve an understanding (as distinguished from admiration) of the very existence of the Ashkenazi Jew within the entire rubric of Jewish history. He viewed Jewish persistence and continuity with awe despite the fearful carnage, the continual martyrdom experienced by his people, and the prolific profundities expressed by rabbis and sages. Despite numerous self-appraisals, he could not imagine himself surviving such stress either spiritually or physically.

The region where Samuel lived was not distant from Mezibezh, where, in the early eighteenth century, simple people as well as great talmudic scholars had flocked to hear the pronouncements and experience the mystical visions and revelations of Israel Baal Shem Tov ("Master of the Good Name"). This popular leader eschewed the prevalent asceticism in favor of ecstatic behavior and spiritual awakening. Overcoming stiff opposition and its own mystical excesses, the Chasidic movement soon pervaded Jewish thought and religious practices throughout Eastern Europe and, disregarding excesses of practice, provided a sense of joy, inner satisfaction, and opportunity to worship as an individual creative activity.

Samuel was certainly influenced by these elements in religion, but could not easily find them in his surroundings and current existence. He did not agree with Rabbi Akiba of ancient times or with the medieval church that suffering is somehow ennobling. Nor would he ever accept or live by the idea, attributed to the ancient academy at Yavneh shortly following the destruction of the Second Temple, that Jewish continuity can be ensured primarily by forbearance, intensive study, and compromises with, and continual adjustment to, the secular world. However, by the same token, he abhorred precipitous action, rebellion, or aggressiveness without considering their effects. He was to transport a healthy "realism" of the type found in Harkabi's 1983 book, *The Bar Kochba Syndrome*, wherein the Hasmonean revolt was examined and found to have malignant (and for centuries unappreciated) consequences for the existence of the Jewish people.

Since we have alluded to Samuel's living immersion in the ideas and traditions of his religion and people, it may be permissible to understand him as influenced (or inspired) by several illustrious progenitors. One must understand that the East European Jew of that era could not reasonably identify a famous statesman or member of the royal family in his genealogy. Fame and greatness almost always stemmed from being a surpassing scholar and teacher (rabbi). Such a person was Isaiah Horwitz of Prague, born about 1555. In comfortable circumstances, he devoted a great portion of his income to good works and scholarship. He was one of the most respected leaders in the communal affairs of Polish Jewry and held a succession of rabbinical posts. A prolific author, his major work, the *Shenei Luhot ha-Berit* ("Two Tables of the Covenant"), delivered a compendium of the Jewish religion and enjoined the faithful to rigorously observe the Law. It also delved into complex discussions of religious ethics and stressed kabbalistic mysticism. The book was reissued and frequently abridged by Horwitz's descendants over the next two hundred years. The book and its author quickly came to be known by the acronym *Shelah Hakodesh* ("Holy Shelah"). It became a source of consolation and instruction for generations of pious Jews. Some nine years before his death in 1631, Rabbi Horwitz emigrated to Palestine, first settling in Jerusalem and then in Safed. He was buried in Tiberias close to the tomb of the great rationalistic philosopher Maimonides. The facts linking Samuel Wohl to the Shelah are complicated and beyond the purview of this book. But he recalled the disapproval of the village elders as they reproved his father, Mordecai, for allowing him to have a secular education: "That you, a descendant of the Shelah, should permit this," and so on. Like the fact of his early life near the birthplace of Israel Baal Shem Tov, the source of Hasidism, this information creates links to Hasidism through the enthusiasm and positive determination that were inner characteristics of the movement and, indeed, of Samuel himself. The Shelah's emigration to the land of Israel may be regarded as a symbolic precursor of Zionism.

Like the Shelah Hakodesh, Samuel was powerfully drawn to the land of Israel. His devotion can only be described as "intense."

He was to become intimate with its most influential people and was one of the outstanding Zionist leaders of the Diaspora, imbued with the labor idealism of the founders of the Jewish state.

Samuel deliberated slowly and carefully. He loved his immediate family dearly and wondered whether he would really be able to leave. He suspected that his brother, Maurice, only two years younger, would soon be on his way. The family communicated with a distant cousin, a jeweler in Akron, Ohio, who agreed to serve as a sponsor and provide living arrangements. Samuel carefully planned every detail of his journey, finally booked a second-class passage aboard the *Graf Waldersee*, and arrived at Ellis Island in October of 1913. In stark contrast, several years later, Maurice journeyed in an easterly direction and managed to arrive in New York via sprawling Siberia, China, and the western coast of the United States. A year later brother Jack spontaneously joined a group of freed Polish prisoners and eventually reached the United States by way of Warsaw, Bremen, and Liverpool. In each case, and later with the rest of his family, Samuel assisted with all manner of arrangements in the United States and was usually on the dock to receive them.

Part II
Cleveland: Formative Years

Chapter 3
Ethnic Potpourri

John Gunther, in his widely acclaimed book *Inside U.S.A.*, written in the 1940s, refers to Cleveland as "having all the charm of a boiler factory." In the years between 1870 and 1900, immigration and urbanization transformed Cleveland into an industrial city. Burgeoning industrial activity demanded hundreds of thousands of new immigrants, swelling the city's population to 510,000 by 1910. Campbell and Miggins note that progress was costly and stressful. Many factory workers worked long hours in dangerous and unsanitary conditions. Those who survived the working conditions were vulnerable to sudden plant closings and lay-offs. The early decades of the twentieth century in the Cleveland area are punctuated by famous industrial names and families—Rockefeller, Chisholm, Sherwin-Williams, Grasselli, White, and Winton were but a very few. For the most part they flourished. Many of their industries were merged into national or international mega-companies. Some, due to the economic life-cycle, simply expired. Campbell and Miggins speculate that "given its location, labor force, transportation and climate, Cleveland might have been another Pittsburgh or Detroit, if Carnegie's family, like many Scottish families, had only found its way to the banks of the Cuyahoga instead of the banks of the Allegheny, or if Henry Ford had been born in Elyria [Ohio] instead of Dearborn, Michigan." They go on to note that instead of a single-sector economy, "Cleveland was able to remain a national headquarters for many industries and a regional center for distribution." At the same time, a wide range of commercial enterprises, powered by banking and insurance, helped the city maintain "entrepreneurial momentum."

By the time Samuel arrived in the Cleveland area, dozens of immigrant groups were contributing to the growth and cultural diversity of the city. The population was somewhat in excess of 200,000 and growing rapidly. Each nationality group huddled together, often locating within walking distance of employment. The many varieties of Slavs (Ukrainians, Czechs, Slovenes, Serbs, Macedonians, Bulgarians, Poles, etc.) were numerically predominant, with considerable additional representation of Italians and Hungarians. There were also, by this time, 8,000 blacks, who are discussed here as immigrants because they were largely recent migrants from the South. The various Slavic groups differed from each other culturally and religiously. Many were primarily adherents to Eastern Orthodoxy, but the majority could be considered Roman Catholic. A surprising 60 percent of Cleveland was foreign-born at this time, and at least 80 percent of the recent immigrant groups were laborers who provided the muscle for the descendants of earlier British and Northern European immigrants who had the creative vision and planning to build a major and lasting metropolis.

Jews were viewed in reference to their country of origin and thus were often counted as belonging to one or another of the nationalities named above. Yet there were, and are, many pervasive differences. The Jewish rate of population increase in Cleveland exceeded the growth rate of the city as a whole. Cleveland's economic conditions encouraged this influx, but the major driving force was the need to escape tsarist Russia, poverty, and the cynical governmental manipulations resulting in continuing tragedy and distress. Following the world-publicized Kishinev pogrom of Easter 1903, the torrent of Jews leaving Eastern Europe dramatically gained momentum to assume the proportions of a flood.

The Jewish population of Cleveland owed much to those who came before. Unlike the other immigrant groups, the Jews were welcomed by German Jews from Bavaria and Bohemia, who had prospered and were able to help settle the newcomers by a well-developed network of fraternal and religious community organizations. This resettlement was not without its conflicts. The traditions and religious customs of the Russian Jews competed with the more Americanized traditions and viewpoints of the welcoming Jewish Americans. In this, they certainly resembled the process occurring within other, non-Jewish immigrant nationality and religious groups. At the same time, while frequently quarreling and fractious, they lacked the deep enmities and rivalries existent among the European nationalities. Jews were always able to appreciate an underlying bond and a common language (Yiddish), and thoroughly understood their strong mutual interdependence. This can be contrasted to the various Slavic groups, which, so Miggins and Morganthaler suggest, "lacked a mutual empathy toward Pan-Slavism."

Two of Mordecai Wohl's brothers had already proceeded to American shores. Samuel therefore found in New York a plethora of knowledgeable cousins who were willing to be helpful and offer counsel. After several weeks, they dispatched him, still innocent of the English language, to Akron, where still another cousin was to identify him by means of a placard around his neck containing the word "Wohl." It is probably correct to say that his arrival did not cause a ripple in the oily waters of metropolitan Cleveland, but figuratively, he immediately dove in and started swimming vigorously. Under the aegis of the Cleveland Board of Education, he studied English, took several literature and composition courses, and did very well on examinations. He was pronounced fit to enroll in the senior class of venerable Central High School, the first secondary school west of the Alleghenies. An imposing gothic building, it had been located on East 55th Street (then regarded as a wide boulevard) since 1877. The teaching and course offerings were of the highest caliber, while the student body changed from the city's elite to a variegated mix representing the ethnic spectrum of Cleveland. As Samuel successfully accomplished his senior year, he was completely unaware of his wife-to-be, little Belle Myers, who timidly became a freshman two years ahead of others of her chronological age. Another youth laboring in anonymity at the time in the classrooms of Central was the now famous and respected African-American poet Langston Hughes.

Chapter 4
Early Professional Development:
Idealism Translated into Action

For several years Samuel maintained residence in Akron but easily spent most of his time in Cleveland, which was approaching its zenith in terms of Jewish population (80,000 by 1920). A young man in his early twenties, he became president of the Akron Zionist council and was apparently an organizing force among Akron Jewish organizations. In the year 1919 he chaired a committee "For the Defense of the Jews in Ukrainia" representing all of Akron's Jewish organizations. These were the years of the Russian Revolution, the formation and disappearance of European national boundaries, the extinction of tsarism, and the presumed liberation of Russian Jewry. Almost as a last convulsive shudder of a dying order, Jews were again massacred in Poland and Ukraine. He was extremely concerned for his family. He knew they had survived but also had personally witnessed these disturbances.

Samuel was still under twenty when he was elected a delegate to the recently formed American Jewish Congress and was indeed the youngest delegate. The presence of the American Jewish Congress at the Versailles peace conference greatly increased the political strength of world Jewry and brought together Jewish representatives from other countries to form the Committee of Jewish delegations. In addition to his leadership role in Akron, Samuel had taken on the post of executive secretary of the Cleveland Zionist District, a time-consuming responsible position he assumed the very same year, 1917, as the stirring news that Great Britain, as stated in the Balfour Declaration, looked with favor on the Jews settling in Palestine. He willingly threw himself into a nationally orchestrated effort to mobilize U.S. government action and public awareness in behalf of his threatened people. As a Zionist leader, Samuel recognized these events as confirmatory evidence that the Jews of the world urgently needed a refuge and a symbolically meaningful rallying point, Palestine, to restore their vitality. It cannot be specifically documented, but we must conclude that in 1919 he played a major role in organizing the first protest parade in Cleveland Jewish history. Songs and cheers accompanied the 20,000 marching people, proudly led by at least 500 recently returned Jewish soldiers. That evening an overflow crowd at Gray's Armory listened to renowned local and national speakers decry the worsening barbarism.

Samuel's activities that year reached a furious crescendo. However, he managed to fuse the ubiquitous need to support himself with the highest goals of communal life: Zionism and Jewish education. Almost immediately he marketed himself as a private Hebrew tutor and teacher, riding the crest of a steadily rising interest in Hebrew fueled by the recent arrival of traditionally oriented East European Jews. The Zionist-inspired awakening to the renaissance of Hebrew as a new modern language also contributed to the growing pool of potential students.

At the same time, working closely with the recently arrived Rabbi Abba Hillel Silver, Samuel was in day-to-day contact with local and national Jewish notables as well as important government officials. As time passed he developed a profound respect for and personal relationship with the powerful and charismatic Silver. Samuel was executive secretary during Silver's presidency of the local Zionist district. In this capacity he capably followed and implemented Silver's policies but also initiated actions for which credit was attributed to others. Silver, together with several other prominent Cleveland rabbis, strongly urged Samuel to pursue a career in the rabbinate.

As the year 1919 extended, however, Samuel was almost totally occupied with letters, meetings, monitoring international events, and, of course, his work in Hebrew and Jewish education. His major concern was the plight of European Jewry and the steadily brightening hope that somehow Palestine might serve as a refuge and cultural center for world Jewry. He determinedly invited to the Cleveland area such men as Secretary of the Navy Josephus Daniels, chairman of the Senate Foreign Relations Committee, Senator Henry Cabot Lodge, former mayor of Cleveland and Secretary of War, Newton D. Baker, as well as prominent local lay and religious leaders. His ultimate goal was to encourage these men to clarify government attitudes and, by later actions, protect Jewish lives overseas. Despite or perhaps because of the recent involvement of the United States in the World War, isolationism was a force to be reckoned with, and the country was occupied with developing and rebuilding its postwar economy. The world, it seemed, was still safe for democracy, and immigration to the United States was eminently possible. The prevalent attitude toward American participation in European affairs was well illustrated by two letters to Samuel from Warren G. Harding, later to be president, but at the time a member of the Senate Foreign Relations Committee. Harding wrote in reply to Samuel's plea for American protection for Ukrainian Jews.

> It is a most regrettable situation that this great republic is in a position of more or less helplessness in doing anything effective, save to make a moral appeal to those in authority in the old world. . . . I will be glad to participate in any consistent course which our government may adopt in effecting such protection. Frankly, the Senate faces a very difficult situation, except as the administration points the way. The unanimous sentiment of the Senate is heartily in favor of protecting the oppressed Jew in every way possible whatever his liberty and safety are.

Harding's words were truly descriptive and prophetic of the American government's willingness to espouse moral positions but unwillingness to take definitive action. In 1924, in response to public clamor that immigrants from Eastern and Southern Europe were "lowering wage scales," the government enacted immigration quota restrictions, basing the number of people of various ethnic backgrounds admitted to the United States on how many of their nationality group were residing here before 1890. This served to effectively shut off Jewish immigration and was to have horrific consequences during the Nazi genocidal efforts of the 1940s.

As the eventful year of 1919 culminated, Samuel began a correspondence with Louis Dembitz Brandeis, a brilliant lawyer and later to be a precedent-setting justice of the Supreme Court. The noted jurist had a significant impact on Cleveland as early as 1909, when he was instrumental in settling a dispute between the International Ladies Garment Workers Union (ILGWU) and the New York Protective Association of Manufacturers. The results of the settlement favorably affected the ILGWU's subsequent attempts to organize nationally (in Cleveland) and the principle of collective bargaining. Further, in a not unrelated victory, he successfully argued a fifty-four-hour work week before the U.S. Supreme Court. The Ohio Consumers League effectively utilized this decision to promote protective labor legislation for women and children. Its efforts, while strenuous, were largely unsuccessful until 1920, when women cast their first ballots.

Samuel was very familiar with all this, but his interest in Brandeis stemmed from the latter's Zionist convictions and leadership combined with his prestige and moral authority. Gartner notes that during his most important speaking tour in 1914, Brandeis appeared at Cleveland's Gray Armory, where he delivered a ringing endorsement of Zionism, spoke of the urgent need for funds, and described Palestine as a protection against Jewish assimilation and demoralization. He had already assumed a considerable measure of national leadership within the Zionist movement, although his formal break with the renowned chemist and Zionist leader Chaim Weizmann did not occur until a Zionist Organization of America meeting in Cleveland in 1921. Considering that the Jews of Cleveland were one day to be the highest per capita givers to Jewish causes, it is ironic that Brandeis's Cleveland visit was a fund-raising disappointment although other objectives were realized. His biographers and historical authorities stress that throughout his judicial career and Zionist activities, Brandeis was "preeminently a teacher and a moralist." However, pragmatism was the theme embodied in his first letter to Samuel, in January 1919, and was to appear with regularity throughout a thirty-year span until 1939, some two years before his death:

1. Secretary Dulles—a good friend would be a most fitting guest; and he should be secured through efforts of his fellow citizens whom he knows individually.

2. I am disappointed that Cleveland proposes to raise only $50,000. You have the greatest advantages . . . of a large Jewish population . . . and able men as your administrators . . . [and] in Rabbi Silver—one of the finest orators in the land. With such a spokesman—and committee, you should raise at least $100,000 and, before the membership drive closes, should equal 95% of the adult donors of your city.

Samuel enormously admired Brandeis's brilliance, commitment, encompassing vision, and his monumental achievement of being the first Jew to sit on the highest court of the land. Although their correspondence steadily became more friendly, Samuel never succeeded in drawing Judge Brandeis from Washington for any reason or function.

He was, however, successful in drawing Dr. Chaim Weizmann to give a much publicized address at the Masonic Temple. The eminent chemist, then the chief rival of Brandeis for leadership of the World Zionist movement, persuaded Albert Einstein to accompany him to tour vital eastern cities of the United States. The young Einstein, shy, reclusive, and clearly uneasy with his international eminence, was introduced by Weizmann and proceeded to "steal the show" with a less than three-minute address. We will elaborate on this event a little later in our narrative.

Chapter 5
Rabbinic Power

The physical presence of a Brandeis, a Weizmann, or any other nationally prominent Zionist leader soon became less vital as the young Rabbi Abba Hillel Silver, already one of the country's leading Zionists by 1920, and a truly gifted orator, educator, and social welfare activist, began to hit his stride. Silver's national and international activities contributed prominently to Cleveland's leadership role in Zionist and Jewish affairs. Like Samuel, he was of East European (Lithuanian) origin. He emerged from the Yiddish- and Hebrew-speaking milieu of New York's Lower East Side and provided a later template for Samuel by graduating simultaneously from the Hebrew Union College and the University of Cincinnati. He was ordained a Reform rabbi the same year.

Abba Hillel Silver was only twenty-four years of age when he succeeded Moses Gries as rabbi of The Temple in 1917, and promptly, over the opposition of many influential members of the congregation, he softened the austerity of the classical Reform tradition by returning Hebrew to the services and emphasizing the congregation's cultural and religious roles. Moreover, he ardently espoused political Zionism, championing it with a fervor that literally steamrolled his opponents. The historian Lloyd Gartner describes Silver as "an orator of overpowering force, brilliance, and persuasiveness [who] appealed powerfully to the rationality and idealism of his hearers while assailing his opponents with withering sarcasm and irony." The Cleveland chronicler and social activist Sidney Vincent notes that "he did not suffer fools gladly."

Samuel particularly marveled at the leonine Silver's record as a positive social force, his founding of the League for Human Rights, his denunciation of the open shop, an arrangement generally regarded as hostile to unions, and his eloquent conviction that fair and enlightened treatment of labor was the road to social justice. Silver's truly outstanding achievements, character, and intellect interacted with one another to produce, in Gartner's judgment, "a position . . . such as no other Jew ever attained in Cleveland."

Samuel was a valued friend and apprentice to Silver during those early years in the careers of both men. Silver's political realism and pragmatism served to leaven Samuel's idealism, often firmly anchoring it to what was realistic and achievable. Several recent biographers, apparently attempting to introduce balance to their evaluations, have noted that Silver was prone to pettiness and implacability toward those he regarded as in error or in opposition. His correspondence with Samuel through the years tends to support such observations, but Samuel himself cannot be regarded as petty, nor was he inflexible in any sense.

Rabbi Barnett R. Brickner succeeded the prominent Rabbi Louis Wolsey as the spiritual leader of the Euclid Avenue Temple (Anshe Chesed). Rabbi Wolsey, in the later years of his career, strongly supported classical Reform Judaism. Like Silver, Brickner had emerged from New York's Lower East Side with a background in traditional Jewish thought and Zionism. He continuously strove to fuse education and social justice as a means of reuniting life and religion, which he viewed as having diverged alarmingly over the centuries. Samuel found him warm and receptive and much more collegial than the sometimes forbidding Silver. Brickner's congregation soon rivaled Silver's in sheer size and proved to be another pivotal force in the community. Samuel's later impact on his own congregation and community was similar to Brickner's in several significant ways—his emphasis on education, social justice and the introduction of the more meaningful and stirring traditional customs into the aseptic sterility of the Reform Jewish worship service.

The third, but by no means least, member of the rabbinic triumvirate that so powerfully influenced Samuel was Solomon

Goldman. He came from the same background as Silver and Brickner but was by conviction a Conservative rabbi, and a graduate of the Jewish Theological Seminary. In 1918 he became rabbi of B'nai Yeshurun synagogue, an earlier Hungarian Orthodox congregation. Goldman was able to enlarge the membership and was successful in "conservatizing" the service, but his aggressive personality encountered substantial opposition when he attempted to transform the synagogue into a Jewish community center. In frustration, he transferred to Anshe Emeth, now known as the Cleveland Jewish Center. Here too his progressive views stirred reflexive hostility among the Orthodox congregants and culminated in a nasty public lawsuit over mixed seating of men and women. Although Samuel had already left Cleveland to study for the rabbinate, he received, in 1925, a letter from a close friend that conveys the ill feelings prevalent in the congregational squabbles of those years. It is arguable whether such disagreement would take a less blatant form today:

> Last Saturday, the first one after the Passover was over, Goldman's opponents finally plucked up courage. Weinberg [fictitious name assigned by the authors], so Goldman told me, had had some drinks before coming to the synagogue. Anyway, he started the trouble, going on the platform and attempting to prevent taking the Sefer [Torah] from the ark. Goldman took it out himself, without Weinberg's making an effort to restrain him personally. Then, about three of Weinberg's friends went on the platform. Goldman began reading, and they began to talk loudly. He continued. . . . Then they stopped talking. And he still continued reading. Thus endeth the second round. . . . No blows were struck and no police were called. . . . The news of the rumpus having gotten about town . . . you should have seen what a good audience Goldman had for his drosha [sermon] at mincha [the afternoon service]. Members of the Center . . . who ordinarily don't see the inside of the place except Rosh Hashanah and Yom Kippur

were all present. My advice to you, Sam, is when you are a
rabbi, if you want to boost your audience, don't give them
fine sermons. Nothing will do it like a first class honest-to-
goodness fight.

Goldman's conflicts with his congregants should not distract us
from his contributions as a scholar, Zionist, and educator. He later
attained national prominence in all three endeavors. He and
Samuel developed an instant mutual friendship and respect. He
appointed Samuel as the principal of his religious school system
and later saw him become a teacher and tutor in the Cleveland
Hebrew schools, a branch of which met at the Jewish Center.
Rabbi Goldman presided over the Center, which in those days was
a unique phenomenon. It was simultaneously a synagogue, a forum
for public lectures, a social and recreational center, a venue for
education, and a library. In short, it provided a coordinating and
centrifugal force that helped the Jewish community attain an identity and kept them together in an integrated presence. Goldman
literally dominated the scene and was at the same time a charming
host, effective educator, religious-change catalyst, and ebullient
scholar.

Myron Guren was a close friend of both Samuel and Rabbi
Goldman. He served and supported the latter when he assumed the
pulpit of B'nai Jeshurun. He soon followed the rabbi to Anshe
Emeth and became his executive educational director. He was a
pioneer Jewish educator and devoted public servant and was seminal to the creation of an active Jewish Center and the vital
Conservative congregation later known as Park Synagogue. He
became, in later years, a sage, whose unpublished reminiscences, as
related to Daniel Polster (1966) and Rabbi Howard Hirsh (1980),
added rich substance to our memory of Samuel's recollections of
the "Goldman days." As Guren told it:

Goldman recruited groups all over the community. . . . and
he was wise enough to see to it that the groups were of different kinds. . . . He tried to make the [individual] groups

more homogeneous. . . . In those days we would meet
Goldman at his study at the end of the day. We would have
a meal in a kosher restaurant and then we would go to his
home, first looking over the new books that he had
received that day, and straightening out his library as well
as amateurs could do it, and then we would have a session
of reading and we would always devote at least an hour of
reading from things at hand; Bialik, Ahad Ha'am, or, if we
didn't have the book at that moment we felt interested in
reading, we would talk over with Goldman subjects for
future sermons. He would often show us his contemplated
sermons for the coming week.

Samuel found himself part of this cabal or inner circle of very
intelligent and searching young people who positioned themselves
protectively around Goldman while drawing from him continual
sustenance and support. Rabbi Goldman's "brain trust," as he often
referred to them, would frequently attend the usual open forum
held after the sermons on Friday night and, in gadfly fashion, ask
questions, harass, and tease their mentor. Guren confesses to having "a great time of it." One might note that in addition to Guren,
these young men were to achieve prominence in diverse fields.
Samuel Beck became a renowned psychologist and pioneer in the
introduction of the Rorschach test and theory in the United
States. Morris Berick directed his energies to the law. He was crucial in breaking the bonds of real estate discrimination in the
Cleveland metropolitan area and eventually became president of
the Cleveland bar association. David Ralph Hertz, admitted to the
group some time later, was to become a judge. His wife, Marguerite,
was also an internationally known psychologist and developed a
Rorschach system that gained respect and prominence.

Young Suggs Garber, while not a participant in the group, came
to know and respect them later on, making large contributions of
time, effort, and money to Jewish education and Zionistic endeavors. His prestigious law firm and engaging personality combined to
make him a sought-after consultant in financing Palestine land

purchases and large-scale land transactions. Ezra Shapiro was a Hebrew student of Samuel's when he taught in the Talmud Torah at the Jewish Center. Ezra became prominent in politics, serving at the city's law director, and was a singular leader of Zionistic activities. In the latter capacity he and Samuel often corresponded, keeping their friendship viable.

Roland Gittelsohn, son of Rabbi Benjamin Gittelsohn, himself a scion of a rabbinic line, was also an early student of Samuel's. Whereas the father, Benjamin, was a quiet scholarly figure, Roland, his son, proved to be a dynamic achiever. Roland Gittelsohn is perhaps best remembered today as the Jewish naval chaplain who spoke and officiated at the dedication of the Jewish section of the Iwo Jima cemetery. This should not obscure his leadership role in the rabbinate as president of the Central Conference of American Rabbis, his expertise in modern Jewish problems, and most of all, the social sensitivity and political activism demonstrated throughout his successful career.

Chapter 6
New Arrivals, Joie de Vivre, and Marriage

Meanwhile, the far-flung Russian lands and people were contorting in agony and confusion. The tsarist regime had been overthrown amidst a welter of slogans and ideological jargon. Before many of these political and social views could be considered or actually tested, open warfare in the form of local contesting armies came to the fore. Jewish young men and women were themselves a part of the overall problem. A not insignificant number turned their energies and ideals to one or the other of the groups struggling for power. A reasonable portion cast their lot with the victors and so assumed prestigious leadership positions in the ruling party of the newly created Union of Soviet Socialist Republics.

The content of letters reaching Samuel took an alarming turn. His family had narrowly escaped injury or death in a recent pogrom. It was clearly time for them to leave. Hasty planning with brothers Maurice and Jack resulted in the rest of the family disembarking at Ellis Island, where father Mordecai, mother Rachel, and siblings Sophia, Alexander, and Zioni (Ted) successfully persevered through the interrogations, observations, and bureaucratic routines of that tiny but significant entry point to the welcoming mainland. The experience was not without its anxious moments. The medical personnel, after cursory examination, noted that Mordecai appeared consumptive (tubercular) and promptly placed him in quarantine. It seemed eminently possible that the whole family group might be sent back to the port of embarkation. However, after four extra days of strained waiting, the patriarch was allowed to rejoin his family and begin life anew in the United States of America. Frail asceticism would never again cause consternation and alarm. Mordecai's quarantine could properly be regarded as the most stimulating and challenging situation of his life.

The authors, in retrospect, believe that Samuel, and indeed all of the children, erred in the manner they chose to settle their parents in the New World. Both parents were in their fifties and had considerable commercial skill. Instead of helping them to prepare for autonomous living, they were encapsulated in a cocoon of tender affection and securely buffered from the outside world. They always lived with one of the family members in a homogeneous Jewish neighborhood (the Glenville area surrounding 105th Street) and expended the rest of their lives in a variant of genteel poverty.

Samuel's younger sister and brothers all confronted the new environment squarely and made important life choices with varying degrees of success. Of the recent arrivals, only the youngest brother, Ted (Zioni), eventually left the Cleveland area. Sophie, Samuel's vivacious sister, vowed that she would not have anything to do with Jewish men who were products of the Old World shtetl, that is, ascetic and intellectual. She would marry an American boy; and indeed she did, Louis Jaffe. She lived a life of joy and laughter, even if less than financially rewarding. Whimsically, she was never able to turn her back on knowledge and learning, because her only daughter and her granddaughter turned out to be extremely intellectually gifted and at the same time comfortably and enthusiastically Jewish.

In the years preceding his family's arrival, Samuel pursued a dynamic course that included teaching, lecturing, and nourishing Judaism and Zionism. The renaissance of the Hebrew language throughout the area facilitated his efforts. His activities were to bring him prominence and friendship, particularly from the intellectual "young Turks." He was very effective with small groups as well as with larger gatherings. Fifty years later, letters exist from contemporaries recalling his idealism, his passionate energy, and, most of all, his ability to motivate them. They allude to him as a singer of songs and a raconteur adept at supplying anecdotes and witticisms. We have speculated that the latter quality, which we hardly believe, may have subsided along with the general turbulence of his youth.

Samuel observed that the Jewish community of Cleveland had barely attained late adolescence in terms of goals and communal development. The small band of German Jews who arrived on the shores of Lake Erie in 1837 had managed to establish a German-speaking community in the Central Market District. They had expanded their presence along Woodland and Central Avenues, fusing with the Jewish immigration from Eastern, Southern, and Central Europe. Russian Jews first settled in the Haymarket area to the south of Public Square and lower Woodland in the district near Broadway Avenue (Campbell and Miggins). After the turn of the century, the Jewish population exploded to the east, entering the Glendale–Kinsman Road areas, and very soon afterwards, Cleveland Heights, Shaker Heights, and Beechwood. Other immigrant groups, even as they moved to the suburbs, left sizable bastions of compatriots remaining in their earlier neighborhoods. Jews, on the other hand, emigrated as a massive wave leaving a trough or vacuum. The situation caused authors Lipman and Vorspan to describe Cleveland proper in 1962 as a city almost without Jews. Samuel lived on Woodland Avenue in 1914 and found it burgeoning with life, but by the early twenties, some eight years later, it had already started to decline with an accelerated outflow toward the Glendale and Kinsman Road areas.

In Chapter 3 we referred to Belle Myers, who entered Samuel's life as a student in one of his Hebrew classes. Her uncle, R. H. Myers, was the first of her family to emigrate from Marionpole, Lithuania, in the early 1890s. He established himself solidly in the Cleveland community and is still loved and respected by his living descendents. The firstborn of Jacob and Rachel Myers was Belle, followed in succession by Harry, Milton, and Rupert (Ruby). They struggled to find equilibrium in a large extended family whose members communicated with each other and were quick to offer aid and encouragement in times of crisis.

Jacob, fresh from the tsar's army, had earlier ambitions to be a talmudic scholar. He quickly surrendered this dream in order to be a providing father in the New World. Like many others at that time, he worked in the family grocery, labor that Jacob found unrewarding. He concluded that he would be much happier with outdoor work. He then became part-owner of a barrel company, where he achieved some measure of success and happiness. One of the authors can remember, as a small boy, seeing his grandfather Myers in gartered shirt sleeves; a man in his late fifties or earlier sixties, tossing steel drums over the tailgate of one of his trucks. Hardworking and determined, his outward demeanor was mild, but his views and perceptions were fixed by his background and the times. He was not tender or emphatic in manner, and when his wife died, it seemed that no one could fill the nurturing role with the four children.

As the eldest, Belle, now age ten, attempted to assume her mother's role and was credited by her brothers with raising them well into their high school years. Belle was not ill-equipped for this task, because her mother had earlier imparted to her the domestic arts, particularly seamstress skills. Belle entered Central High's freshman class two years ahead of her age group. She was shy, introverted, and had an overdeveloped sense of responsibility. Despite constricting obligations at home, she was a consistent cum laude honor student. She produced creditable poetry and art. She enjoyed languages, mastering them far more thoroughly than today's secondary school children. German, offered in the public schools through eight grades, was complementary to the Yiddish spoken at home by her family. In high school she was introduced to French and Spanish. Belle achieved very high grades and a reading mastery. Although others seemed to welcome her intellectual forays, she was socially stressed and uncomfortable, being two years younger than her classmates. She did not find acceptance in the social life of the school. Her light brown hair was worn long in a

single thick braid ending just short of her shoulder blades. By this
period in American society, the emancipation of women had
begun with a vengeance. Sophisticated adolescent girls and young
women bobbed their hair and began to indulge in the time-hon-
ored activities of smoking and "petting." Belle had the "distinction" of being the smallest girl in a class of 140. Throughout high
school her hair remained modestly long. By the time of her senior
year, she was memorialized in the high school annual as "a quiet,
truthful, helpful girl—we never tire of seeing or hearing our little
Belle Myers." Somehow, this did not seem to help matters. Even so,
she managed to complete a year in a Pennsylvania normal school
(teachers college). Education was one of the few professions generally open to women of that era. Jacob, who did not believe higher
education was important for women, convincingly argued that her
help was urgently needed at home. And so Belle returned to
Cleveland and a different destiny.

While in high school Belle attempted to improve her mastery
of Hebrew by taking a course with Samuel, who had formed a con-
versational group for young adults. He also created a Young Judea
group, the first chapter of this Zionist organization in the area.
Belle was elected secretary. The group continued to meet for two
years. During this period Belle completed several business courses
together with Spencerian shorthand. This proved to be fortunate,
because she was able to obtain a solid supporting job after marriage
requiring a combination of business and foreign-language skills. As
they experienced the interweaving of their lives, Samuel's recollection of how he became aware of Belle is touching in its simplic-
ity.

> I had read the compositions in class, a rather superior one,
> and among them I discovered a rather unusual composition
> in Hebrew. Each work was good, even better than the last.
> I was eager to know all the students in the class, but partic-
> ularly the one who wrote such fine Hebrew themes. She
> was among the youngest in the group. She graduated from
> high school at the age of 16. She was in *Cleveland;* not a

shtetl. Here among the children born in the United States was an excellent group of young people who *wanted* and *were eager* to learn Hebrew. It so happened that the little girl who wrote such fine compositions later became my Belle.

Belle seemed to enter Samuel's life easily and with grace despite her relative youth. She and Samuel were constantly together and Belle was consistently accepted by Samuel's circle of friends. Samuel's mother was not one to bestow compliments easily. "A wonderful girl but I can't always understand her speech" (referring to her Lithuanian Yiddish).

Belle quickly achieved a vivid insight. She correctly understood that Samuel had the power to lead and inspire. He was fiercely loyal to people and causes. Life with him would never lack interest or meaning. She knew deeply that she was already an integral part of his being. The second stage of this insight was that he very much needed her. She could organize the details of his existence while he soared to the heights of noble purpose and abstract goals. She could provide the healthy concreteness and common sense to manage life's problem situations and conditions. At the same time, she was more in tune with the subtleties of the American experience. She often served as a sounding board for his ideas, and, although it was seldom perceived by others, she had a fine, critical mind and often made solid contributions to Samuel's presentations and projects.

The lives of Samuel and Belle began to converge and coalesce into a certain unity. Samuel discerned that others in his circle were also developing relationships and acquiring spouses, perhaps illustrating that rarified intellectuals and militant idealists need love and understanding as well as companions to share their visions. Indeed, these young couples seemed to affect themselves and their group synergistically. However, Samuel and Belle were able, wisely, to forgo the overload of intellectual stimulation and took pleasure in simple activities, such as family reunions, small parties, and dinners. During the sometime severe winters, they walked long dis-

tances and talked reflectively about / their future lives. During
spring and summer, they enjoyed picnics at Gordon Park, a small
strip of greenery within the northeast lakeside boundaries of the
city.

Their marriage was both a culmination and a new beginning.
Belle and Samuel were formally united by the beaming Rabbi
Silver in June of 1921 at the B'nai Yeshurun Temple, then located
at Scovill and East 55th. They enjoyed a brief honeymoon at
Geneva-on-the-Lake, a bucolic collection of small lakeside cot-
tages some 40 miles northeast of Cleveland. This was, of course,
well before more recent times, when the same locale evolved into
a meeting place for herds of hedonistic adolescents.

Back in their very first apartment, Samuel, as he was often
wont to do, paused to reflect on the past and carefully consider the
future. With no lessening of idealistic drive or intellectual activity,
he factored his newly achieved marital state and recently arrived
family into the equation. Using a rational exploratory method sug-
gestive of talmudic pilpul, he examined all aspects of his current
life and prospects for the future. He must, he told himself, restrict
his thinking to personal needs. Jews, Judaism, and Zionism were
always in the forefront of his awareness, and there was little ambiguity there. He felt keenly responsible for his family, only recently
established on American soil. In addition, he was now a married
man, and the accumulated weight of these responsibilities pressed
heavily upon his slender frame.

Only a year earlier, Samuel's mother, his fiancée Belle, his sister Sophie, and his youngest brother Theodor (Zioni), variously
suffering from scarlet fever and flu, had been quarantined to con-
valesce in the Majestic Hotel, the largest building in the
Woodland area and well known throughout Cleveland. A major
fire engulfed the building, raging out of control. The next day, the
Cleveland Plain Dealer and the *Cleveland Press* proclaimed the
tragedy in front-page inch-and-a-half headlines. It was noted that
members of Samuel Wohl's family, rescued by heroic firemen, had
been carried out in unconscious or stuporous conditions. These
events were shocking and disturbing to Samuel, impressed once

again by the fragility of human existence, but, characteristic of his future coping style, he reacted with increased determination to help and protect, and grimly determined to gain future control over the events leading to and resulting from such catastrophes. He must prevent future occurrences and ameliorate unpleasant effects on those he cherished.

Samuel considered other forms of livelihood, evaluating them for greater satisfaction and security. He enrolled in and graduated from the Cleveland School of Advertising. As those knew him might reasonably have predicted, he completed the year-long course successfully but found it incompatible with his needs, particularly in the area of interaction with other people. Providentially, the invited commencement speaker was John Watson, an eminent psychologist and successful corporate executive. His speech that evening stressed the theme that people could be effectively molded and manipulated by skillfully utilizing aspects of their environment. At this time, parents were relying on the Watsonian system of "habit training" as the central method for raising children. Watson's ideas were widely interpreted to mean that the emotional life and relative intangibles, such as striving for love and respect, had little role in influencing behavior. Metaphysical concepts like morality and philosophy of life were also not deemed to provide much value. Yes, Watson's speech did not "motivate" Samuel in the slightest and seemed antithetical to his beliefs and basic personality.

Chapter 7
A Watershed Decision

Samuel's mind harkened back to 1919, when all three members of the triumvirate of famous Cleveland rabbis, Silver, Brickner, and Goldman, had recommended that he enter the rabbinate. Goldman was probably the linchpin in persuading Samuel to apply to the Hebrew Union College in Cincinnati to prepare for ordination as a Reform rabbi. It was unquestionably true that Samuel could be far more effective in accomplishing his goals centered around the fusion of Jewish destiny with Jewish nationhood or the land of Israel (Eretz Yisroel). He was greatly impressed by the fact that these three forceful personalities (loosely translated, "great egos"), who were already beginning to quarrel about a large range of topics and events, could unanimously agree that he should leave Cleveland for Cincinnati.

Of course, Samuel was familiar with the writings of Isaac Mayer Wise, the proverbial founder of American Reform Judaism. Arriving in Cincinnati in the late 1850s, Rabbi Wise had immediately begun to craft a more liberal contemporary Judaism, one suited peculiarly for the American Jew. From this impact, ripples spread concentrically to include the state of Ohio and Cleveland and very soon the country as a whole. Wise was an activist, paternalistic, sometimes a stormy, petrel. Preaching only in German, he was eagerly sought after for counsel, information, and inspiration. He proposed and inspired a magnificent edifice: the Plum Street Temple (K.K. B'nai Yeshurun). A little later, he accomplished the construction of the Hebrew Union College, which he conceived as a needed institution to train American-born rabbis. Gartner explains that to Wise, American Judaism was synonymous with Reform Judaism. Never one to shrink from confronting religious orthodoxy, Wise was exasperated as he lectured to a quasi-Orthodox Cleveland congregation, admonishing them not to cling to the past, and castigating their prejudices and old customs. "Many of these [customs]," he said, "are simply not religious or contained in Jewish writings."

Although he deeply admired Wise's attempt to help Judaism evolve nobler goals and purposes, Samuel did not concur that one had to be more American (whatever this might convey) in order to take full advantage of American freedom. Rather, the air of freedom should be deeply inhaled, utilizing elements from the past that would energize and beautify modern belief and worship, and creating a faith that would benefit the Jewish people.

Samuel did not look forward to moving from northeastern Ohio to the southwestern portion of the state. He felt comfortable with his friends, family and the life he had built in the Cleveland area. Cincinnati was a place, after all, which had only about a quarter the number of Jews in Cleveland and was a smaller city with few very distinct ethnic groups. Somehow, the move seemed like an excursion to Middle America, which, like the rest of the great American heartland, Samuel viewed as strange and vaguely hostile. His urge to emigrate began to diminish as he nostalgically considered the multitudinous small shops and businesses and the Yiddish-English hubbub that characterized the main arteries of the Woodland Jewish section.

His family, the intellectual stimulation, and even the streetcars and interurbans, which normally terrified him because of what he considered the unsafe lurching speeds of the long gondolas precariously perched on white cobblestone streets, assumed an almost cloying sentimentality and substantially weakened his resolve. He brought his doubts to Belle and asked her opinion, remarking that he felt as if he were going into the *golus* (exile), and feeling sure that the things that weighed heavily on his mind would also trouble her.

Belle, who, was then coping with a full share of stressing problems, nonetheless amazed herself by her reaction. She did not
respond, like the biblical Ruth, "Where thou goest, will I go." She
sensed this was be a watershed decision that would irreversibly
change their lives. Her observations were insightful and to the
point. She offered a clear synthesis of what Samuel's three eminent
rabbinic friends and mentors had proposed in loftier language.
More specifically, she said, he was suited for the Reform rabbinate
(about which he knew very little) in every way. It was a profession
that perpetuated the role of leader, teacher, and sage in Israel,
which now and in the future would realize the best aspirations of
the Jewish people. With uncharacteristic fervor for a shy young
woman, she stated that she was strongly in favor of their moving
and that she would support him and love him even beyond the limits of her ability.

Samuel was moved and decisively swayed by Belle's observations. He had reached the critical point in the decision-making
process and began the process of applying to the Hebrew Union
College of Cincinnati and its president, Julian Morgenstern. The
"uprooting" and subsequent explanations to family and friends
proved difficult but achievable. It was with mixed feelings pervaded by a sense of eagerness and anticipation that he awaited word
from the two institutions that would soon be his dual alma maters,
the Hebrew Union College and the University of Cincinnati.

Cincinnati was the cradle of Reform Judaism with its "mother
church," known as the Plum Street Temple. Isaac Mayer Wise had
powerfully affected the city's developing congregations, and
Samuel was to become aware that Cincinnati differed significantly
from Cleveland in a number of respects. It was spread out charm-
ingly over hilly prominences, in contrast to Cleveland's relatively
flattened location on the lake plain. It was an older city, an Ohio
River town, which served as a Midwestern springboard for those
who wished to advance their fortunes in the country's West or
South. The people were ethnically homogeneous and were already
assimilated to the cultural norm.

Chapter 8
A Precious Gift

Samuel received word of simultaneous acceptance by both Cincinnati institutions and became acutely aware that somehow he had to condense eight years of undergraduate and graduate education into four. During the apprentice period for entry into the rabbinate, Samuel was to learn many things and to absorb considerable wisdom and knowledge from a distinguished group of scholars. However, he possessed a precious gift which he would soon present to his mentors and to the Cincinnati community. This gift comprised his Zionistic beliefs and his love of Hebrew.

The renaissance of ancient Hebrew into a modern tongue accompanied the Zionist awakening of East European Jewry in the late nineteenth century. Zionistic policies began to take form and substance while Jews in massive numbers emigrated—a few to the land of Israel (Palestine), and many others to the distant countries of the West. The Zionist movement was nourished by the emerging freedom while Hebrew burgeoned and evolved subtly into a viable modern language.

At first Yiddish, too, blossomed after its transplantation to America. It was, after all, the language of the Diaspora: the *mama loshen*, or "mother tongue." Almost all of the first-generation immigrants spoke and read it fluently. Several Yiddish theaters in Cleveland, including the Perry and its resident company, provided the local Jewish population with their favorite entertainment. Yiddish newspapers and journals flourished, and, for a time, Yiddish crowded out the teaching of Hebrew in Jewish parochial schools.

Of course, Yiddish was the language routinely spoken in Samuel's early home, together with lullabies, jokes, and witty tales. He was familiar with the works of the great Yiddish writers of Europe and the United States. To him it was a beautiful, expressive language impregnated with the suffering and strength of Jewish survival through the centuries.

The reader will recall that it was the Haskalah, or Enlightenment movement, in Eastern Europe that first awakened a keen interest in Hebrew. Then the rise of Jewish nationalism in the last quarter of the nineteenth century transformed it into a language that could be used in everyday life. Soon, in the 1890s, modern Hebrew found its way into the Baron de Hirsch schools in Galicia. The Zionist congresses also led to increased interest in Hebrew cultural and educational efforts. The Mizrachi organization, representing the Orthodox trend in Zionism, disagreed with the majority. It was not initially enthusiastic about the increased utilization of Hebrew, but eventually realized that an accommodation might be possible. In light of all this, it is not surprising that the Jewish educational establishment in Europe and America decided to adopt both Yiddish and Hebrew in their schools.

The arrival of the East European immigrants in the United States clearly conveyed the need of these people to continue and educate toward their traditional beliefs. They successfully resisted the Americanization urged upon them by the earlier Jewish community. The established German Jews hoped that the new immigrants could be weaned away from both Yiddish and Hebrew, with the greatest emphasis focused on the specifically *religious* aspects of Judaism. The established Talmud Torahs were staffed by newly arriving trained teachers inspired by the vitalizing power of Hebrew as a living language. In 1910, these efforts culminated in the organization of the Bureau of Jewish Education in New York City. Other "bureaus" would soon be founded in cities throughout the northeastern United States having large Jewish populations. At first they attempted to represent the wide spectrum of the Orthodox faction of the traditional Jewish community. They gradually became schools for the study and teaching of Hebrew in the modern idiom. Hebrew became the dominant language of the Jewish school because the second generation of Jews was drastically less familiar with Yiddish. Samuel did not need to read the survey by Dr. Mordecai Kaplan of New York City to understand the educational inefficiency of the existing Jewish schools. Although they were increasing in number, their financing was shaky and the teachers were paid pitiful salaries. Samuel was also of the opinion that the teachers should possess the qualifications required of public school teachers and should divest themselves of the century-old pedagogy that tended to choke off interest and understanding in the American Jewish child.

Samuel loved Hebrew and Yiddish literature. In addition to biblical literature, talmudic and rabbinic literature, he devoured nineteenth- and twentieth-century literature from Europe, Palestine, and the United States. At an amazingly early age, he was familiar with such writers of Hebrew fiction as Judah Katzenelson (Buki ben Yogli) and Abraham Friedberg, the poets Chaim Nachman Bialik and Saul Tchernichowsky, and essayists like Eliezer Perelman (Ben-Yehuda).

As Yiddish literature expanded in all directions, Samuel embraced it. He was captivated by the influential romantic trend discerned in the writings of Sholem Asch, I. J. Singer, and his brother Isaac Bashevis Singer, and by the gentle storyteller Sholem Aleichem. Amazingly, there were still Yiddish and Hebrew schools and publications in Eastern Europe, and despite the economic and political cataclysms and the pervasive endemic anti-Semitism, Yiddish literature and poetry were flourishing. To Samuel, Hebrew and Yiddish were two founts which inspired and slaked his burning thirst for knowledge. He viewed them as an integral and inseparable part of Jewish nationalism and religion. In Palestine, he recognized the seminal catalyst and beginning fruition of the noblest aspects of Jews all over the world. Moreover, as the chalutzim (pioneers) drained the swamps and built communities in Palestine, Samuel viewed them as creating an even greater miracle—uniquely resurrecting the ancient and sacred language of Hebrew and

transforming it into a rich modern tongue. Years later he expressed
his sense of awe about this revival:

> I have seen the miracle of the revival of the Hebrew lan-
> guage, the language which was first taught in the little
> "cheder" by translating Hebrew words into Yiddish. . . . My
> father always wrote his letters to me in Hebrew but now I
> hear the language spoken by little children in kindergarten.
> I hear it spoken by soldiers in the army of Israel. I hear it
> spoken from university platforms. I hear the vivid words of
> great plays given in the timeless language, and I have seen
> the man who, by his tremendous courage and great idealism
> established the first Hebrew speaking family in Jerusalem.
> Eliezer Ben-Yehudah withstood malicious attacks upon him
> because he used the "sacred language" for everyday speech.
> This same Ben-Yehudah left us a great legacy, not only to
> the modern venture of living Hebrew but also the example
> of one man, who, with his own resources, created a great
> Hebrew dictionary and gave the world a Hebrew language
> model that will sustain itself and meet every requirement.
> It was a privilege indeed to see Ben-Yehudah working in a
> little room in the New York City public library on 42nd
> street. When he returned to Palestine he was received with
> great acclaim and given a newly built house. . . . a rather
> unique person was the first child whose language was
> Hebrew alone from his infancy. He was the first son of Ben-
> Yehudah and he called himself Ben Avi (son of my father).

Ben Avi was an eloquent speaker, and after the First World
War, he visited the United States and spent considerable time in
various communities. When he arrived in Cleveland, Samuel
attended his address, which was delivered in Hebrew. Some minutes later the address was concluded in English. It became a stirring
and moving event when Rabbi Abba Hillel Silver, a young man,
and a leader of a classical Reform temple, responded to Ben Avi,
concluding *his* address in Hebrew.

During this time Samuel gave many hours to Hebrew and Zionist activities and organized the first modern Hebrew-speaking circle in Cleveland, Haivri Hatsair ("Hebrew Youth"). The young men and women in the group represented many strata and divisions of opinion within the Jewish community. Some were senior high school students or university and college students, and others were working to earn a livelihood. Yet there were no barriers to attending these periodic Hebrew-speaking meetings. Attendance was excellent and steadily grew to almost unmanageable proportions.

A few years later, Samuel organized the first school for adults that was devoted solely to the study of the Hebrew language. He named it the Tarbut School after the Russian Zionist movement, conceived in St. Petersburg in 1917, which furthered the spread of Jewish and Hebrew education throughout Eastern Europe. Attending the school were some 200 students who came three evenings a week to study the Hebrew language. Among them were a great number who later distinguished themselves in various fields of science, law, the rabbinate, and literature.

In 1929, two years after he entered the rabbinate, Samuel expressed his thoughts on Judaism through nationalism and its finest manifestation, Zionism:

> Without Jewish nationalism, Judaism as we have it today in all of its phases could never have come into being. Judaism is the collective expression of the Jewish people, not of any other people. It is not merely a religion but the Jewish religion. There can be no Judaism without Jews, for it is more than a religion. It includes the sum total of Jewish life and Jewish experience. If all Frenchmen who are Catholics would disappear, Catholicism might have fewer followers but it would remain. If all Norwegians who are Protestants would disappear, Protestantism would remain elsewhere in the world. But can you conceive of Judaism without Jews? . . . I claim that every prophet was first and foremost a Jewish nationalist; that their noble and matchless utterances are a

result of a most exalted love and fervor for their people, —
for their national verities. They never advocated the giving
up of Israel's nationhood for that of the Babylonian,
Assyrian or Egyptian. Their impassioned utterances are
universal because they express that which was intensely
national within the Jewish soul; righteousness, love, mercy
and goodness. . . . We love Eretz-Yisrael [Palestine] because
it is the land where our creative spirit blossoms, bringing to
fruition our greatest and noblest cultural heritage. . . . [it] is
holy because of the promise it holds for the Jew of a new,
free and full life. It is holy because of the glorious Jewish
renaissance nourished by the spirit of the blood and marrow
of our Halutzim. We need it as the great spiritual center so
that we may live as Jews unfettered by physical ghettos and
spiritual prisons. . . . Israel made unperishable contributions
to life and thought of the world through the spoken and
written national language. The products of Israel's creative
power bear the indelible impress of its people's native
genius. Its national literature is that alone which is written
in its national language. . . . Twenty centuries of life in the
diaspora have not stunted the Jewish creative spirit. The
reintegration of Hebraism with its people has given us a
Bialik who expresses the soul of the Jew with a prophetic
voice. In Hebrew we have our greatest wealth, the noblest
of the creation of Israel's genius.

Samuel Wohl, so young in years, looked through timeless eyes
on the perceived redemptive power of the British mandate of
Palestine. Could it transform the Jewish people? He thought so. He
recalled the words of Theodor Herzl as he declared that the nationhood of Israel had never ceased, that the Jews of the entire world
are one people, that Jews and Judaism cannot be separated, and
that, like all peoples, Jews must have a homeland where their
genius, devotion, labors, and sacrifices will create a model land in
accordance with the teachings of the prophets. The people themselves were transformed. They stood proud, motivated, ready to

accomplish the task ahead. The tragedies of Kishinev and the hundreds of violated Jewish communities only intensified their effort.
Samuel repeatedly resisted the view, popular in early Reform
Jewish literature, that Jews are merely a religious denomination
and nothing else.

> We are one people, a unique people, a God centered peo-
> ple which has, out of our experiences in history and our
> heart and mind, evolved a faith in God, justice, mercy and
> love. We have therefore created ideas and ideals that have
> gone beyond the boundaries of Israel and have been
> accorded universal recognition. We are seldom credited for
> giving Universalism to the world. But universalism was not
> born and nurtured in a vacuum. It had to have a soil.
>
> It had to be transmitted by a people. Who were these
> people? The Jews. Where did the prophets give utterance to
> these high ideals? In Palestine. What was Palestine then
> when the prophets and Psalmists taught and spoke? It was
> a Jewish state sometime free, sometimes dominated by a
> conqueror. From whom did these prophets draw their suste-
> nance, their faith, their wisdom and their understanding?
> From their brethren who lived in the kingdom of Judea.

Part III
Cincinnati: Significant Accomplishments, Nobility of Purpose, Rabbinic Modeling

Chapter 9
Ordination and Graduation

L
ate in the summer of 1922, Samuel departed for the Queen City of the West considerably bolstered by a scholarship award granted by Rabbi Silver and the sisterhood at The Temple. This handsome bequest was given each year that he attended Hebrew Union College. However, it was not nearly enough to sustain a married student. In this respect, Samuel considered himself extremely fortunate. As was well known, President Julian Morgenstern and his board did not look on married applicants kindly. Apparently several married students had been accepted in the past and had eventually posed "great difficulties" for the institution. To add insult to injury, Samuel was of East European origin and an ardent Zionist, two factors that predictably generated little enthusiasm in the president and the largely American-born German-Jewish board members. President Morgenstern was at that time firmly opposed to Zionism as a political expedient for American Jews, while the board reflected a rising concern that adherence to Zionism would cast doubts on the loyalty of Jews to America. Dr. Morgenstern's letter to Rabbi Silver explained, in the reserved formalities so typical of that time in academia, that "Mr. Wohl" impressed the committee very favorably and had been accepted for the fall term."

Samuel unhesitatingly alighted from the New York Central passenger car at the tiny Winton Place station in Cincinnati. He quickly surveyed the rather dingy landscape and grimaced inadvertently in response to the aroma of Procter & Gamble's soap-making activities. The Hebrew Union College was only a few minutes

distant by automobile, but Samuel knew that he had to board a
number 47 orange-colored streetcar and transfer to a Clifton-
Hughes bus in order to reach the College. Since he had been
accepted enthusiastically as an advanced student, he had to check
his schedule of courses both at the College and at the University
of Cincinnati, find a temporary small apartment for himself, and
finally, obtain lodgings that would permit Belle to join him.

The relatively new buildings then comprising the Hebrew
Union College were first put on the drawing board in 1903 but
were completed some years afterwards. Samuel mused that Isaac
Mayer Wise, like the proverbial "wandering Jew," had not lived to
see the actual embodiment of his dreams. The College was constructed during the presidential tenure of Kaufmann Kohler, whom
Michael Meyers has termed "the foremost expositor of Jewish
thought in the ranks of Jewish Reform" at that time. Kohler was
named a candidate for president by the Board of Governors and the
parent Union of American Hebrew Congregations (UAHC).

Kohler held that Prophetic Judaism should be established by
flexibility of attitude and intelligent criticism. A deeply religious
man, he perceived the Jews as obliged, despite their international
small numbers, to uplift the nations of the world. Moreover, Meyer
observes, he paternalistically attempted to shape the character and
outlook of his rabbinical students. His accomplishments have
exceptional weight in view of the oft-expressed approval of the
homogeneous German-Jewish Board of Governors and individual
wealthy donors.

After Kohler's retirement, Julian Morgenstern enthusiastically
began his work as the first American-born president of HUC. He
was probably also the first real administrator to lead the college. In
marked contrast to his predecessor, he welcomed all forms of opinion from both faculty and students. He adroitly guided the college
between the rocks of the Zionist dilemma. During the debilitating
Great Depression of the 1930s, he managed to revitalize the curriculum, vigorously added new faculty, and expanded the academic program. Morgenstern was certainly not short on academic credentials (summa cum laude in Semitic languages). He systemati-

cally developed an innovative methodology for applying historical and sociological factors in analyzing biblical texts. Always he stressed the moral and religious message of Israel's historic role.

Julian Morgenstern and Samuel Wohl became close friends, the friendship being ignited, as Morgenstern subsequently recalled, during the hour interview preceding Samuel's acceptance into the college. One may speculate that Morgenstern perceived in Samuel qualities complementary to his own. Slicing through the accumulated personal correspondence of years, it appears that Julian greatly admired Samuel's positive outlook in championing the peoplehood of Israel. By the same token he realized that Samuel could bring creativity and achievement to American Judaism.

Samuel, without guile, proffered his loyalty and friendship, not only to Dr. Morgenstern, but almost to all the distinguished faculty then in residence. This included but was not limited to the scholarly and world-renowned historian Jacob Mann and the witty Israel Bettan. Bettan was an excellent lecturer. From the Midrash and homiletics, he drew modern practical applications for American life.

Abraham Cronbach had been appointed to fill the void in Jewish social studies at HUC. He had more than a few idiosyncrasies, but consistently presented an example of personal commitment and the ability to choose ethically. He was totally nonviolent and possessed unquestionable integrity. Cronbach helped Samuel remember his own early idealism, and Samuel was deeply impressed by the scholar's consistency and the courage of his convictions. Yet he could only shake his head at Cronbach's "naiveté and stubbornness." The professor held rigidly to his faith that good would ultimately triumph. He often opposed needed social and political change.

Samuel S. Cohon was appointed professor of theology in 1923. Students and faculty alike respected his encyclopedic knowledge of Judaism. He was to have an extraordinary impact on the development of Reform Judaism through his scholarship and by cogently conceptualizing future goals and directions for the Central Conference of American Rabbis, Reform Judaism's governing

body. Professor Jakob Petuchowski refers to him as "in his day, *the*
Jewish theologian on the American scene." Cohon edited a new
revision of the *Union Prayer Book* that was widely acclaimed.
Samuel and he developed a deep and lasting friendship, based on
their mutual appreciation of modern Hebrew, their modern view of
the role of tradition in Jewish worship, and above all, their conception of the fusion of religion and peoplehood. Cohon was an
avid book collector, and we are sure that much of Samuel's later
collecting was at least stimulated by several "significant finds" for
Professor Cohon.

The faculty continued to expand with the addition of Sheldon
Blank, instructor in Hebrew and Bible, and Jacob R. Marcus, who
had been an instructor during the Kohler years, and had obtained
a doctorate in Berlin. Dr. Marcus was appointed assistant professor
of Jewish history and in time narrowed his interests to American
Jewish history, an area in which he was generally regarded as the
world's outstanding authority. Samuel enjoyed associating with
both of these young men, appreciated their excellent but quite dissimilar humorous remarks, and consulted frequently with them in
subsequent years.

Solomon Freehof was ordained in 1915 and immediately
became an instructor at the college. Michael Meyer depicts him as
"a broad, but focused, scholar." He continued the work of Jacob
Lauterbach in attempting to maintain the traditional and legal
(halakhic) support of Reform Jewish practice. Freehof left to join
the active rabbinate in 1924, and with his formidable intellect,
searching wry humor, and scholarly prominence, quickly became
one of America's outstanding Reform rabbis. He persisted in his
interests, centered on the interrelation of halakhic tradition in current Reform Jewish practice. His responsa are uniquely scholarly
and profound. Freehof more or less befriended Samuel, and the two
men recall in their correspondence their many walks up and down
Clifton Avenue discussing all manner of "pretentious subjects."
Slightly older in years and quite experienced in the rigors of HUC,
he was able to counsel Samuel regarding the academic challenges
ahead and the comparative idiosyncrasies of his future professors.

Under Morgenstern the faculty of Hebrew Union College became a precisely functioning system within the overall rubric of the Reform movement's educational needs. Meyer refers to them as "well balanced," but even by today's standards, they must be considered a truly outstanding group of scholars and teachers, favorably comparing with the theological luminaries of other religions.

As an aside, one of the authors (Ted) can remember his brother Amiel, then (1950) a student at the college, urging our father to compare the faculty of his day with the current teaching staff. Samuel cautiously noted that it would be inaccurate to give a single label to either group, continued diplomatically to describe the strengths and weaknesses of *any* group in academia, and concluded, with the inevitable bias of the old grad, that today's HUC's professors relied too much on their teaching methodology and might even be viewed as martinets in their adherence to discipline, study, and assignments. On the other hand, the faculty of the 1920s were far more inspirational, persuading their students by consistent example, thereby facilitating the effect of a rabbinic role model.

Other elements cementing the bond between Samuel and his friends among the faculty were the strengths and personas of their wives and the outstanding ability of their high-achieving children. Indeed, these ladies were far more than a support for their husbands. It is regrettable that limited space prevents us from even minimal consideration of their lives.

The students at HUC had to find lodgings in the surrounding community. All but Samuel were bachelors, and they seemed to respect him immediately because of his "special student" status (he was excused from certain course requirements) and because he was (gasp!) married. He secured a small apartment on Eden Avenue near the large General Hospital and then moved to a more comfortable apartment ("Glencoe") amidst the red-brick burgher-built buildings of Corryville. Several years passed rapidly, and Samuel considered himself to be fully challenged by the academic menu presented to him by the university and HUC.

Meanwhile, Belle very quickly sought and obtained employment in the B'nai B'rith office, directed by Boris Bogen, whose title

at the time was superintendent of the Cincinnati United Jewish
Charities and School of Jewish Social Agencies. Dr. Bogen also
taught several courses in sociology and Jewish philanthropic organizations. He hired Belle as a general secretary with a significant
amount of time devoted to the translation of foreign (German,
French, Spanish, and Yiddish) correspondence. She was to hold
this job for three years until she resigned in the face of impending
motherhood and her husband's first post after ordination.

Despite the pressures to surmount each academic hurdle as
quickly as possible, Samuel acquired a command and a true love of
contemporary and past great German writers. He found himself
enthralled by his courses in philosophy and English. However, his
smooth-sailing craft foundered on the rocks of scientific zoology,
where he admitted ruefully that the laboratory requirements were
repulsive and almost beyond his ability to cope. Laboratory science
was a general category that lay far beyond his experience. He found
it extremely difficult to shackle his imagination and thought
processes to the revolving capstan of experimental method and
procedure. Despite this he persevered and survived with generally
acceptable results.

During this period, the age and educational level of HUC's students steadily progressed upward. Most of the students at this time
were children of Russian-born immigrants. They were allowed
almost complete intellectual freedom, but were also expected to
conform to a certain code of appropriate social behavior. Some of
the professors insisted on conventional attire (neckties and jack-
ets). Miss Cora Kahn stated in well-enunciated words that proper
appearance and manners were necessary and (years before
McLuhan) that "the medium is the message."

For whatever reason, if a young man wished to enter the
American rabbinate, his acceptance by the Hebrew Union College
of Cincinnati almost guaranteed an increase of stress.

Dr. Morgenstern was much more permissive of individuals and
ideas than his predecessor, Kaufmann Kohler. During his tenure,
more than half of the Board of Governors, the wealthy German
Jews who supported the institution, and the majority of the facul-

ty were of non-Zionist persuasion, viewed traditional observances as considerably less than eternal verities, and were generally supportive of a "critical Judaism." Those students of East European immigrant stock who managed to persevere and who maintained their earlier familial orientation often encountered stress when attempting simultaneously to lead and adjust to their first congregations. There was a certain temptation to become militant in activist causes. For example, there was an increasing segment of the student body, and even a few faculty, who had Zionist sympathies or convictions.

Samuel, however, concentrated only on the attainment of knowledge, clearing the barriers to ordination, and pursuing well-conceived goals and ideals in his typical enthusiastic fashion. Both Zionism and American Jewish theological development, since the time of Kohler, had emerged into the light. We can debate whether Samuel's presence significantly accelerated the change in perspective toward a Jewish homeland, but the steady growth of the Zionist movement allowed him to assert his ideas freely and further educate both faculty and students. A majority of the students viewed him as more mature, somewhat older in years, and almost infinitely better grounded in Jewish concepts and lore than they. His idealism and strength of conviction impressed everyone who knew him. He was elected chairman of several student committees, culminating with the presidency of the student body in 1926–27.

Life was hectic, but Samuel availed himself of opportunities to introduce diversity into his training. During two successive summers, he attended the University of Chicago's prestigious divinity school. Later, as HUC student president, he was instrumental in arranging a program of exchange lectures with the same institution. Samuel was later to draw upon this source of liberal religious thought by inviting many of its distinguished faculty for lectures and workshops. As chairman of HUC's literary society, he compiled a formidable dossier of speakers and ideas to serve as programs for the HUC students and faculty. Some forty years later, several of his colleagues wrote to us about their sense of awe as they listened to a reading by the great Hebrew poet Chaim Nachman Bialik.

Samuel's determination to solidify his scholarship and his ubiquitous concern with the personal hurdles standing in the way of ordination did not, of course, blind him to the world without. He continued to participate in and contribute to causes. In a letter written to the president of the National Student Federation of the University of Cincinnati:

> I am directed by the student body of the Hebrew Union College to solicit your kind offices in support of a movement of protest against the atrocities in Romania committed against the Jewish people and especially against the Jewish students. . . . Important organizations in our land have sent resolutions of protest to our State Department. . . . I feel that a protest in the name of the National Students Federation would be very helpful and effective. . . . I shall try to get in touch with you during the week and arrange for a conference to discuss this matter in more detail.

Actually, this makes one mindful of Samuel's sensitivity and militant attempts to alleviate Jewish suffering all over the world.

Morgenstern strove to create a modern and systematic institution of higher Jewish learning. However, his major interests were colored by his focus on biblical research. The student body perceived a laissez-faire vacuum in which the stress of academic requirements and expectations clashed with professional needs vital to functioning in a temple pulpit and the necessity of obtaining the experiences and insights of rabbis and leaders in the community. In Samuel's day, this need only was partially served by participating in bi-weekly placements where students would serve very small or rural congregations throughout the Midwest.

Shortly after his arrival in Cincinnati, Samuel was shocked to receive a letter from Dr. Morgenstern informing him that he had been appointed to conduct services for the High Holy Days at Sault Ste. Marie in northern Michigan. There were no positions nearer Cincinnati at the time and apparently no prospect that any vacancies might occur. Mercifully, Samuel was soon recruited by the Ione Jewish congregation in Portsmouth, Ohio, and, by the end of 1926 he was commuting there every week. He was dragged roughshod over the coals of congregational controversies and emerged unscathed, so to speak.

The congregation was on the brink of disintegrating under stress and disunity. The many factions could not develop a sense of purpose or direction. Samuel quickly reorganized the "Sabbath School" and apparently created a consuming interest in Jewish education while opening lines of communication with the volunteer teachers and parents. His sermons compelled listeners to think while educating them and providing a role for emulation. One of his congregants, a reporter for the *Portsmouth Morning Sun*, felt that the young man's message needed wider circulation than it could possibly receive "within those four walls." Thus the Portsmouth pulpit became much more than a typical "bi-weekly," and the trauma of final separation was mutually wrenching both to Samuel and the congregation.

Before his ordination, the student rabbi was approached by a committee of three Cincinnatians: Charles Schaengold, I. E. ("Ike") Levine, and Nathan I. Fleischer, who were the first to talk directly with Samuel about the pulpit at the Reading Road Temple in Cincinnati. The Portsmouth experience was actually the beginning of his professional life of service.

Samuel was in a not unpleasant quandary regarding future career goals within the ministry. A close friend, Abram Sachar (later to be a renowned historian and founder-president of Brandeis University), was attempting to interest him in Hillel Foundation work in the college town of Champaign, the site of the University of Illinois. Almost light-heartedly, Samuel wrote another friend, Beryl Cohon (then a respected rabbi in Pensacola, Florida, and Professor Samuel Cohon's older brother), asking for the "fruit of your wisdom." Rabbi Cohon's response was both entertaining and insightful in the manner of Mark Twain.

Advice is cheap, but I am learning that it is extremely dangerous.

Don't let anybody advise you too earnestly; advise yourself. But this too is advice. . . .

If you want to be a preacher, and I am using this evan-
gelistic term deliberately because (from my years of experience) I have found out that we are not rabbis—we are just
kidding ourselves when we say that—but preachers,
magidim, then go into the pulpit; if you want to be an organizer and fuss with fraternity-sorority politics, and be a
macher [important personage], and talk in all the sophistries
of the day with a lot of bombast, then go into Hillel work.
I cannot back up these views . . . I [only] have a notion. . .
. As for the pulpit, if you can preach a decent sermon, and
forget all the homiletic tricks, and if you have some insight
into the stuff of which life is spun, and are willing to forget
most of what has been preached at you at College—then
the pulpit is the place for you. You will have to get yourself
a good book on logic, disabuse your mind of most of the
academic stuff contained in your system, and learn to look
at life with clear intelligent eyes. That's all you need. I'm
becoming convinced that most of us fail as preachers
because we fail to grab life by the roots and talk straight.
Most of us are either too dull for that or too stuffed with
dead theologies.

It is worth mentioning that Dr. Cohon became the founding
rabbi of a dynamic congregation in Brookline, Massachusetts. He
began to write prolifically, succeeding in lightening up the "dead
theologies" mentioned above, and, in fact, was greatly in demand
on college campuses throughout New England for years, holding
positions on the faculties of Boston and Tufts universities.

Samuel had already, in fact, decided to accept the position
offered by the Reading Road Temple. One could speculate that this
decision had actually been made five years earlier during his fate-
ful discussion with Belle.

As Julian Morgenstern laid the hands of consecration upon
Samuel's head during the ordination ceremony, he was ordaining

not only a rabbi but a recent father. Letters of congratulations glowingly referred to the new rabbi in Israel and the birth of a healthy baby boy, Theodore Herzl Wohl. For months, in anticipation of this event, the young couple had referred to approaching events as Belle's "graduation." Samuel subsequently described her graduation as "magna cum laude."

Chapter 10
Early Ministry

The Reading Road Temple was eager to obtain the services of the energetic young rabbi, and Samuel could barely restrain his eagerness to begin his ministry. His congregation had been organized by German Jews in the West Side basin of the city in 1847 and was originally Orthodox. The membership of the congregation increased rapidly, and in keeping with this its buildings became larger. Over the decades the congregation evolved through several mergers and spurts of growth. At the same time, the proselytizing spirit of Dr. Wise had induced an irrevocable move toward Reform observances. Finally the Reading Road Temple, more properly Ahabath Achim–Sherith Israel, moved out of the city's West End to a new location on Reading Road in the South Avondale section of the city.

The leadership of the congregation viewed Samuel as a leader who could revitalize the temple, give its members a sense of purpose, and, with a firm hand on the helm, guide the craft between the perils of ennui and indifference. Letters sent to congregational members stressed the need to welcome the new rabbi and "support his work." The curve of new member applications surged suddenly upward. Almost in anticipation of his first officiating event, Saturday morning, May 7, three days after the birth of his first child, Samuel received a letter from his perambulating good friend, Arthur Reinhart, soon to become executive director of the National Federation of Temple Brotherhoods, and typical of a cadre of unaffiliated young men. Reinhart declared, "You can count on

[me], and you, as [its] rabbi, may know that you will have at least one person who will work with you whenever he is in town."

Enthusiasm and interest grew to heightened levels by November of the same year, when installation services for Rabbi Wohl were held at the Reading Road Temple. Samuel himself played a somewhat limited role, sharing the principle "address" on Friday evening and giving a special prayer during the Saturday morning service. The general order of the service was conducted by Drs. Jacob Marcus and Abraham Cronbach, there were special messages and addresses by Dr. Julian Morgenstern and Professor Samuel Cohon, and Dr. David Philipson, honorary "dean of the Reform rabbinate," delivered the major installation sermon. Professor A. Z. Idelsohn, noted musicologist and professor at the Hebrew Union College, wrote and organized the music for the services. The president of the congregation, Sidney Weil, was the only lay participant in the services. More will be said about Sidney a little later in this narrative.

"A Festival of Joy" was the apt topic of Samuel's sermon, given on the first day of Succoth, the Harvest Festival, in early October. The sisterhood of the Temple erected a succah for the first time, beautifully decorated with flowers in celebration of the occasion. This was only a continuation of the solemn High Holy Days, when record numbers had attended the Rosh Hashana and Yom Kippur services. Over 1,000 people attended each evening and morning service. This was viewed as a remarkable attendance in consideration of the congregation's size and Cincinnati's total Jewish population, which was probably only slightly above 20,000 souls. At least it was a rousing welcome for Samuel, and thus his first High Holy Day officiation confirmed to the congregational leadership that they had chosen wisely.

Samuel was pleased by the reception he was given. He commenced to inspire and to widen the horizons of his congregation, much as he would later (in the words of Dr. Marcus) "work to widen the horizons of American Reform Judaism." He searched assiduously for new directions and new applications while at the same time emphasizing the solidity and beauty of Israel's heritage traced back before the dawn of recorded history.

Samuel understood what we have already termed the basic sterility of Reform Jewish life, however intellectually pretentious it may have been. Just a few months after his ordination, in keeping with this understanding, he created the beautiful consecration service, which he linked to the venerable Hakofos ceremony, commemorating the transmission of the Torah over the generations. Samuel's instinct for drama produced a Succoth service that not only imprinted itself on the minds of five-year-old children but, of equal importance, stirred the emotions of their parents. Major congregations like Temple Emanu-El in San Francisco and Brickner's Euclid Avenue Temple in Cleveland adopted it eagerly, following Samuel's original outline completely:

I. Entire school marches in a processional into the temple, bearing fruits and flowers while the choir sings appropriate Succoth music. Special shelves, from the floor to the elevation of the pulpit are built, so the entire length of the pulpit is covered with harvest fruit and flowers.

II. A number of (brief) recitations and addresses are given by members of the religious school classes interspersed with hymns.

III. Three sets, consisting of a grandfather, his son and his son's son ascend the pulpit. . . . president of the congregation hands one Torah to the first grandfather, who in turn hands it to his son and he hands it to his son (etc.) . . . and a third Torah is handed to the grandfather who keeps it for himself. This is done with three sets of grandfathers, fathers and sons. The last Torah is handed to the rabbi, altogether making ten Torahs. The choir sings Hakafoth music.

The three sets . . . descend from the pulpit, one set walks up the right aisle [of Plum Street Temple], the second . . . the left aisle, and the third, led by the rabbi, the center aisle. Those in the two side aisles join the center aisle, walk down single file and return to the pulpit, where they form a semi-circle holding their Torahs.

Then:

IV. The little kindergarten [consecrants] march, clad in white, in a processional (two by two) and ascend the pulpit. The little ones [then] recite in Hebrew and English "Torah tzeeva lanu Moshe" ("The Torah as given to us by Moses"). Then the rabbi places himself in front of the Ark (facing the congregation and the children, two by two, step forward and the rabbi consecrates them . . . walking back. . . . Violin and alto solo is played during the consecration service.

Samuel's first venture proved strikingly successful, and the new ceremony was adopted by his own congregation and also by the nationwide Reform and Conservative movements. It is today a moving annual event, much welcomed and anticipated.

In the autumn of 1930, Samuel developed a lively and informative forum series, no doubt inspired to some degree by what he had experienced in Cleveland. Lay and religious lecturers of national renown discussed interesting subjects before large audiences and replied to questions in lively fashion. Important and prestigious people from the community often presided over these meetings, adding their own opinions and ultimately enthusiastically supporting the series throughout the Cincinnati area. The forum's visibility was such that nationally renowned organizations and individuals took the initiative in contacting Samuel in order to participate. Everett R. Clinchy, founding director of the National Conference of Jews and Christians, wrote requesting a conference in Cincinnati to "talk over your forum series and the possibility of a symposium in Cincinnati." These plans came to fruition the following year and proved highly successful.

Still another significant enterprise was launched. Sarna and Klein note the emerging paradox of the economic acceptance and social rejection of American Jewry during the early and middle seg-

ments of the twentieth century. Even today, this remains a disturbing factor influencing the total adjustment of Jews to their social
environment. The country's economic pulse began to quicken
uncontrollably as the decade of the twenties came to a close. Anti-
Semitic thinking and behavior virulently affected public attitudes.
The use of stereotypic jokes and labels increased exponentially.

All of this led Samuel to introduce the Institute on Judaism for
the Christian Clergy. The purpose here was to educate and not
offer banal apologies. He believed strongly that Christian religious
leaders would leave with new respect for Judaism and possibly with
a will, verbally at least, to support it within the rubric of their individual congregations and national denominational associations.
The project proved so successful that it was adapted by the Union
of American Hebrew Congregations. It is today present in various
replicated forms all over the country.

Samuel was quick to point out that Reform Judaism, since the
time of Isaac Mayer Wise, had always confronted the country's
majority population with confident hope and an outstretched
hand. In the Cincinnati area, Rabbis Max Lilienthal, David
Philipson in the early twenties, and Samuel's future colleague,
James G. Heller, had actively collaborated with ministerial groups
and stressed the importance of appropriate communication with
the gentile world.

Samuel's successes were not lost on the Cleveland triumvirate
of mentor rabbis. However, Rabbi Goldman was soon to leave for
more challenging and equally contentious fields of battle, nor did
he have much access to developments within the Reform Jewish
community. Silver and Brickner, despite their mutual antipathy,
both maintained close and friendly contact with Samuel. Silver
was to enlist Samuel's aid in several national/international political projects, while Brickner's continuing association seemed at
least partially based on his ever present collegial spirit and open-
ness to new ideas. We have noted that Brickner was among the
first to adopt the consecration ceremony, thereby giving it added
rationale and impetus.

The congregation, too, under the leadership of Sidney Weil, offered continual support and augmented the progress already made by such public relations successes as "Ask the Rabbi," held at the Cincinnati Club. Samuel, seated in a large room, held court, facilitated discussions and responded to any questions or opinions rendered by the attendees. All of this was garnished by "suitable refreshments."

Sidney and Florence Weil were exceptional people in their own right and were typically representative of the congregational support and loyalty experienced by Samuel during the early years of his tenure at the Reading Road Temple and subsequently, after its unification with the Plum Street Temple. Cincinnati-born Sidney had literally been a horse trader early in his life and through his First World War army days, and remained one figuratively throughout the rest of his life as an astute businessman and communal leader. Not surprisingly, he had abundant "horse sense" but only a fourth-grade education. His early childhood in an extended German-American family had firmly grounded him in traditional Jewish observances but also provided the flexibility needed to conquer the streets of Cincinnati's West End with decision-making business acumen, monumental stubbornness, and determination. No amount of gruffness could conceal the kindness and compassion extended to his own family, his congregation, his people, and many friends and admirers.

Shortly after the end of World War I, Sidney both charmed and swept away his Charleston, West Virginia, bride-to-be, Florence Levy. The gentle and gracious Florence was the legal secretary of Congressman Littlepage of the U.S. House of Representatives.

Sidney used the 1920s as a staging ground for the first of several fortunes that he was to attain and lose. Early in that period, he became the general agent for Ford, and subsequently acquired a controlling interest in banks, garages, cleaners, and other business establishments in the Cincinnati area. He was inevitably drawn into the vortex of speculative excess that culminated in the stock market crash of 1929. Rising from the nationwide debacle, he took on new projects and managed to rebuild his fortune through the insurance industry.

One of Sidney's noteworthy early projects was his ownership of the Cincinnati Reds baseball team. He was probably the first Jewish owner in professional baseball. Loving the game passionately, he was respected by fans and players alike, but the times were not conducive, and Sidney surrendered the club five years later. Nonetheless, he remained enthusiastic about this peculiarly American sport. Indeed, it was the only sport to claim his interest continually. He understood the spectacle and drama occurring both on the playing field and in the stands. Seated in the Weil box, he was surrounded by friends who were more than eager to explain the many aspects of the game.

Samuel benefited greatly from his friendship with Sidney and with most of the succeeding congregational presidents. They were a conduit to the faithful and, at the same time, forceful men of vision usually knowledgeable in the martial arts of congregational politics. Sidney's son Irwin inexplicably asserted and perhaps emancipated himself by entering the academic world as a Slavic (Russian) expert. Much earlier, however, he and his wife-to-be, Vivian Max Weil, were outstanding representatives of the next generation of bright and involved congregational youths reaching for Jewish purpose and simultaneously reshaping and reconceptualizing what their eager minds had captured.

Irwin was the source of many perceptive opinions regarding "Rabbi Wohl." In a recently completed unpublished biography of his father, he notes that "Rabbi Wohl soon felt the helping hand of his new friend in many different practical sides of life. . . . Above all he . . . valued the life force and sometimes child-like aspect of Sidney."

As their relationship progressed, these two men, so dissimilar in many ways, proved catalytic to the Isaac M. Wise Temple and the development of Cincinnati's Jewish community.

Chapter 11
A Major Merger, Cincinnati
Developments, Jewish Arrivals

I t was not until June of 1931 that the Plum Street and Reading Road temples responded to the favorable recommendations of their committees and almost unanimously ratified an agreement to merge their respective congregations. The fused congregations were to be known as the Isaac M. Wise Temple. Rabbi Samuel Wohl at the Reading Road Temple and Rabbi James G. Heller of the Plum Street Temple were to jointly to serve the institution. Efforts to sell the Reading Road Temple were begun, and meanwhile the congregation continued to utilize both major buildings as well as a newly constructed award-winning modern structure located at North Crescent and Reading Road in Avondale.

The amalgamated Isaac M. Wise Temple had a total membership of approximately 900 families, or more than 3,500 persons. The religious school attained an enrollment of approximately 650 children. Rabbis Wohl and Heller announced that the two congregations desired to broaden their scope of activities and enlarge their fields of service. Presidents Sidney Weil of the Reading Road Temple and Louis Ullman of the Plum Street Temple were widely quoted in all three Cincinnati daily newspapers as they spelled out the essential similarities in composition, goals, and function of the two previously independent congregations.

Samuel found that events were moving almost too quickly. The evening after the announcement he and Belle hosted an informal celebration at their Cleveland Avenue home for members of both boards, the committees, and their rabbis. The very next morning he was due to leave on a long-planned international foray, principally involving the countries of Central and Eastern Europe. These events constituted a meaningful and symbolic means of marking the beginning of increased contribution and activity. His ideas, past and present, coalesced into principles, hopes, and dreams for local, national, and international concerns. This journey was to be the first of many such quests where he was to develop expertise in Jewish and global events and issues. He became an admired authority through his travel and personal encounters. It seems to us that he embodied the true responsibility of a Jewish leader—the need to actually know.

In later years, Samuel was to serve as a columnist and community expert. When it came to contemporary Jewish affairs, there were few as conversant and articulate as he. However, before describing his first major journey and considering his ideas and achievements in depth, we will once again pause and introduce the Isaac M. Wise Temple congregation, the Cincinnati Jewish community, several background facets of Cincinnati itself, and several groups of clergy, Jewish and Christian, that proved to be nodal points as he pursued his goals as rabbi and Jewish communal leader.

We have described Cincinnati as largely homogenous and heavily settled by Germans, mainly from Bavaria. Soon after its founding, the city extended several miles into the neighboring hills, and, with its position on a mighty river, continued to be visually pleasing to the discriminating traveler. Located at the congruence of three states, Kentucky, Indiana, and Ohio, Cincinnati expectedly was the beneficiary of major inland waterway commerce via a web of canals that could transfer goods to major distribution cities on the Great Lakes. Very early in its existence, the city drew economic sustenance mostly from the exchange of various commodities from the Southeast and West whereas the second half of the nineteenth century witnessed the rapid growth of railroads and the development of diversified light and heavy industry.

In contrast to many Midwestern communities, Cincinnati seemed to be built chiefly of red brick, giving a sense of solidity and complementing the stereotype of the industrious, conservative

German worker and businessman. In 1788, when Cincinnati, then "Losantiville," had been a collection of rude log cabins, it was accurately depicted as a brawling river town with an astronomical number of saloons and a wide-open red-light district. Imitating Chicago, hog butchering caused the feeder canals to become deeply tinted with blood; the canal beds much later became the sites of major highway construction.

Until about 1870, Cincinnati's population exceeded Chicago's, and it led all other Midwestern cities, to quote James Heller, in "making amazing strides in population and establishing a life in which culture side by side with industry might prevail." At the turn of the century, however, the river traffic rapidly declined. Chicago and other Midwestern cities, fed by rail lines and absorbing wave upon wave of immigration from Southern and Eastern Europe, became major distribution points for goods.

These trends notwithstanding, Cincinnati became and continues to be "more than just another Midwestern city." It is generally and broadly cosmopolitan and retains remarkable stability in times of economic turmoil. Despite its conservative traditions, it has been innovative and even progressive in political and governance matters, proportional-representation voting, and so on. It is a "major league" mecca for a broad spectrum of activities, such as art museums, a major symphony, and professional sports and amusement parks.

The first permanent Jewish settler in Cincinnati, an English Jew by the name of Joseph Jonas, arrived in 1817 and established a business as one of the city's 6,000 inhabitants. In the succeeding years, 1820 to 1870, German Jews appeared in greater numbers. Sarna notes that even then there was a "promised land" vision among the early Cincinnati Jewish community. He notes that Cincinnati appeared to be a shining vision on the "American frontier" where Jews could settle as citizens, succeed economically, practice their religion freely, and coexist happily on equal terms with their Christian neighbors. This was perhaps the real "American dream" that caused people to endure inconceivable hardships to reach their destination.

Starting as itinerant peddlers, the Jewish settlers, half of whom were from Bavaria, became successful and quite influential citizens with phenomenal ease. By 1860 they were involved in many other occupations. They came to dominate the distribution and sales of men's clothing and had strong representation in dry goods, liquor, and, of course, Fleischmann's yeast. By 1931 Jews were also very well represented in the professions and were disproportionally represented as white-collar workers in the clothing trades, and in real estate, pawnbrokerages, and large department stores. They were highly visible in the city's insurance businesses and were on numerous banking and civic boards. Sarna maintains that they were well integrated in the city's economic structure as a whole.

The philanthropies of Cincinnati's Jews, directed toward both Jewish and general causes, became legendary. Numerous Jews were very similar to Julius Freiberg, who was elected an "honorary member" of the Chamber of Commerce—the highest honor it could bestow. He was praised in death for his "cosmopolitan citizenship . . . ever ready to serve the best interests of the municipality, supporting liberally every measure for the advancement and improvement of the settlers of his city."

Jewish philanthropists, in their support of Jewish and non-Jewish causes, were not content to simply help the deserving poor. They reformed, honed, and improved delivery systems. The immigrant community's health, welfare, and happiness were their constant preoccupation. Membership on the Cincinnati Board of Education led to exemplary achievements for public education and influenced practices to an extent belying the small number of Jews in the general population. A watershed event was the enactment of a new city charter in 1924 heralding what might be called the beginning of "good government." Jews threw their support behind their own Murray Seasongood, whose Charter Party ended county corruption and provided a positive program for local government.

The Jewish presence in Cincinnati preceded their arrival in Cleveland. However, the similarities between the two cities were quite striking. Jewish settlement in the basin of the downtown area of Cincinnati first centered in what were later known as the West

End and "Over the Rhine" districts. The Jews were largely Germans from Bavaria. They were joined after the 1880s by Romanian, Polish, and Russian Jews who congregated according to their country of origin. The newer arrivals were, of course, Orthodox and generally poverty stricken. They brought with them the entire bundle of ethnic strengths and weaknesses that had been their heritage for the last several hundred years. As in Cleveland, they were helped and patronized by the already Americanized German-Jewish groups, and they strongly resisted pressure to Americanize as fast as possible.

The German Jews led the migration to the then independent suburb of Avondale, which became the center of Jewish life until the mid-1950s. Wealthy German Jews maintained a rather homogenous enclave in the northern sections of the area, while the East Europeans gradually worked their way north along Reading Road, becoming a solid group in the southern and central areas of Avondale. A small group of Turkish Jews, more commonly referred to as Sephardim, arrived in Cincinnati around the turn of the century and chose to settle in the western section of the city, effectively cut off from their co-religionists. Their religious observances and customs were significantly unique and had very little in common with those of the other Jewish groups in Cincinnati. Hence they found themselves isolated and had very little communication with their co-religionists.

It was inevitable that tensions and divisions would occur between the German and East European groups. Polk Laffoon IV points out correctly that Fleischmann's yeast and gin, Fechheimer's shoes, and Friedlander clothes were widely distributed. The German Jews maintained a patronizing attitude and clearly regarded the new immigrants as "foreigners" and dependent. Most of the social distinctions were soon to break down. This was accelerated by the Second World War, following which East European Jews became wealthier as the second- and third-generation children of immigrants strove successfully to realize their share of the national destiny.

The German Jews interacted freely with the gentile community. Largely of Reform persuasion, their services were in English and, stripped of ancient traditions and liturgies, seemed abbreviated and sterile. By the same token, they clung to their Jewish identity, contributed and worked for community arts and institutions, and founded or helped to found most of the area's important social agencies. They were hostile or indifferent to Zionism, emphasizing that Judaism was a religion and that other elements of the Jewish ethos were outmoded or no longer needed.

The East Europeans, poor and preoccupied with the struggle for survival, tended to identify with traditional religious precepts. In 1927 their religious observances were underattended, and there seemed to be little sense of community within this 80 percent of the total Jewish community.

It seems to us, some sixty-five years later, that Cincinnati's Jewish community is no longer schismatic in terms of identification with the State of Israel, cultural-ethical identity, or even religious beliefs. The East European Jews have not only assumed positions of leadership in civic and communal affairs, but also have infused their idealism and vitality within the Reform movement and its congregations, where they are undoubtedly now a statistical majority.

Samuel always felt that the community's rabbinic leadership should be credited with having steadily improved the German and East European Jewish rapprochement while at the same time diligently creating communication and mutual respect with the gentile majority. The particulars of these achievements will be easily grasped from our account, in the next chapter, of the Plum Street Temple and the Cincinnati clergy of the 1930s and 1940s. These Jewish and gentile leaders had a major impact throughout the Cincinnati area and especially on its Jewish community. They constituted a critical mass, so to speak, with whom Samuel found communication, understanding, and empathy.

Chapter 12
Bricks, Mortar, and Leadership

As the pedestrian approaches the intersection of Eighth and Plum Streets in Cincinnati, his or her discerning eye is greeted by a soft skyline interstitching of towers, spires, and horizontal planes. Crouched protectively in the foreground is a Scotch Presbyterian church built of rough-hewn stone. The imposing Romanesque City Hall building, which quite broadly represents our civil liberties and the secularism of a major city, stands on the northwestern corner. Across the street on the southwestern corner stands the graceful Greek Revivalist St. Peter in Chains. Constructed within the last century, this was and again today is the archbishop's cathedral, that is, archdiocesan headquarters. If we turn once again toward the southeastern corner of the intersection, and here we must quote from the *Israelite* of 1869, "There stands the gorgeous temple of K.K. B'nai Yeshurun, a monument to 3,000 years of history, pointing heavenward with its two minarets, Boaz and Joachim, nodding compliance to the emblem of liberty and the progress of humanity."

The Plum Street Temple was opened to the public and dedicated in 1866. James Keyes Wilson was a prominent architect and the first president of the Cincinnati chapter of the American Institute of Architects. He collaborated closely with Rabbi Wise and, over a five-year span, completed a majestic structure that was to serve its congregation well and the total Cincinnati community.

Many descriptions of the temple note that its physical appearance has changed very little over the years. The original most

81

excellent organ was in use until relatively recently, and the original chandeliers and candelabras are still present. Although there is ongoing disagreement as to whether the complex design of the temple reflects primarily Moorish or Gothic elements, the exterior, with its two minarets rising 50 feet above the roof, suggests the "golden age" of Moorish Spain. Merkel points out that it is the interior abstract decorations emerging from the eclectic mix which should claim the public's admiration. Simonson, a renowned German-Jewish architect of the nineteenth century, called attention to the flowering of Judaic culture in Muslim Spain during the Middle Ages, thereby inspiring the construction of several "Moorish" synagogues in Germany.

Lewis Kamrass, the youngest elected senior rabbi in Yeshurun's history, confirmed Simonson's view in a statement quoted in an *American Israelite* article. Kamrass opined that the decision to build the temple had great symbolic importance. "The temple was Wise's prophetic statement of faith that America would provide a golden age for American Jewry. Imagine the optimism, vision, almost sheer audacity to build a building like that." Kamrass added that the temple has served the community continuously, providing thousands of congregants over many years with a strong sense of personal identification.

There are, indeed, families that have celebrated several generations of bar mitzvahs, weddings, High Holy Day attendance, and other meaningful ceremonies and events in the same pews. We have already referred to the temple with mild levity as the "Mother Church of Reform Judaism." The *American Israelite*'s term, "wellspring," is more accurate. Rabbi Isaac Mayer Wise used his pulpit as a sounding board and presided over the founding of Reform Judaism's Central Conference of American Rabbis, the Union of American Hebrew Congregations, and the Hebrew Union College. It is from this pulpit, too, that Wise, sometimes by simple fiat, introduced ritual and custom changes that immediately and significantly affected the way many American Jews practiced their religion. Every year the combined Hebrew Union College and

Jewish Institute of Religion ordination of Reform rabbis is held at the Plum Street Temple.

Mr. Joseph Stern, Jr., a former congregational president, spoke movingly of an experience that was common to almost all of the temple's congregational children. He told how he sat with his grandfather in their reserved pew, counting the hundreds of lights or only those that were burned out. "The pew that my great grand-father owned—I still sit in it. I won't sit in any other pew. I'm not religious, but when I'm in the Plum Street Temple, I feel at ease with the world," he said. Nevertheless, another board member was overheard telling a representative of the Union of American Hebrew Congregations that "the temple is a millstone around the neck of the congregation."

Well before the turn of the century, increasing numbers of the congregation began their move to the suburbs. Even the Isaac M. Wise Center, on Reading Road in South Avondale, proved only to be a temporary solution. Eventually, the "new" Isaac M. Wise Temple Center was dedicated in 1927. A striking building, it was given the annual award of the architects of Cincinnati. The "Wise Center," as it was called, became, even more than formerly, the working muscle and sinew of the congregation.

The Plum Street Temple was now used at most seven or eight times a year and underwent two major renovations, in 1950 and 1974. After 1974, the temple was maintained on a "patchwork" basis. Rabbi Alan Fuchs, Rabbi Albert Goldman's successor, after consulting the past congregational presidents, formed a group to ensure the survival of the Plum Street Temple building. Joseph Stern, a captain of industry and participant in an almost unbeliev-able number of general civic and Jewish projects, became the mov-ing force behind "Friends of the Plum Street Temple" in 1983. David Joseph, Harris Weston, Edward Saeks, Stanley Chesley, and others successfully raised an endowment fund to help preserve the temple. James Magrish, a brilliant attorney, even earlier had uti-lized his congregational presidency to elicit concern regarding the physical condition of the temple. He was also the power behind

obtaining a national historical landmark designation for the building. Herbert Bloch and Robert Goldman, Isadore Berman and
Sidney Weil were all presidents of the congregation who assumed
major roles in the furtherance of the temple. Stern reminisced with
unfeigned horror, "When they [congregational members] talked of
tearing it [the temple] down, it was as if they drove a stake through
my heart."

Joseph Stern is a blunt and candid person who does not mind
expressing his feelings. His three-word summation of Samuel Wohl
was, "a real pastor." Along with all the interviewed congregational
presidents, he was extremely supportive and favorably disposed
toward Samuel Wohl. Therefore, when Samuel joined James G.
Heller as co-senior rabbi, the fates were foretelling that he would
perform well throughout the tenure of his position. It is our opinion that Samuel was to forge a vital link stretching back to Isaac
M. Wise and to Wise's successor, Louis Grossmann. We were particularly struck by Heller's quotations from the eulogies of Dr.
Henry Englander and Rabbi Louis Wolsey delivered at
Grossmann's memorial service:

> There was in him something that appealed alike to old and
> young, to man, woman and child, something that made us
> feel his presence fully at home. It made even little children
> feel intuitively that he was their friend . . . in interest, in
> studies, in service, in scholarship. Louis Grossmann was
> representative of all that was best in Jewish life . . . one of
> the worthiest disciples of Isaac M. Wise, who built his
> thought and vision into the imperishable structure of
> American Judaism.

The authors perceive these statements as quite descriptive of
Samuel Wohl as well. As we have noted, he was ready and able, in
concert with an exceptional group of dedicated laity, to pursue his
own ideals for the greater good of the congregation and community.

Chapter 13
Vital Friends and Religious Persons

J ames G. Heller, born in New Orleans in 1892, was the scion of a Reform rabbinic family. His father, Maximillan Heller, was ordained by the Hebrew Union College in 1884. "Max" was reputed to be an excellent speaker and writer. He was certainly an independent freethinker as judged by his very early adherence to Zionism. He led a long and rewarding rabbinic career in New Orleans. Among many honors and positions, he was president of the Central Conference of American Rabbis. It is clear that he bequeathed more than a genetic pattern to his son, who was to pursue similar pathways.

Jim Heller, after contributing four years of war service as a World War I army chaplain, and briefly holding rabbinic positions in Philadelphia and Little Rock, was elected senior rabbi of the Isaac M. Wise Temple of Cincinnati in 1920, a post he held for the rest of his professional career. He was a magnificent speaker, debater, and orator, treating listeners both to erudition and sincere conviction. This greatly impressed the B'nai Yeshurun committee headed by Herbert Bloch. How could it not?

James Heller possessed other qualities that were to serve his newly adopted congregation well and nationally elevate him to the foremost ranks of the American rabbinate. Like his father, he was an ardent Zionist. This fact alone certainly did not greatly impress the congregational search committee. However, his patrician manner, his presence, his beautiful command of language, his American birth and heritage (it is asserted anecdotally that Heller's mother was a member of the DAR) proved irresistible to the search committee and later to the Plum Street congregation. The young man was also a gifted musician and composer. He proceeded to graduate from the Cincinnati Conservatory of Music and devoted long hours to the Cincinnati Symphony Orchestra and to his composer's muse.

It is an interesting fact that several past editions of the *Union Hymnal* were almost overloaded with the liturgical compositions of Rabbi Heller and C. Hugo Grimm, congregational organist and choir director. Heller used to reminisce that he often wrote his sermons after writing program notes for the symphony. A beautifully designed ex libris reveals a Torah scroll and musical instruments obviously symbolizing Heller's rabbinic and musical careers. Jim Heller did not see any conflict between his musical and religious vocations. In his view they complemented each other.

Rabbi Heller's congregants and the Cincinnati Jewish community perceived added depth in a man who seemed conscious and confident of his ability to lead. In the earliest days of his service, Heller organized the rabbis of the city into a Board of Jewish Ministers, the forerunner of the current Board of Rabbis. Shortly thereafter the temple constitution was revised to allow more flexible use of women and to bring forth a number of provisions that allowed the board and the rabbi to work together as collaborators and not in splendid mutual isolation as had previously been the case.

One accomplishment followed another as James Heller parented the building of the Isaac M. Wise Temple Center on the corner of North Crescent and Reading Road in Avondale, which quickly became the administrative nerve center of the congregation. By the same token, he assumed national prominence in many of the principal facets of mainstream Jewish activity. As already mentioned, he was president of the Central Conference of American Rabbis and was in continuous demand as a speaker for almost any worthwhile cause and organization.

In a real sense, Jim Heller's first contacts with Samuel took place during the deliberations, over several years, on the proposed unification of the Plum Street and Reading Road temples. Samuel Wohl was an active participant in the deliberations as part of the

Reading Road Temple's negotiating committee. After the merger in 1931, the new congregation, under its co-rabbis and enlarged board, began to shake off the lethargy of the national economic depression and embarked on ambitious programs to strengthen itself internally. At the same time, it ambitiously attempted to broaden and deepen understanding within the general community. Rabbi Heller created the Cosmic Club, a society of liberal ministers. In 1929, Samuel conceived and carried out the already described annual Institute of Judaism for several hundred Christian ministers of all denominations who listened to scholarly expositions on the history and principles of the Jewish faith. According to Professor Jacob Marcus, institutes for the Christian clergy represented one of Rabbi Wohl's most enduring contributions to the American scene.

We have already mentioned that the forums begun by Samuel while at the Reading Road Temple attracted many educators, clergymen, and civic leaders to presentations covering a broad range of crucial and timely topics. Heller, in his concise history of the congregation in the centenary years of 1842–1942, summarized realistically that "through the efforts of the rabbis in many civic and religious organizations, both locally and nationally, the reputation of the congregation was enhanced and its tradition of a generous interpretation of its function in life carried forward."

Rabbis Wohl and Heller continued to work and achieve in collaboration, and, to the astonishment of most observers, were genuine friends who held each other in mutual high esteem. The editor of the *National Jewish Post*, a great admirer of Rabbi Heller, wondered in print how it was possible for anyone sharing the same pulpit with him to escape submersion and anonymity. He reasoned that Rabbis Heller and Wohl were different personalities, and if one overshadowed the other, it was because the gifts which Rabbi Heller possessed were such that claimed attention, whereas Rabbi Wohl's activities and interests, although not less important, led in other directions. He concluded that the secret strength of "quiet spoken Sam Wohl was that he was true to himself. . . . Therein lay his power."

We wish to advance a somewhat different opinion. As Harry Kemelman observed in his series of rabbi-detective books: "A clergyman's relationship with his congregation is usually very delicate and easily disturbed." Rabbi Heller was a gifted human being, but perhaps a little "too human" for the decades of his rabbinate. He had very little patience with some congregational groups and individuals, firmly insisting on time to travel, to engage in national and international activities, and to devote himself to his music and other arts. There is much evidence from the recollections of older congregational members that while he was not a failure at his pastoral duties, they were simply difficult for him, and congregational disenchantment and dissatisfaction grew.

At this point it should be noted that many other congregations, such as those of Rabbi Abba Hillel Silver in Cleveland, Stephen Wise in New York, and Solomon Freehof in Pittsburgh, were content to permit their rabbis to exploit their strong points. It is a truism to say that every congregation has its own needs, and that, of course, a rabbi or any clergyman is evaluated within the particular time in which he lives. Rabbi Albert Goldman, Samuel's successor, stated:

> While each rabbi throughout his career develops his own form of talent, no rabbi can be equally great in all areas in which he is called upon to serve. . . . all any rabbi can hope to do is fulfill himself in those areas in which he brings his own inner genius. Some men are scholars, others are preachers, some are activists, others are contemplators. Some are practical, others are mystical. . . . Few are rabbis who have fulfilled themselves in so many areas as Rabbi Wohl. He has been as equally adept in the minute affairs of the congregation as he is in the panoramic sweep of world affairs.

Goldman points out that Sam Wohl's "concern for people has been a foundation stone not only in his career but in the development of the 'pastoral' rabbinate." Moreover, "He has entered into the lives of people . . . has been a mainstay and support for the failing and hurt."

In our view, Samuel took over many of the unrequited needs of the congregation. In many respects he was the temple's "executive director," shielding Heller from undue pressures, and allowing him to concentrate on ceremonial speaking and national and international leadership activities. When Samuel himself went on a prolonged trip, Jim Heller's letters betrayed joy at his return and barely concealed relief. Heller seemed to support all of Samuel's projects and ideas and often, by his prestige and convincing oratory, helped Samuel achieve strongly cherished projects and goals. Furthermore, the two thought alike regarding every major problem confronting the Jewish people in the Diaspora.

Samuel, like James Heller, was an excellent speaker. As co-rabbis they delivered speeches and sermons that together constituted the best "one-two punch" in the American rabbinate over a period of two decades. When it came to Zionism, Samuel could espouse the cause with his heart and with his intimate detailed knowledge of the movement's development and of the men and women who were succeeding against impossible odds in bringing the concept of a Jewish state to fruition. Heller frequently integrated Zionistic concepts with multiple levels of meta-analysis. He greatly accelerated the acceptance of Zionism among the Reform rabbinate and the Reform congregations throughout the country. Such was the power of Heller's melodious voice and intonations that even the temple's gentile choir (Conservatory of Music students with a sprinkling of older professionals) would always listen raptly to his sermons. One was overheard to say in the hush between the final syllables of the address and the organ postlude, "I have no idea what he said, but I loved hearing him say it."

Samuel was disturbed and saddened when in 1952 Rabbi James Heller drew futilely from his bankrupted account of the congregational board's good will. Aspects of his personal life had surfaced that today would probably have much less impact on the congregation and even then could conceivably have been worked out and forgiven if Heller himself had been more contrite or there had been more liquidity in the reservoir of good will tempering the board's reflexive anger.

After Heller resigned, Samuel was instrumental in helping him obtain a leadership position with the Labor Zionist Organization of America. The LZOA was centered in New York, and its leadership was heavily weighted with men honed in the visionary idealism of the ghettos of Eastern Europe. Many were Yiddish-speaking and not overly familiar or, in some instances, even sympathetic with Reform Judaism. Although Heller seemed eager to accept the post, Samuel agonized over "casting him to the wolves" in this manner. Nevertheless, despite his major "cultural handicap," Heller continued for years in his new work, followed by an even longer position with State of Israel Bonds. We believe that pragmatic Labor Zionists appreciated the basic value of this man to their cause. Shortly before his death in 1965, he published a final book, *Isaac Mayer Wise: His Life, Work and Thought.*

Most of the changes in the Cincinnati Reform services and liturgy were proposed and easily accepted under the stewardship of Isaac Mayer Wise, such as the use of an organ, mixed seating of congregants, utilization of English as the primary language of worship, and regular use of a professional choir. In 1910, a gangling twenty-year-old was hired as an organist at the Reading Road Temple. In 1922, he joined the rabbi-composer James G. Heller as organist and a year later also as choir director. Even in 1931 when Samuel first met Dr. C. Hugo Grimm, one might have thought that he had been a religious music director forever. His craggy countenance seemed severe until a radiant smile would suffuse any social situation with warmth and humor. Dr. Grimm was not a member of the Jewish faith. As he explained the circumstances of his hiring:

> Back in the nineteenth century, when the Jewish Reform movement began, organs were added to the temples for the first time. Actually, there weren't enough trained organists. So the temples had to borrow gentiles to be organists and to serve in the choir. That's how I got into the act.

As Samuel ascended the pulpit of the Plum Street Temple in 1931, Dr. Grimm was appointed to teach composition at the Cincinnati Conservatory of Music, quickly becoming head of the department, and from 1944 to 1952 he conducted the conservatory's symphony orchestra. He was an extraordinarily fluid and flexible composer for orchestra and chorus. His symphonic works and his cantata, *The Song of Songs,* won large cash awards from the prestigious National Federation of Music Clubs and the McDowell Club of New York.

Over the years, Dr. Grimm's regular choir numbered from twelve to sixteen and was generally made up of Conservatory of Music students, almost always talented and gentile. In his role of choir director, Grimm would most often seat himself at the organ. As his arms and feet flew nimbly over the keys and pedals, his head and neck proved marvelously expressive, cuing the singers in their musical duties. What could not be conveyed by cranial code, he supplemented by shouted directives in German. His knowledge of the service was complete and detailed. He easily anticipated and compensated for unexpected deviations and miscues committed by both the rabbis and lay participants.

It is difficult to objectively evaluate Dr. Grimm's contribution to Reform music, service, and liturgy. From a historical perspective, he fits impressively into a long array of musicians and musicologists who, beginning in the latter part of the eighteenth century and continuing in the present day, reconstituted the synagogue liturgy.

As is so often the case, the pendulum swung startlingly to the right. In the late eighteenth century, several large old urban Jewish congregations in Germany massively shrugged off what they regarded as conditional restrictions and adapted a service that was Christologic (Lutheran) in form if not in content. Idelsohn, the historian of Jewish liturgy, points out that these people were enthralled by German nationalism and no longer perceived themselves as living in the *golus* (exile). Therefore, they rejected what they saw as Semitic and oriental elements in themselves and in their liturgy.

It was the grassroots laity, rather than cantorial or rabbinic sources, who introduced these concepts. In the early years of progressive reform, almost all of the composers were Christian. The liturgy became increasingly in the church style, and even cantorial performances of traditional prayers and melodies seemed patterned after great European composers. The pendulum, in swinging back, has assumed a steady state. Traditional elements of the service are no longer rejected simply because they are traditional or "too Orthodox." But all aspects of inclusions in the service should be held to the criteria of beauty, meaningfulness, conformance to aesthetic rules, and the dictates of musical harmony and composition.

In the nineteenth century, Salomon Sulzer reigned over Central Europe's chazzanim (cantors). He had the greatest influence and most powerful impetus in the development of what we describe today as Reform Jewish liturgy. He contributed in basic ways to the work of subsequent great Jewish cantors, musicians, and composers such as Solomon Weintraub, Samuel Naumbourg, Louis Lewandowski, and Maier Kohn. These men flourished under his benevolent dictatorship, but owed allegiance to the Germanized Mendelssohn and, of course, Handel's magnificent oratorios.

Sulzer and other composers, gentile and Jewish, self-consciously attempted to create a "Jewish liturgy." They brought a certain amount of dignity and structure to the service. They stressed brevity and conciseness, serious and dignified melodies, and admittedly based much of their writing on classical harmonies and style. Idelsohn further comments that they attempted to make "music modern in form and Jewish in character." However, they did not, and to this day do not, impress the traditionally oriented Jew. They emphasized the "phase of exultation and holiness in synagogue song, neglecting the no less important emotional (sentimental strain) which is an important feature in Semitic-oriental music."

It became apparent very early in the process that Germanic gentile and Jewish composers and musicians were giving a significant number of people what they wanted. Dr. Grimm probably represents the last chapter of musician composers who significantly shaped modern Jewish liturgy, allowing it to sustain Jewish faith and worship. Samuel always viewed Grimm as a "bedrock" whose labors helped sustain the congregation for almost six decades. The bedrock metaphor contrasted nicely with the fact that Dr. Grimm and the choir were located, inevitably, in the balconies of both temples, above and behind the heads of the worshipers. They were, so it seemed, closer to heaven, as the sonorous organ and beautifully timbered professional choir alternately enveloped, inspired, and comforted the congregation below.

The early German reformers and Rabbi Wise in America attempted to bring order and understanding into the centuries-old arrhythmic cacophony of traditional Judaism. These goals were fully realized, although we feel compelled to state that much of the emotion and "character" and sense of Jewish continuity was strained by the welter of intellectualism, resulting in congregational worship that was essentially passive, even sterile. Prayers were offered self-consciously, and congregational singing was almost non-existent.

Samuel was appalled by this state of affairs. Even while a student at the Hebrew Union College, he systematically and consciously attempted to reintroduce what he considered meaningful ceremony, music, and content. Together with Rabbi Heller, he culled the then newly revised *Union Prayer Book* and attempted to devise an interesting, "motivating" service. At the same time, Samuel progressively introduced more Hebrew into the service, confirmed the relatively recent congregational agreement that the rabbis should wear robes, and persuaded the board and Rabbi Heller with surprising ease that a modified talis (prayer shawl) creatively sown into the frontal lapels of the robe would be particularly appealing.

Marcus emphasized Samuel's continual attempts to dramatize the Jewish heritage and to make it more intelligible. In the early forties, Samuel established an annual liturgical festival, usually held at the beginning of Sukkos, the autumn festival. Typically, the festival's music was orchestrated by Dr. Grimm and sometimes included liturgy from other Jewish holidays. It was accompanied by members of the Cincinnati Symphony Orchestra and augmented by the temple's professional choir. Samuel was not a musician, of course, but he knew that a rich Jewish liturgy and music could inspire, could reflect the joy of communal worship, and above all, could give the public a full understanding of the synagogue ritual.

Following the resignation of Rabbi Heller in 1952, Chicago-born Albert Goldman was chosen by the temple board, with Samuel's concurrence, for the position of co-rabbi. Goldman had been ordained at the Hebrew Union College in Cincinnati in 1940, spent four years as a World War II army chaplain, and served several additional years as assistant rabbi to the Boston congregation of Joshua Loth Liebman. During the sudden illness of this famous rabbi, the full weight of a large prestigious congregation fell squarely on Albert's shoulders. Subsequently, he served Temple Emanuel of Yonkers, New York, for five years.

Albert plunged into the affairs of the Isaac M. Wise with vigor and intensity and at the same time managed to pursue his own agenda of studies and social action by establishing thoughtful beachheads with Cincinnati's local Catholic educators. He was well received as a Jewish Chautauqua lecturer at Xavier University, which ultimately conferred upon him the honorary degree of Doctor of Laws. He was also prolific in his attention to the relationship between dynamic psychology and religion. These insights, together with his militant participation in human and civil rights movements, were sincerely offered to the sometimes reluctant congregation in the form of sermons and newsletter messages.

In style of sermonizing and public speaking, Rabbi Goldman contrasted somewhat with Heller and Wohl, and similarly in content, but it was always obvious that he organized and crafted his talks with care. In our opinion, his appeal was to the intellect, and there was never any ambiguity as to the message he wanted to deliver.

We believe that Albert Goldman's most valuable contributions were couched in the context of social activism on behalf of human rights. He was quick to exploit television and radio. After conducting his own radio show, *Dialogue*, he was instrumental in the creation of a weekly WKRC-TV program also called *Dialogue*, where a priest, a rabbi (usually Goldman), and two Protestant denominational representatives (generally one white and one black) would discuss all manner of social and religious issues. This program proved unexpectedly popular and continued many years beyond its projected demise.

At the same time, throughout the 1960s, Goldman consistently attempted to promote harmony between the increasingly restive Avondale black community and what he termed the "white, liberal, Jewish presence." Concurrently, he supported the national civil rights struggle, marching shoulder to shoulder with Fred Shuttlesworth, a local minister and well-known lieutenant of Martin Luther King, Jr. Albert never wavered in his opinions and general pattern of activities, carrying them on in unbroken form after he assumed the post of senior rabbi in 1965. Following his retirement in 1980, he ministered to the needs of a congregation in Washington, Pennsylvania, while reaching out to the community, lecturing, and conducting workshops on grief and bereavement issues. He also served in the role of chaplain in mental hospitals, jails, and institutions for the retarded.

Bene Israel, founded in 1824 and later known as the Rockdale Temple, is generally credited with having been the first organized Jewish congregation in the Cincinnati area. Both Bene Israel and Bene Yeshurun, founded somewhat later, were determinedly Orthodox, intent on preserving the Jewish ethos in the American land of opportunity. However, with the arrival of Isaac Mayer Wise as spiritual leader of Bene Yeshurun, both congregations, in parallel fashion, easily began the process of instituting Reform observance and practice. They prospered greatly, increasing in size and influence. During this period, as we have already noted, Cincinnati became the location of several enduring institutions and organizations, such as the Union of American Hebrew Congregations, Hebrew Union College, the Central Conference of American Rabbis, and the *American Israelite*, a weekly English-language newspaper founded by Rabbi Wise. To complement or perhaps compete with Bene Yeshurun, Bene Israel's Rabbi Max Lilienthal joined Wise in supporting Cincinnati's burgeoning Jewish philanthropies and a multitudinous host of social and educational activities.

David Philipson graduated with the first group of Hebrew Union College rabbis ordained in 1883. He became rabbi of Bene Israel in 1888, served the congregation for fifty years until 1938, and maintained an emeritus status until his death in 1949. Dr. Philipson taught for many years at the Hebrew Union College, where he was influential and respected. He was most productive in a broad number of scholarly works that were well received by the educated laity. His autobiography, My Life as an American Jew, aptly personified what historians have referred to as the "optimism of the prospering Midwest Jews." Since he outlived all of the early reformers, he became, as observed in Alfred Segal's "Plain Talk" column in the Cincinnati Post, "an institution in the city like the symphony, the art museum, the university, and other cultural and spiritual monuments of which the city was proud." He also became the major proponent of classical Reform Judaism and helped organize the Pittsburgh Platform, whose precepts held that "Jews are a religion and not a people." He was, by any definition, an important anti-Zionist.

When Samuel appeared on the Cincinnati scene in 1927, however, Zionism was already being accepted by an increasing number of the Reform rabbinate. By 1938, the date of Philipson's retirement, and, manifestly in the 1940s, Zionism was a cause supported by a great majority of American Reform rabbis. It is ironic that the venerable Dr. Philipson, who helped bring about monumental changes in American Jewish thought nourished in a new land of freedom and opportunity, could not permit flexibility or evolvement of his own early optimistic dicta. Even during his lengthy post-retirement years, his influence, like his physical presence on the pulpit each Saturday, prevented his congregation from obtaining a "world perspective" and reduced the spectrum of what could be viewed as legitimate Jewish interests. With the exception of superficial collaboration on community affairs, neither Samuel nor

James Heller had much communication with the venerable rabbi.

Victor E. Reichert became Philipson's associate at Rockdale in 1928, and, of course, he was not a Zionist. He was also, in our opinion, somewhat confined in his opinions and public pronouncements by Dr. Philipson's omnipresence. Yet he was much beloved by his congregation, cooperated freely with other congregations in community affairs, and very early took up the varied skeins of interfaith relationships. His very good friend, the Jesuit priest Edward Brueggeman, described him as "a great ecumenicist" who "believed all religions should talk *to* one another and not *about* one another." Reichert, a very engaging person, fulfilled the dual roles of teacher and active religious leader. In addition to teaching in several east coast and New England colleges and universities, he taught creative writing and Bible for more than forty years at the University of Cincinnati. He was also a well-read man who enjoyed poetry and was an expert on the writings of the great American poet Robert Frost, with whom he had a close friendship for many years. He and Samuel were able to ignore the fact that they headed "rival" congregations, and despite somewhat different patterns of interests, they maintained a fifty-year cordial relationship based on mutual respect and affection.

Rabbi Stanley Brav was an exceptionally personable young man who served Victor Reichert and the Rockdale Temple as an associate in 1948 and shortly after became a co-rabbi until 1954, when he helped found a new liberal congregation, Temple Sholom, largely made up of younger congregants from the Rockdale and Wise Center temples. He apparently was looking for a smaller, more intimate congregation where the members and the rabbi could achieve true communion and reciprocity. He was an ardent pacifist and consistently projected an image of realistic wholesomeness to the Jewish and general communities of Cincinnati. He seemed to be involved in almost every issue related to peace and justice, and, like his colleague Albert Goldman of the Wise Temple, he was militant in the local and national civil rights movements. For example, he made timely and important efforts to assist blacks in the South, when it was dangerous to do so. Both

Rabbi Brav and Rabbi Goldman worked continually and closely with Jewish communal agencies like the Jewish Community Relations Committee during the late fifties, sixties, and seventies to bring about local social change for the common good.

Brav's rabbinic position at Rockdale was soon filled by Murray Blackman, a dedicated, perceptive young man, who had a love for and knowledge of Jewish literature. One suspects that his book, *Jewish Themes in American Fiction, 1940–80*, implemented Victor Reichert's interest in American poetry. Blackman demonstrated leadership and organizational skills that were portents of his later appointment to the committee on Jewish education of the Union of American Hebrew Congregations and the Central Conference of American Rabbis. With the exception of Zionistic values, he shared a wide range of interests and opinions with Samuel. During Blackman's eleven years serving the Rockdale congregation, he and Samuel remained warm friends.

As already noted, the more traditionally oriented component of the Cincinnati Jewish community was preoccupied with matters of earning a living and coping with the ongoing challenges of existence. They did not respond to the apparently unrealistic expectations of many of their more fortunate co-religionists that they "see the light" and sever their links to more than 5,000 years of history and embrace what seemed to them to be customs and beliefs similar to those of the gentile majority. The Jewish community remained fractionated, as it had since their arrival, between Jews from different European communities and of varying shades of belief. There was little unity and much quarreling over almost incalculable problems of custom, religious observance, and education.

Sarna and Kline, perhaps a little too histrionically for sober historians, trumpet "Rabbi Silver to the rescue." They are referring to the invitation extended by several groups of Orthodox Cincinnati Jews in 1931 to Rabbi Eliezer Silver, the president of the Union of Orthodox Rabbis (Agudath Israel). Silver's organization was dedicated to the newly arrived legions of Orthodox rabbis who were struggling in a strange land, which they considered *treife* ("unclean"), and attempting to assist other immigrants in achieving a traditional Judaism.

Rabbi Silver immediately provided the sorely needed leadership and energy by organizing creating an Orthodox city council (Vaad Ha-Ir) in Cincinnati. He was the goad and driving force behind this governing body's establishment of organizational structures, educative activities, and continual stress on the observance of Jewish law, or halakhah. He certainly fulfilled the role of authoritative spokesman for Orthodoxy, which until then was often locally in the shadow of the national Reform movement. Rabbi Silver carried on the fight aggressively. He had unbounded confidence in himself and in his beliefs. Autocratic, he often ran roughshod over his opposition and at times seemed, in the manner of Jews for hundreds of years, to turn the focus of his preoccupations inwardly within the body of his people, ignoring the reality of the world without.

A major exception to this observation was Silver's laudably successful attempts to rescue Jewish scholars who were among the first to be persecuted by the Nazis. Later, during the Holocaust, his efforts were expanded to include thousands of other Jews by means of the Emergency Rescue Committee (Vaad Hatzalah) which he founded in 1939. In these activities, he was in curious parallel with Dr. Julian Morgenstern, the president of HUC, who carried on a copious correspondence with the U.S. State Department aimed at relaxing immigration laws to allow Jewish academics to enter our country.

Silver, either through guile or overarching belief, remained in splendid isolation and almost never collaborated directly with Reform Jewry. Samuel viewed Silver's presence as strengthening the entire Jewish community, and he advocated compromise with Silver whenever possible regarding actual or potential conflicts with traditional Jews. He was convinced that the traditionally minded could not, without violating internal codes and beliefs, make even small concessions, whereas the more flexible liberal religionist could achieve large compromises without reducing self-worth or religious tenets.

Samuel also greatly respected Rabbi Silver's talmudic prowess, but noted that he spent far too much energy on preserving his authoritarian control. In this, Samuel anticipated Kraut, who stated that Silver "often made life difficult for other (presumably less assertive) Orthodox rabbis officiating at other synagogues." In actuality, Samuel had as little interaction with Rabbi Silver as with Archbishop McNicholas, who reigned over the Roman Catholic archdiocese, the largest single religious entity in the Cincinnati area. According to an anecdote told to one of the authors, Rabbi Silver rewarded Rabbi Wohl by terming him the "least goyische [gentile] of all of them [Reform rabbis]."

One cannot help but wonder whether the "rescue" of Orthodoxy might have occurred in 1918, preceding Rabbi Silver's arrival by some thirteen years, when Rabbi Louis Feinberg, a graduate of the Jewish Theological Seminary, the educational institution of the Conservative movement, was invited to serve as rabbi of Adath Israel, an Orthodox congregation in Cincinnati. The "gentle scholar," as we will call him, immediately instigated rescue operations, refined almost every aspect of congregational activity, promoted significant forms of educational endeavor, and reached out to the community's youth to form the Adathean Society. Under his leadership, an imposingly beautiful new synagogue was constructed, fronted by six huge Corinthian columns. The completion of the synagogue in 1927 seemed to finalize the integration of the disparate groups comprising the congregation. Rabbi Feinberg's immersion in the study of Jewish law located Adath Israel on the spectrum of observance closer to traditional Orthodoxy.

Samuel appreciated Louis Feinberg's scholarship, firm convictions, and sincerity, and, like a good portion of the Adath Israel congregation, resonated to the "sweetness of character and sincerity which was so uniquely part of Rabbi Feinberg." Samuel repeatedly and somewhat prophetically observed. "The Reform movement will founder without the sustenance of thousands of years of study distilled in Feinberg's [collection of] essays entitled, 'The Spiritual Foundations of Judaism.' "

Indeed, the gentle scholar's personal example and literary skill accomplished a vital purpose in strengthening and clarifying the religious peoplehood of Israel in a manner more basic and lasting than leadership squabbling could ever accomplish. As early as the late forties, Samuel anticipated that Conservatism would gradually position itself for a measured change, resulting in the overall development of its own movement, and eventually providing powerful inspiration to and influencing Reform Judaism.

When Samuel arrived at the Reading Road Temple in 1927, Rabbi Feinberg, despite his scholarly and artistic inclinations, had already clarified and energized the faith of his rapidly growing congregation. Samuel Wohl and Louis Feinberg had the highest mutual respect and cooperated closely on various community and Zionistic committees. Coinciding with the hegemony of Rabbi Silver, Rabbi Feinberg spent his last years as a concerned spiritual leader of his flock while continuing his scholarly pursuits. After his death in 1949, his former assistant, Rabbi Fischel Goldfeder, was chosen to succeed him. Goldfeder was young, dynamic, and American-born. Overall, the congregation prospered under his ministry, and he discovered a close identification with Samuel in their mutual love of Zion.

The small but significant Jewish population of Greater Cincinnati belied its numbers by powerfully contributing to the professional, business, social, health, and government of the city. Reform Jews and the Reform movement constituted the interface between the ancient entity of Judaism and the various strains of Christianity. Samuel proved adept at communicating with and influencing the majority gentile population. Jews cannot exist in a vacuum, he often commented.

> We have so much to contribute to world culture and should continue our often futile mission of monitoring the world's conscience. Self-preoccupation and turning inward can only deform us and lead to spiritual stagnation. Even survival and self-preservation dictate that we be eternally sen-

sitive to external events in the trends and currents of the gentile world.

Samuel's combination of integrity, determination, compassion, and worldwide sagacity never failed to impress the community's power structure, the media, and regional thinkers of all types. We referred earlier to his founding of the Institute of Religion, bringing together ministers of all faiths on a regular basis. This was Samuel's first of many significant enhancements of Isaac Mayer Wise's original conception of the role that his congregation was expected to play in the community. It was to extend beyond the walls of the temple and the bounds of sectarianism. Samuel continued to meet frequently and consult with members of the Christian clergy on matters of local, national, and international interest. In time, as a result of such endeavors, he and the tall, imposing Bishop Henry Hobson of the Southwestern Episcopal Diocese of Ohio become close friends.

Bishop Hobson was an exceptionally perceptive and caring person who consistently embraced the larger, more encompassing view rather than narrow self or sectarian concerns. Since his congregants were clearly the social elite and represented the highest and most effective levels of society, his opinions and actions conveyed considerable influence and moral suasion in all of Cincinnati's mainline Protestant churches. An examination of several items of correspondence between the two men is both fascinating and instructive. The letters reflect utter sincerity, sharing of personal events and convictions, and, at the same time, transient perceptive assessments of current issues. The "Hobson Committee" proved to be a rallying point for responsible, thinking people who were horrified by the Nazi ideology and excesses abroad and the increasing isolationism, anti-Semitism, and shrill pro-German pronouncements verbalized throughout southwestern Ohio.

Hobson's enlightened policies and social outreach were continued after his retirement by Bishop Roger Blanchard, a continual force in his own right. The Rev. Richard Isler, on assuming the chairmanship of the local chapter of the Council of Churches, strongly emphasized democratization and social action as significant principles on the national, international, and local levels. Samuel forged strong relationships as well with other clergy who possessed social consciences and were friendly to the Jewish community. Such ministers as G. Barret Rich of the First United Church (Presbyterian), Lynn Rattliff of Hyde Park Community Methodist Church, and Edward Chandler, director of St. Michaels and All-Angels Episcopal Church of Avondale were very active in interreligious and interracial causes.

Samuel powerfully supported and maintained constant communication with the Jewish Community Relations Council, particularly with its early presidents, Robert E. Segal, Dr. Jacob R. Marcus, and C. E. "Mike" Israel. One might well say that the aforementioned network of activists were able, in synchrony, to afford the media cogent syntheses and analyses of the hate peddlers and pro-Nazi mercenaries in this country. Constant light was shed on such clerical mouthpieces of evil as Father Coughlin and Gerald L. K. Smith.

The National Jewish Community Council became sequentially involved in a much broader series of issues impinging on Jewish welfare and development. Samuel continued to support the JCRC and maintained close personal relationships with members of the City Council and with more than two decades of Cincinnati mayors: Russell Wilson, James Garfield Stewart, Dorothy Dolbey, Ted Berry, Carl Rich, Charles P. Taft, and the media's Carl Groat, Brady Black, Joseph Sagmaster, and William Hessler. He advanced certain goals and provided integrative cement much more effectively than community emphases on continuous fact-finding and dry protest.

Before the accession of Pope John XXIII, American Catholicism was represented locally by Archbishop John McNicholas, who headed the Cincinnati archdiocese from 1925 through 1950. The archdiocese in this period numbered well over 400,000 Roman Catholics of largely German descent. McNicholas was a strong and nationally prominent leader, said to be the force behind many of the collective statements issued by the United States Conference of Catholic Bishops. His flock alone numbered more than all the local Protestant denominations and Jewish groups combined.

McNicholas was an authoritarian leader with a tremendous power base, hierarchically dominating, inaccessible, and aloof to non-Catholics. Samuel was no more successful in communicating with the archbishop than were any of the Jewish community's other leaders, whether lay or clerical. He attempted to bridge the gap by inviting Catholic laymen to participate in his Open Forum programs but was easily checkmated in this regard, since in all such situations, and even after an initial acceptance, he would receive a sometimes apologetic negative "reconsideration" accompanied by the explanation that the topic being discussed was either directly or tangentially contrary to official church doctrine. Catholic isolation was enhanced and completed by the prohibition of clerical or lay participation in any event having even a minimal religious coloration or held in any non-Catholic religious edifice. The Avondale church of St. Andrews and its friendly priest, Father Sherry, interacted in a cordial manner with their Jewish neighbors, but only informally and unofficially.

Very recently, an archdiocesan spokesman stated that the leadership of Cincinnati's bishops has been in the forefront of the many changes in American Catholicism. From our viewpoint, only Vatican II grants credibility to that statement. Even before Vatican II, however, Archbishop Karl Alter heralded a welcome change in attitude toward and cooperation with the rest of the community in nineteen southwestern Ohio counties. Archbishop Alter and later Archbishop Paul Liebold strongly championed social justice and often threw their full weight behind communal efforts to better race relations and to develop ecumenical programs for minorities and the poor. Vatican II provided the climate within which frictional relationships—for instance, between the clergy and laity—were reduced, and there was a marked increase in reaching out to Jewish and Protestant leaders on social and even religious issues.

Of course, Protestantism was the area's dominant religion until about 1820, when large numbers of German and Irish Catholic immigrants appeared on the scene. Baptists and Presbyterians arrived first and seemed to spend a good portion of their lives defending themselves against hostile Native Americans. The various denominations formed a complicated mosaic. Each denomination formed and reformed, redefining creed and dealing differentially with its internal or social problems.

As we have noted, Samuel freely participated on social action committees and had personal friendships with many prominent ministers, particularly those with a scholarly or humanistic bent. Joint (interdenominational) Thanksgiving Day services were always heavily laden with Unitarian/Universalists, along with Rattliff's United Methodists and G. Barret Rich's Presbyterians. Samuel participated conscientiously in the Cosmic Club for clergy, but we would guess that he found great intellectual stimulation there but little desire to achieve actual interreligious cooperation. We would further surmise that there was little real communication with the vast majority of Protestants who belonged to churches adhering to the fundamentalist or more Calvinistic doctrines.

As the floodgates of pent-up Catholic desire to understand their own church and communicate with their neighbors opened, there was a reflexive reaching out by Protestant leaders and organizations as well as by the Jewish community. Samuel quickly became friendly with Archbishop Alter, whom he genuinely liked and respected. He gave a well-attended and truly precedent-setting luncheon in honor of the prelate as a tribute to his "civic, religious, and cultural achievements."

As was widely reported in the press, Archbishop Alter decried religious bigotry and heatedly denied the frequent false rumors that the American Catholic bishops were plotting to usurp political power by promoting U.S. representation to the Vatican. As chairman of the administrative board of the National Catholic Welfare conference, he repeatedly denounced the "infection of anti-Semitism" and called for vigorous public repudiation of this ancient evil. Introducing the archbishop at the luncheon, Samuel said, "Men of religion are the greatest asset of our democracy. . . . dedicated men have ministered to our people. During generations, they kept the vision of human fellowship under God before their eyes."

Even more significant and influential were Samuel's relationships with prominent and articulate church-related lay persons of all persuasions who held important positions in industry and politics.

In the eyes of Samuel Wohl, Charles Phelps Taft was a man deserving of great respect. "Charlie" was known by all, rich and poor alike, as an indefatigable public servant, sometimes acerbic, sometimes loveable, but always seeming to strive aggressively for the highest goals. Taft was mayor of Cincinnati and had served in the council for sixteen terms. A son of President William Howard Taft and brother of U.S. Senator Robert A. Taft, Charlie had led a childhood enriched by several years residence in the White House and had received an Eastern Ivy League education. Together with Murray Seasongood, Charles Taft was one of the founders of the Charter Party in 1925 which secured nonpartisan good government for the people of Cincinnati. From his early stint as Hamilton County prosecutor, he was continuously involved in local, state, and national affairs. He held several high posts in the Roosevelt administration during World War II, in spite of, or perhaps because of, his label as a "progressive Republican." Charlie Taft usually left his local Charter Party leanings at the Hamilton County line and was clearly a "moderate" Republican when it came to general philosophy and the support of national political figures, such as the presidential aspirations of his brother Bob. Space does not permit us to adequately chronicle the many anecdotes, the idiosyncrasies and, above all, the attainments of this very tough but sensitive man.

It was sometimes said that Charles Taft held higher offices in religious circles than as an elected official. He served as the first and only lay president of the Federal Council of Churches, now the National Council of Churches, and was an Episcopal delegate to the first assembly of the World Council of Churches in

Amsterdam. As an active member of Christ Church (Episcopal), he functioned under the aegis of Bishop Henry Hobson, and it was in this manner and through frequent interactions with the National Council of Churches board that Samuel and Charles formed a friendship and toiled jointly in the vineyard of a multitude of causes.

The correspondence between Charles and Samuel is characterized by rambling good humor, great determination, simple tastes, and basic identification with almost everybody. In at least two letters, probably in response to Samuel's condolences regarding an earlier tragedy concerning a daughter and the death of his wife Eleanor in 1961, Charles reflected a touching picture of gratitude and serenity hereto unsuspected. Moreover, he accurately perceived Samuel as entirely and unreservedly candid and empathic in his words of encouragement and support.

We have already briefly noted the important role of the media in helping to integrate and enhance the efforts of well-meaning citizens. Samuel's contacts with editors and editorial writers, and his rapport with the three Cincinnati area dailies, the *Enquirer*, the *Times Star*, and the *Post*, helped circulate and dignify many of his activities and attainments. Brady Black, vice president and editor of the *Enquirer*, typified Samuel's media support. Black, as an editorialist and editor, did not agree with Samuel's humanism and what he termed his sometimes "democratic-socialistic leanings." Yet the man whom his peers considered a "model of journalistic objectivity" developed a considerable respect for Samuel's grasp of local, state, and international political/economic issues, and many times publicly lauded his humane wisdom.

It is certainly no surprise that Samuel's institutes, forum series, and "good neighbor" awards were given editorial and front-page coverage over a period of twenty-five years. All three were major conceptual achievements, tremendously facilitating Samuel's communication with and influence on the surrounding community. If one conceives the Isaac M. Wise Temple forum as an avenue of communication and influence on the surrounding community, Samuel succeeded brilliantly. By the second decade, well over a hundred famous personalities had ascended the rostrum of the Wise Center. Recalling the forum's history, Samuel related that it had brought to Cincinnati "lords and ladies, Freudians and non-Freudians, radicals, liberals and conservatives, debates and symposia." He added: "My concept of a religious institution is not merely a Reform institution for worship but a repository of ideas which impinge directly upon the lives of people." Thus, he continued, anything that "reaches out for a better life—that helps human life to be unharnessed and to grow, is within the province of religion." Religion is the great unifier of ideals, he said, and the purpose of the forum is "the liberalization of the mind and the development of better thinking. We are not interested in any particular creed. We have no axe to grind."

Russell Wilson and James Garfield Stewart represented a succession of mayors who publicly thanked Rabbi Wohl for the internationally famous forum. Roger Ferger, editor and owner of the *Cincinnati Enquirer*, was typical of the many prominent citizens who attended forum series meetings over the years.

A singular highlight was the visit of Mrs. Eleanor Roosevelt in 1938. Arriving by Pullman at the downtown Union Terminal, the First Lady was distressed to hear that her commitment to address the forum involved at least two days of reporters, interviews, formal and informal meetings with representatives of various organizations, the receipt of many honors, and conferences with many individuals. Mrs. Roosevelt was later to muse in her nationally syndicated column "My Day" that she was "always a little overwhelmed by these . . . attentions because I feel the hosts have put themselves out so tremendously and nothing you can say or do can really repay them."

After detailing many more of the day's happenings, Mrs. Roosevelt acknowledged the cakes produced by the "Bake Shop" (Jewish social agency) and a "delicious box of candy" given to her by Judge Robert Marx, who "told me that it is made by a little shop that refuses to be commercialized, remains the same size, keeps the same saleswoman and will not acquire a large clientele . . . and is the best candy I have ever eaten."

The theme of Eleanor Roosevelt's forum address, held at Emery Auditorium, was that cultural understanding between the Americas was the touchstone for economic and political unity. Cultural relationships are the harbinger of other desirable results. "These relationships lead us right out into what all of us are thinking of—the strength and defense of our nation." Further tracing the development of cultural relationships with our southern neighbors, she spoke of music as a universal language and praised South American shortwave broadcasts featuring the Cincinnati Symphony Orchestra. On the economic front, she stated, the United States must realize that if it wishes to sell goods to South America, it also must buy goods. She then defined the policy of "good neighborliness," explaining that it was not just a policy of government, but also "must be carried out by every one of us in our own communities."

Mrs. Roosevelt went on to speak of many other issues, commenting on the withdrawal of Philip Murray, president of the Congress of Industrial Organizations, from the Defense Mediation Board. She admitted to being rather conflicted about this event, stating that she could understand the feeling for a closed shop but that it seemed very serious to take the CIO out of the Defense Mediation Board. She concluded that she had great respect for Murray and felt he was "calmer" than John L. Lewis, the fiery president of the United Mine Workers.

Mrs. Roosevelt's ideas apparently registered deeply with Samuel. Later, he was to visit the countries of Central and South America on two major fact-finding and good will expeditions undertaken at the behest of the State Department and the Joint Distribution Committee. Shortly after Mrs. Roosevelt's visit, he inaugurated the Isaac M. Wise Temple "Good Neighbor Award" to recognize each year a Cincinnatian who had labored to make the Queen City a better place to live or whose community service had gone far beyond the limits of his faith or his economic, political, or social interests. An *Enquirer* editorial put it well when it noted:

Those responsible for selecting the recipient of the annual Isaac M. Wise Temple Good Neighbor Award . . . are speak-

ing for all of Greater Cincinnati. . . . [It] has served the eminently worthwhile purpose of embodying the community's
gratitude to men and women whose service has gone far
beyond the limits of selfish interest. . . . in receiving the
Good Neighbor Award tonight, Archbishop Alter takes his
place among an impressive array of other Cincinnatians
similarly honored—Right Reverend Henry Hobson, retired
bishop of the Episcopal church for Southern Ohio, former
city Councilman Dorothy Dolbey, Councilman and former
mayor Charles P. Taft, former Councilman Carl W. Rich,
and Councilman Theodore Berry.

The yearly selection of a recipient to be honored with the
Good Neighbor Award was accomplished by the mayor's Friendly
Relations Committee (now the Human Relations Commission)
and its chairman, Marshall Bragdon.

In 1972, Councilman Theodore Berry became Cincinnati's
first black mayor before the largest inaugural audience ever assem-
bled in the City Council chambers. As his first official act as
mayor, even before delivering his acceptance speech, Berry asked
the audience to rise in silent tribute to Neil McElroy, former board
chairman of Procter & Gamble Company and secretary of defense,
and to Rabbi Samuel Wohl, both of whom had died within the last
twenty-four hours. The two had contributed richly to the religious
and industrial life of the city, Berry noted.

By means of writing, public addresses, and sermons, Samuel
demonstrated a significant understanding of the scars and hurts
racism had inflicted on African-Americans and the pervasive, terrible injustice of it all. His call against racism and scapegoating at
the onset of the Second World War was urgent and focused. He
proclaimed the story of millions of Americans who had been set
aside, denied their rights of freedom, justice, and economic opportunity.

Today these millions who have lived, worked and suffered
for over three centuries are a permanent factor in

American life. Confronting poverty and prejudice, they have made great contributions to America in agricultural and industrial labor and notably in the arts of music, dance, literature and the stage. Many are successful doctors, lawyers, businessmen, teachers, and scientists (remember George Washington Carver who did more for the South, white and black, than all the philanthropists and even government agencies). All of this in a short period of 75 years since Lincoln's emancipation proclamation, Negroes remain to this day disenfranchised, segregated, subject to Jim Crow laws, denied educational facilities and the object of economic discrimination. They are the scapegoats of hate and suspicion. . . . Demagogues rise to power, become congressmen, governors and senators and fight bitterly for poll taxes, employment and discrimination and malpractice within the armed forces in the midst of war. Such is the strength of hate, of injustice, and blind intolerance that, even now, we cannot come with clean hands at a time when we fight for the Four Freedoms of all mankind.

He went on to emphasize that the basis of racial equality before the law were the Thirteenth, Fourteenth, and Fifteenth Amendments stemming from the Civil War.

Samuel considered Nobel Prize winner Martin Luther King "a man of great spiritual qualities" and was convinced, as was King, that the conscience of the white man would finally assert itself and blacks would obtain justice and the opportunities denied them for so many years. He frequently identified the similarities and analogies between European and American-style racial attitudes. Quoting Nazi Labor Front leader Robert Ley, "An inferior race needs less food and less culture than a superior race. Never can the German man live in the same way as the Pole or the Jew."

In the course of his reading, Samuel discovered what he termed a "striking statement" by a black student and suggested that millions of Americans should take it to heart.

If you discriminate against me because I am uncouth, I can become mannerly. If you ostracize me because I am unclean, I can cleanse myself. If you segregate me because I am ignorant, I can become educated. But if you discriminate against me because of my color, I can do nothing. God gave me my color. I have no possible protection against race prejudice, but to take refuge in cynicism, bitterness, hatred and despair.

On the occasion of Lincoln's birthday, Samuel lectured:

There is so much that is superb and beautiful in the personality of Lincoln. . . . a generation suffering and disillusioned desperately needs his guidance and his message. . . . a timely word penned to his friend Joshua Speed: As a nation we began by declaring "All men are created free and equal." As a practical matter, we may read it "All men are created equal except Negroes." When "know-nothings" get control—"All men are created equal except Negroes, foreigners and Catholics!" When it comes to this, I shall prefer emigrating to some country where they make no pretense of having liberty . . . to Russia, for instance, where despotism can be taken pure, and without even the base alloy of hypocrisy.

Pointing out the irony of fighting authoritarianism abroad and succumbing to bigotry in our own country, Samuel early emphasized the obvious and still relevant fact that the white race is losing its worldwide dominance and is outnumbered by non-whites. "They may justifiably view themselves as a minority and had better quickly decide to join the human race. Soon it may be too late."

The ending of a sermon delivered during World War II is still a lasting ringing endorsement of mankind's need for brotherhood.

We know that no people can claim superiority over another people, that *no* race is an inferior race, that the ugly outbursts of intolerance and chauvinism are a disease and crime against humanity. To be a friend of humanity is to be a friend of *every* race and every group. It is to *appreciate*, not merely to tolerate differences. In a world in which medieval barbarism is again on the rampage, no longer in the name of God, but in the name of blood, when racial intolerance is pouring its poisonous fluids into the stream of life, all good people must band together to save civilization from darkness and degeneration. . . . Men will be free *not* through uniformity, but through a *unity* that rises above historic differences.

If one scans the list of famous Wise Center Forum speakers, one can identify four African-American speakers: Mordecai Johnson, president of Howard University; W. E. B. Du Bois, the noted sociologist and author of *The Souls of Black Folk*, a founder of the NAACP, and the editor of *Crisis*, its magazine; James Weldon Johnson, author of the Negro national anthem, "Lift Up Your Voice and Sing," and a charter member of the NAACP; and A. Philip Randolph, president of the Brotherhood of Sleeping Car Porters. During the thirties and early forties it was rare indeed for African-Americans to appear on such a platform.

As schoolchildren, we were taught that Cincinnati had been the light at the end of the tunnel for fleeing slaves before the Civil War and an economic promised land for migrating blacks after the two world wars. Was it not on the way to Cincinnati that Harriet Beecher Stowe had Eliza of *Uncle Tom's Cabin* cross the ice on the Ohio River one step ahead of her villainous pursuers? Yet the Cincinnati of the 1930s and 1940s, like so many other northern and northeastern locales, continued to display the Reconstruction-Era-induced bigotry and segregation that was a national fact of life.

Among the easily viewed and conceptualized outward manifestations of the discrimination against blacks was the city's sprawling West End, which author Paul de Kruif is said to have labeled "the worst slum he had visited in America." There was the usual discrimination in industry and labor unions, segregated schooling, exclusion from the city's main recreational facilities, and the unwillingness of its best hotels, restaurants, amusement parks, and theaters to accept guests of color. In such a climate, racial better-ment and was very difficult to achieve, although conditions were not as bad as in cities farther south. Quite symbolically, it was in Cincinnati where black railroad passengers at Union Terminal were compelled to change cars in order to implement the Southern practice of segregated seating. This practice prevailed also on the city-owned Southern Railway.

Samuel was quite proud that Jews had participated in the founding of the NAACP. However, he was not blind to the fact that prejudice against blacks pervaded his own congregation and could scarcely be ignored. He chose almost every opportunity to criticize and expose racial bigotry and hate. It galled him more than one can describe that he had great difficulty in finding acceptable hotel accommodations for the aforementioned distin-guished forum speakers, nor could he comfortably entertain them at any well-regarded downtown restaurant. As a matter of fact, on at least two occasions, Belle was pressed into service to afford a "wonderful home cooked meal" to Mordecai Johnson and William E. B. Du Bois.

Du Bois was a fascinating guest but an even more interesting forum speaker, because he was the foremost proponent of main-streaming the Negro into higher education—that is, of educating blacks the same way one would educate whites who had intellec-tual educational potential and a propensity for learning. This had been a divisive issue in the black community ever since Booker T. Washington of the Tuskegee Institute had strongly advanced the concept that it was to the Negro's best interest to accomplish a grounding in practical or vocational subjects in preparation for a worker's role in society.

Samuel respected his invited speakers not only because of their manifest achievements but also because he could strongly identify with the apparent hopelessness of their situation as men of indomitable spirit who surely must sometimes have felt that they were shouting into the wind. From his understanding of the worldwide and historical situation of the Jew, Samuel was able to empathize with the inevitable frustrated anger of the American black when confronted with the gap between his lofty ideals and the current stark reality pressing on his shoulders.

We remember an occasion when we were children and our father took us to a baseball game within the "friendly confines" of Crosley Field ballpark. The baseball arena was located in the previously mentioned scabrous West End. As we traversed several blocks to reach the ballpark, Samuel stopped abruptly and directed our gaze toward a small five-year-old boy, dirty faced and barefooted, sitting on the front stone stoop, paint peeling from the apartment roof above him. His chin resting in his small hand, he pensively regarded the garbage strewn about the bare earth of his small front yard. The scene was almost identical with the ones recently displayed in a *Life* magazine series "Poverty in Appalachia," utilizing a white child as protagonist. Samuel, calmly but with great emotion, gestured with his hand, stating, "No one should have to live this way." This reminiscence is made even more poignant when one considers that hundreds of thousands of Cincinnatians over the years were confronted with such sights and yet managed to deny them and relegate them to the background of their awareness.

It took considerable courage for Samuel to invite A. Phillip Randolph as one of his well-publicized forum speakers. Allen Howard, a columnist for the *Cincinnati Enquirer*, recently noted that Randolph was able to "claim more civil rights victories than any other person because whatever he did, he went straight to the top with it." Beginning with his public opposition to World War I, he successively and aggressively championed the causes of all underprivileged and mistreated peoples. Howard notes that some whites regarded Randolph as "the most dangerous Black in America." In 1925, he founded and organized the Brotherhood of Sleeping Car Porters. It was a powerful union, and the first black union to be granted an international charter by the American Federation of Labor. Randolph was a gadfly to both Franklin Roosevelt and Harry Truman, and is credited with causing both presidents to sign vital civil rights executive orders. In 1941 he threatened a march on Washington in order to urge Roosevelt to strike down a ban on hiring blacks in war plants. Ironically, twenty-two years later, when he helped organize 250,000 people in a march on Washington for the civil rights bill, he received much less acknowledgment than did the Southern Christian leadership of Martin Luther King and Ralph Abernathy.

In any event, Samuel utilized a mixture of persistence, love, and moral certitude to attain his goals. He found it expedient, at whatever level he was dealing with, to address and question those who had power and authority. For example, reasonably and without rancor, he called almost every major hotel, restaurant, and theater owner in the Cincinnati area and utilized his personal credibility, rationality, and "appeals to their sense of decency." It amazed him that a few prominent restaurants and three major hotels, the Gibson, the Netherland Plaza, and the Hotel Alms of Walnut Hills, simply agreed to change their policies. It was probably not a coincidence that in the late forties the social prohibition against blacks, at least in downtown Cincinnati, lapsed considerably.

Samuel maintained consistent interaction with individuals and organizations in the black community for years despite his all-encompassing primary concern with the status of world and local Jewry. Only recently have substantive books and essays treated the history of Afro-Americans in the Cincinnati area. There was a single book in Samuel's day entitled *Cincinnati's Colored Citizens*, published in 1926 by Wendell Philips Dabney. The multi-talented Dabney was a politician, composer, historian, hotelier, and the very first black appointed city paymaster. Self-described as a "stormy petrel" and "active in every branch of human endeavor," he bluntly informed Samuel that he very much admired what he was accomplishing for the black community with his forum series.

Dabney expressed great pleasure when invited to participate in the welcoming committee for Du Bois. Shortly after Du Bois's forum presentation, Samuel was pleased to receive from Dabney a signed first edition of his book along with the cryptic message "in honor of the birthday of W. E. Du Bois." He was convinced that the words and actions of several of the Cincinnati clergy during the years just preceding the watershed Supreme Court decisions and subsequent sweeping civil rights changes had played an important part in bringing about the needed changes in race relations. Hobson, Alter, Wohl, Rich, Rattliff, and Isler were among those who convinced the black community that they "mattered" and who established a foundation and reservoir of good will that would soften the stress of revolutionary pain and lead to planful improvement.

First in 1927 and then with the merger of the two temples in 1931, Samuel sought to focus his congregation within the overall rubric of the worldwide aspirations and tragedies of the Jewish people. On his retirement in 1965, he mused that over the years his rabbinic colleagues had been exceptionally notable and able. He noted, too, that clerics of other faiths had proved indispensable for the betterment of the Jewish and human condition.

Part IV
Global Knowledge and Travel, Congregational Developments, Ideas and Discussion

Chapter 14
Early World Perspectives:
Identification of European Totalitarianism

The reader will recall the 1931 merger of the Reading Road and Plum Street Temples. Samuel and Belle hosted a spontaneous celebration for leaders and rabbis, and the following morning Samuel departed from the haven of America and embarked on his "first trip to the outside world." His itinerary included Germany, Central Europe, Poland, and eastern Russia, culminated by attending the World Jewish Congress in Basle as a delegate. We have already remarked that Samuel's forty-year span of crisscrossing oceans and continents was consistent with the Jewish leader's need to know—pleasure always secondary to discovery. He revisited Germany and Central Europe the very next year. His reminiscences, lectures, and interviews given to the foreign and domestic press emphasized the malignant threat of German fascism and his very saddened and horrified preoccupation with Eastern Europe.

After arriving on the continent of Europe, Samuel realized belatedly that he was abroad for the first time since his departure from his former Ukrainian homeland. The leaders of the Russian Revolution had done their work well, but he noticed a considerable amount of the old culture, customs, and places left intact. As he traveled through Byelorussia, Russia, and Ukraine by rail, he noticed that in large city enclaves and smaller towns where the Jewish people formed the majority, they were permitted to have their own schools. The language of instruction was Yiddish, and

121

even in a relatively large city like Berditchev, there were Jewish courts of law. The old newspaper, *Emmes* ("Truth"), was still published daily, except that it was printed utilizing the Cyrillic alphabet and told of reactionary Jews and the "wonderful" campaign of the atheists against the religious reactionary forces.

A visit to his birthplace, Novaya-Ushitsa, moved him greatly, for many of the town's Jewish inhabitants, who remembered him as a child in his family, met and greeted him a mile outside the city limits. He walked back into the town accompanied by literally hundreds of people. He was still able to recognize homes, synagogues and the Roman Catholic and Russian Orthodox churches. He was free to see anyone. For almost twenty-four hours he held court in the homes of friends, while the people of the town visited one by one, relating personal and family anecdotes and relaying information to relatives in various parts of the United States. After his return to the United States, he contacted most of the relatives of the people who had visited him. He was able to convey to them the first bit of knowledge about their kin, about the turbulent civil war, the revolution, and the many violent changes.

Samuel toured the large population centers of Moscow, Leningrad (St. Petersburg), Kiev, and Odessa. He was impressed with the elimination of the restrictions that had once caused Jews by the many thousands, to flock to the major cities to obtain bread and jobs. Thus there was still a pulsating Jewish presence in these areas. At that time, there was no prohibition against Jews assembling for Jewish affairs or causes, although, paradoxically, he was told that the famous Brodsky Synagogue in Odessa had been transformed into a communal club (a place where the story of Lenin was told). He was told also about the anti-religious museum that occupied the most famous Orthodox cathedral in Leningrad. Samuel found the museum fascinating, but "frightfully shocking because of the unmitigated falsehoods and distortions told to thousands of sightseers linking every Jewish and Christian object with czarist reaction and medievalism."

In Moscow and Leningrad Samuel visited such places as the Kremlin and the many historical museums and other edifices inherited from the old regime. He wondered at the new mausoleum before which thousands of people passed by from morning to night to view the embalmed body of Lenin. The ballet, then as now, was superb, as was the theater. The flush of pleasure and nostalgia brought on by these events was gradually dispelled when he read notices in the newspapers by children renouncing their parents for being middle-class or bourgeois and wanting nothing whatever to do with them.

All printed material, and particularly religious printed material, was under strict censorship. Not even a Jewish calendar could be printed. Nowhere was one able to buy a Jewish book even by one of the very well known Russian Jewish writers. For a very short time, between 1931 and 1933, the Soviet regime, accepted (extorted?) from people who hoped to emigrate a sizeable amount of money forwarded by their American relatives in return for exit visas.

Samuel observed that the position of the Jew in the Soviet sphere of influence was still very vulnerable and quite tinged with irony. Jewish intellectuals had played a tremendous role in conceptualizing and popularizing the revolution. They had fought in the Red Army, and Leon Trotsky, a renegade Jew, had been one of its principal organizers. In fact, many became generals, and thousands lost their lives fighting the Whites and the reactionary forces. Jews were represented in the highest echelons of the Foreign Ministry. Maxim Litvinov was paid no heed during the last sessions of the old League of Nations when he declared that war was imminent. He later became the first ambassador from the Soviet Union to the United States. Later, the same Litvinov, after years of high achievement, became foreign minister, only to be removed and thus forgotten by Stalin.

For a time, it seemed that talent, distinction, and ability counted more than racial or national origins. Indeed, the Soviet constitution (subsequently drastically rewritten) posited anti-Semitism as a legal crime subject to significant penalty. From the period of the late twenties until about 1936 or 1937, the Jewish people in Russia felt that they had helped to achieve drastic but important changes. There was a place for them, and they could continue striving to adapt to the living conditions in the country.

The purges begun by Stalin in 1937 effectively dispelled these notions. The extinction of Jewish identity, religion, and culture ensued. Samuel exhibited his usual prescience when, in conference with reporters, he noted that there was no future for the people to live and breathe as Jews. The Soviet government, of course, closed its borders not only to Jews but to people of all ethnicities, and no one was allowed to emigrate. Only those on special missions were permitted to leave the country. Most of them returned because they had families in their home country. They were confined within boundaries even stricter than those of the old Pale.

Samuel, at this point, had no trouble selecting Stalin as the arch-villain responsible for uncountable crimes against humanity and the Jewish people. He viewed him as promoting the destruction of the Jewish community of the Soviet Union. He was clearly responsible for the liquidation of Jewish generals from the Red Army. He caused the execution of Jewish writers. He closed all Jewish schools and stopped the printing of publications that had appeared for more than a decade under Lenin. He was responsible for the terror and fear of every human being in the Union of Soviet Socialist Republics, including those who were close to him.

By 1932, there were only two surviving Old Bolsheviks who had been members of the government with Lenin; the rest had been executed. Before Nazism's murderous excesses, it was difficult for Samuel to imagine that one barbarian could mobilize the power of an entire army and secret service and destroy so many suspected opponents of the regime, including large segments of the people.

Samuel mixed easily with the populace during this visit, wearing a Russian blouse and speaking the language fluently. He found that the clergy as a group were outcasts. A clergyman walking on the street in priestly garments was a laughing stock. Churches had been converted into clubhouses for the education of workers. Children were systematically taught atheism in the schools, although the elderly still attended the few churches permitted to exist.

Within the wreckage of old faiths, he thought he saw a new one arising. The images of the saints had been replaced by Marx and Lenin. Whereas traditional religion raised the eyes of the people toward a heavenly paradise, the new faith filled the eyes of the people with visions of an earthly heaven. This new deism produced "the martyrdom of people willing to make sacrifices to lay down life itself for an idea." In a front-page article in the *Cincinnati Times Star*, Samuel was quoted as asking a high government official in Moscow: "Is not this misery of the people a frightful price to pay for the success of the Soviet idea?" The official answered:

> It is a high price, but still not as high as what the capitalistic countries paid for the last war. You killed off a generation in that war, some 20,000,000 men. You submitted millions of others to hideous suffering. But to what purpose? . . . what did you gain? . . . This was aimless suffering. . . . Yes, we suffer, but we at least suffer for a great purpose. We hope our sacrifices to establish the nobler social order that is our ideal. You Americans are suffering today also, but to what end?

While standing in one of those endless lines on which Russians had to wait hours for the meager supplies they were permitted to buy, Samuel observed:

> The sadness of a woman in rags reading Shakespeare in Russian. Probably nowhere in the world can one see such hunger for knowledge as in Russia. Youth attends universities in rags; the 95% illiteracy of Czarist Russia has been reduced to 40%. Today, standing on Soviet land, one is not by any means converted to the goals of world Communism.

He was impressed, however, and sympathetic to the introduction of the Five-Year Plans. A *Times Star* reporter asked, "Why not a Five-Year Plan here?"

"Let's call it a Five-Year Plan to abolish poverty," Samuel
replied: "—a plan to which we shall give all the intelligence, the
holy zeal, and scientific ingenuity we gave to winning the war
(World War I). Now we drift and don't know where we are going."

During this first visit, Samuel visited the Baltic states and was
impressed by the still great city of Vilnius (Vilna). Even then he
regarded it as a promising center of Jewish culture in the Diaspora.
Vilnius was still the "Jerusalem of Lithuania." He visited several
important synagogues and also the prayer room and study of the
Gaon of Vilna, a great sage of the eighteenth century. He perused
books in the Strashun Library, which had the greatest collection of
Judaica in the country.

The next year, 1932, he visited Warsaw for the first time. He
seemed to be transported to a poor approximation of medieval
times. The clothing fashions of many of the Jews he encountered
seemed to be medievalism blended with modern poverty. He met
others, emancipated Polish Jews, who were active in Jewish affairs
and culture, and had liberated themselves from the emotional
regressiveness and rigidity of the majority of the country's Jews. He
registered the fact painfully that an extreme Orthodox wing controlled the Kehilla of the Jewish Communal Organization. He was
fortunate to receive the guidance of two Warsaw newspaper editors
who were generous with information and time. The tens of thousands of Jews in the Nalewki district indelibly impressed his mind.
Walking through unbearable slums, there yet seemed to be a
tremendous Jewish renaissance. Books were published every day,
with poets and writers gathering at their clubs. Samuel had at least
one evening with them and described the discussions as "boister-
ous and informed."

Accompanied by the sports-editor grandson of Rabbi Abraham
Zevi Perlmutter, a prominent Orthodox leader and member of the
Polish parliament, or Sejm, he entered one of a number of Chasidic
shtieblech, or prayer houses, inside which mature yeshiva students
were continually studying.

Samuel relates,

In one of them, we were immediately surrounded by yeshiva students, some already bearded, dressed in kapotahs and the interrogation began. I was asked many embarrassing questions and had to skate on very thin ice in regard to Judaism, Reform Judaism, American Jews, etc. But when I asked one of their spokesmen "Why remain in this place— why not go to a yeshiva in Palestine?", this student pointed to the window and said—"When that window is closed, we hear nothing and see nothing and we do not care about the outside world." . . . When I tried to explain to this particular group what Reform Judaism means, I was countered with the question—"Do you believe in the Torah Min Hashomayim? (Torah from Heaven)." I tried to give an explanation that would not hurt their feelings, but was not successful. Soon I began to hear whispers and a kind of taunting with the words "'Apikorus—Apikorus (heretic)." I managed to give them a friendly Shalom and left their precinct.

Samuel walked and rode the narrow streets of the center of Warsaw. He reflected on the several months of his visits to lands and cities where he had encountered his brethren. His moods swung from periods of exultation to nadirs of gloom and pain. He was often both rebellious and dazed from the misery he had viewed and the agony he had experienced. Once the Nalewki had been teeming with life. Before the war, when it was still possible to do business with Russia, it had been an artery of commerce and industry; however,

Today it is a dark and brooding tragedy. Thousands have been pauperized literally. Business is at a standstill. . . . You see living corpses, hungry men and women, undernourished children. How they maintain life within their bodies, I don't know; how they endure such hardship, I can't understand. I went into the courtyards where life was teeming, where I could see with my own eyes. I made inquiries. "What do you do? How much to you earn?" I saw hundreds of people earning perhaps a zloty or two a day; not enough to buy food.

Samuel harkened back to the great merchants and mercantile activity of Warsaw. He noted that there had once been a great textile industry in Lodz. Now the factories were closed and Lodz resembled a graveyard of chimneys. In the surrounding countryside, conditions were even worse. Samuel noted in passing that Jewish life could not be sustained if not for the thousands of relatives sending a few dollars for the work of the Kasas (small credit banks), which the Joint Distribution Committee maintained in Poland.

In several speeches following his return, he asked the audience to consider the condition of life when the government is focused on the economic extermination of "our brethren." There were, to be sure, pogroms, riots, and excesses. But an unscrupulous government was achieving a much more diabolic method of economic ruination. The Jews in Poland were scrupulous in keeping the Sabbath. A vast majority, in fact, lived by the customs and ceremonies of their ancestors. The government compelled them to close their shops on Sundays, on all Catholic holidays, and on all national holidays. During the month of Nisan, when the Passover occurred, the various Catholic festive and patriotic holidays numbered eighteen days out of the month. This was certainly not because of the Polish government's concern about the religiosity of its people, but was calculated to destroy the industry and businesses of the Jew and to give his competitor a free hand. State monopolies confiscated Jewish businesses and industries, including one incident where 22,700 Jews were dismissed from the jobs. Similarly, Jews were prevented from working at many trades, and the numerus clausus, or quota system, prevented them from practicing their professions.

Considering the situation desperate, Samuel stressed, as he was to do many times in the future, the religious faith of the Jewish people, their iron will to survive, and the messianic dream of redemption. As a second source of hope and strength, he was quick, as always, to empower his audience. He had seen with his own eyes, "the lifesaving work done by the Joint Distribution Committee—aid given to Jewish schools, sanitation, public feeding and small bank credits." When he attended the World Jewish Conference in Geneva, he heard from men who were Jewish representatives in the various parliaments of Eastern Europe that never before, "not since the days of actual slaughter on the battlefield, not since the evacuations of thousands when they were driven from their homes into no-man's land, had there been such suffering as there was at this time."

Following the establishment of the Duma in Russia, the Bolshevik Revolution immediately terminated the process of Jewish emancipation. The Jews suffered more than any other group in response to the war and revolution. Demographics visited them with special misfortunes. During the subsequent civil war, anti-Bolshevik forces perpetrated pogroms in some 900 cities and villages of Ukraine and White Russia. Conservative estimates placed the number of Jewish dead at no less than 750,000. Another 500,000 to 600,000 hundred thousand left their homes and fled. It seemed to Samuel that the entire Jewish population of Ukraine had lived from 1918 to 1922 in constant terror, digging mass graves and reciting prayers for the dead.

As an invited lecturer to the Cosmic Club, Samuel again demonstrated his expertise in contemporary analysis of a people. He explained to the audience that the question of nationality was central to the position of the Jew in the Soviet Union. The Soviets did not recognize nationalities or separate constituent groups unless they occupied distinct territories. Therefore, the manner in which Jews as a group were to be absorbed into the new regime naturally posed a problem. The complete assimilation of disparate groups to the majority culture, frequently predicted by Bolshevik leaders, proved more difficult than had been expected. In addition to religious tradition, which still retained its hold upon the people, there had developed during the last half century, a type of national energy that now claimed expression. Where assimilation occurred, shaped toward the culture of Russia, it naturally strained relations within and between the lesser republics (Ukraine, White Russia, etc.) and their Jewish inhabitants. The million or so Jews who had emigrated to Russia proper were a small minority in the midst of a culturally and socially superior element. As a result, the little bit of Jewish culture they brought with them soon disappeared.

Samuel stressed the fact that Jews in the Soviet Union, at least on paper, possessed equal rights with all other citizens and were not subject to special legislation. At the same time, since they did not have distinct territory, they were not identified as a national unit in the Council of Nationalities. They were continuously subjected to political and other forms of discrimination and were totally without power or recognition.

The future and condition of the Jews in Eastern Europe was very discouraging to Samuel. When he returned home that autumn, he communicated his concerns to his congregation, the media, and the community at large. Soon, without his knowledge, he became persona non grata to the masters of the Kremlin. He found that he could not obtain a Soviet visa for his planned 1932 trip, and it was to be thirty years before he was able to obtain permission to visit Russia from Israel in the early sixties. In the meantime, he never wavered from his opinions, based on continual close study and observation of European affairs. He continued his mastery of the Russian language by copiously reading pre-revolutionary Russian books on Jewish subjects. He once remarked that a Russian newspaper was "the dullest thing on earth . . . it's strictly a propaganda tool."

Samuel's second tour of Russia, in the 1960s, unearthed numerous changes, great and small, since his 1931 visit. The Second World War had receded and the country appeared largely rebuilt. Remarkably, the town of Novaya Ushitsa still had about 6,000 inhabitants. Samuel observed that Jews were notable by their absence. During the war, they had been slaughtered by Nazi troops and the local citizenry. After the cessation of hostilities, the survivors had migrated to large cities where conditions for earning a living were more favorable. The street on which he had lived no longer existed, and he was able to find only two persons who remembered his family. The town was no longer the county seat. Indeed, it seemed dwarfed and insignificant within a surrounding necklace of interlocking, huge collective farms. Samuel's emotions were stirred deeply as he sensed the sterility of this small town and the disappearance of Jewish culture within Soviet boundaries. As an interesting highlight of his trip, he stood with the crowd in Red Square in Moscow and viewed a two-hour military parade marking May Day. He noted that every one of the Russian generals was with the high Communist Party officials as they watched the parade.

In 1934, Samuel provided a profound analysis of the events and forces loosed within the Soviet Union. He initially noted that "what we may consider fruit, others consider poison." He offered a series of contrasts between the American and Russian viewpoints concerning the businessman, profit incentives, individual wealth, and similar topics.

In our country, [the rich man] is often the source of goodness, the subject of praise and imitation. It is not so in that other world that stretches from the Black Sea to the Arctic. . . . A source of evil, it is forbidden to accumulate riches for it may become a weapon of oppression. Wealth belongs to society. Its use must be for all people; to increase their health, protect them from sickness, catastrophes, and old age; to give them education and recreation, to develop the instincts for collective achievement. . . . It was necessary to destroy, to crush all the enemies within, to be merciless and ruthless for the sacred cause of the revolution. Terror and cruelty were employed by the Communist government. Civil war, hunger, epidemics were the results. Millions perished. It was natural for people of the outside world to cry out in horror and to curse those who were considered responsible for the horrific upheaval. Now, however, world statesmanship has realized that a new power has come up upon the stage. Capitalism and Communism must live side by side, or in case of conflict, both of them will perish and sweep away all of civilization. The recent recognition of Russia by the United States established quite clearly that Western powers could not forcefully destroy Communism. It reiterated the principle of "live and let live" among nations.

The potential friendly relationships that might result from formal recognition, Samuel speculated, could be an added force for peace against the menace of Germany. "It means that the counsel and authority of these two great nations should be directed toward the liquidation of war. These may be added to those powers who seek peace, and the Hitler menace of the world eventually may be blocked and subdued."

Chapter 15
The Darkest Hour of Midnight

E very year, Samuel and many members of his congregation intoned the rhythmic poem "And it Came to Pass at Midnight" as part of the Passover Seder service. As one recited the verses, there was keen awareness of the cumulative horror pervading Germany and engulfing all of Europe, sending shudder after shudder throughout the globe.

They have raised the iron fist against humanity itself. No nation is safe from Hitler's madness. The infection is deadly. What is the rape of Belgium, and the Prussian Junker in 1914 compared to the anguish of the Jewish people trapped and degraded? The agony of Germany itself cries out to the conscience of the world. They have already utterly destroyed all of the advances made by farsighted dedicated men. Women have been enslaved again, sent back to the kitchen and to the breeding of warriors. Yes, they can say "Ja" at a Hitler election, but not one woman is permitted in the Reichstag.

Before his projected trip to Europe, Palestine, and the World Jewish Congress, Samuel wrote a brilliant contemporary analysis in which he condemned Nazism and at the same time pleaded for a "New Deal" for the German people. He noted that the contagious disease of Hitlerism apparently had infected the millions of German voters who had cast their ballots for the National Socialist Party, supporting the establishment of the most notorious anti-

Semitic machine of modern times. One hundred and seven Brown Shirts had marched into the Reichstag during the opening session of that legislative body, constituting a victory for the Nazi Party. Concurrently, this was celebrated with a pogrom in Berlin. Department stores and cafes were the particular objects of furious hooligans. These saviors of Germany had amused themselves in the Café Drobkin by smashing every dish and every piece of glassware in the establishment. The Hitlerite press had been carrying on a ceaseless and unrelenting anti-Jewish campaign for several years. Front pages were replete with caricatures of Jews and appeals urging Germans to do away with "Jewish domination." Jews were blamed for the Great Depression and were consistently described as immoral and therefore dangerous to the Reich. In Thuringia, a heavily populated area, schoolchildren were ordered to offer a prayer daily for the destruction of the Jews—the beginning of the mass poisoning of the hearts and minds of children.

The Nazi program or plan could be perceived as having two elements, one foreign and the other domestic. As a major aspect of foreign policy, Hitler demanded the cancellation of the Treaty of Versailles, draconian plans for economy reform, and enlarging Germany's armaments. He asked for an army equal to the French and for a navy equal to the English. He demanded the restoration of the Saar Valley, of eastern Silesia, and all of the former German colonies. Domestic policies were not as complex. Most essential of his demands were the political disenfranchisement of all Jews, the total abridgement of their rights, confiscation of their property, and that banks, newspapers, and theaters be taken away from them. As an afterthought, he demanded that all Jews who had come to Germany after 1914 be expelled from the country.

Samuel viewed the menace to the Jews as also a menace to the entire world and announced that it would destroy world peace. He pointed out that Hitler was not alone in making such a threat. The Communist Party constituted the next-strongest party in Germany.

German moderates deserve the support of the world since conflict is certain to ensue between Hitlerites and the Bolsheviks, throwing the whole land into upheaval and revolution and endangering the world far beyond the borders of Germany. . . . It is simply criminal on the part of the civilized world not to understand and appreciate the causes which are responsible for this state of affairs, and not to alleviate the grave and miserable situation of most of the German people. We do not require Hitler or the Communists to tell us that the Treaty of Versailles is an unjust and iniquitous treaty that may well supply the ammunition and powder for new wars. It is equally well known that the German people cannot, at this time, carry the burden of reparation placed upon them in view of the world depression, high tariffs, and the closing up of commercial markets throughout the world. It is inconceivable that the Germans will bear this terrible load for 57 years and mortgage their future generations. Irritations resulting from the domination of millions of Germans under foreign yoke cannot be dismissed lightly. Germany cannot stand by watching the entire world armed to its teeth and alone remain disarmed according to the provisions of the Versailles Treaty. It seems that Germany has a case before the civilized bar of nations. The present world-wide hunger for bread and employment has caused Germans to demonstrate the extremes of protest in their support of Fascism and Bolshevism. It is imperative that Germany receive a new deal. Our late President Wilson said that there must be peace without victory and that we did not make war upon the German people; and if we are to have peace in the world, now is the time to deal with those forces within Germany who are visible and protect them from catastrophe. Hitlerism must be quelled because of its inherent madness. This would-be dictator has made the Jews the scapegoat for the misery of Germany. He has convinced believing Germans that the Jews are responsible for the German's present economic conditions and when it comes down to plain survival, medieval passions can be roused and the ugliest expressions come to the fore. Moreover, the German, like the Romanian and the Pole, must vent his feelings on somebody and for this purpose the Jew always comes in most handy. Here is a pertinent example: when Paderewski approached the Allies regarding ceding Danzig to Poland after the war, he was met coldly. He explained to the victors the possible consequences. "When the Polish hear of your decision," he said, "they will declare a day of mourning, close their shops and massacre the Jews." The Allies were a little disconcerted at this prediction and asked the question: "Suppose we obtain Danzig for you, what then?" "Ah," Paderewski answered, "That's another story. Poles will be overjoyed. A national holiday will be declared, shops will be closed and they will go out and massacre the Jews." They *did* get Danzig and they *did* massacre Jews.

Samuel understood that in a time of economic unrest, flames of hatred are kindled quickly. Attacks upon Jews might divert the attention of the people from basic issues, but the world would have to pay a price for permitting such insanity.

Let Hitler remember that countries that have done violence to Jews are now in ruins. Let him ponder the fate of the Kolchaks, Denikins, Wrangels, Petluras, and other pogromists of post-war days. To make the Jews a scapegoat for Germany's ills is a dastardly outrage. German Jews have done more for Germany than it is possible to recount. Heine gave them poetry. Ballin and Deutsch gave them commerce and electricity, Preuss—the constitution of the new republic; Walther Rathenau was one of the most significant factors in Germany's reconstruction before Hitler-type fanatics murdered him ruthlessly, and of course the foremost scientist of the ages, Einstein, was forced to flee. They who sympathized with Hitler's criminal anti-Jewish campaign would do well to ponder over the words of Rathenau's mother who wrote to the mother of one of her son's slayers: "In grief unspeakable, I give you my hand. You, of all women, the most pitiable. Say to your son that in the name and spirit of him who was murdered, I forgive, even as God may forgive, if before an earthly judge he makes a full and frank confession of his guilt, and before a heavenly one repent. Had he known my son, the noblest man earth bore, he had rather turn the weapon on himself than on him. May these words give peace to your soul."

Following his initial visits to Germany, in 1931 and 1932, Samuel was featured by Cincinnati writers as "perhaps the only Jew who heard directly the pogrom-inciting speech of Julius Streicher, Hitler's number-one lieutenant in Berlin." Streicher, at that time, was arguably closer to Hitler than any of the other Nazi lieutenants. On Streicher's day of honor in Berlin, no resident Jew dared leave his home. Samuel was warned that the anti-Semitic fury unleashed might not distinguish an American Jew from native co-religionists. Nevertheless, he left his hotel in a cab, which parked in the street near the auditorium where Streicher spoke. For nearly two hours he sat in the cab intently listening to Streicher's venomous gutturals through the amplifiers installed for the benefit of the overflow crowd. William L. Shirer alluded to this German official as possibly the most disreputable of Hitler's lieutenants and a blindly fanatical anti-Semite. He published the notorious *Der Stürmer*, an organ of hatred and lascivious gossip. No one who opposed him was safe from death or prison.

Under Nazi rule, the German nation, which had given the world Heine, Kant, Goethe, Schiller, Bach, Beethoven, and Brahms, quickly transformed itself into a metastatic mass invading and destroying neighboring nations and peoples. Samuel discerned that for almost a century the labor movement had been a major constructive force in Germany. The resulting social legislation of great import had benefited the entire German nation and, as well, had become a model and inspiration for other civilized lands. He described the crushing of the German labor movement, the smashing of its unions, the pillage of its funds, its properties confiscated, its leaders beaten, maimed, and in concentration camps. German universities were also infested with the sadism of the swastika. Courses were decimated and reformulated around fascist pseudoscience and dogma. University faculties, "honest, liberal, cultured men," were driven into exile or locked behind prison bars. The students themselves indulged in orgies of book burning. Artists, thinkers, and intellectuals were prostrate. Samuel accurately assayed Nazi militarism and correctly predicted a cataclysmic destruction of many lands. Early in the 1930s, he stated that

> you cannot isolate the struggle. Nazis in other lands will rise in civil war. Within the sphere of Nazism, every child is trained and taught to hate, every man is frightened and given a bayonet and every voice for peace has been extinguished. Shall every human being anywhere keep still while an abysmal slaughter threatens the world and not do everything in his power to contain the Nazi madness? If this is *not* done, we shall have ourselves to blame. This is not solely a Jewish problem and every Christian ought to know that Nazism is an enemy of his faith; of all Christendom.

James Heller and Samuel Wohl both labored to enable their congregations, their community, and their country to fully grasp the appalling tragedy "spread before our very eyes." Anything less they considered to be callous and disloyal to their suffering brethren. Samuel looked frantically about him. More than 60,000 refugees had already escaped the "inferno." Samuel's early statements referred to the "vigor of certain statements of France, England, Holland, and other powers in expressing concern for the Jewish people." (Such statements, it seems, come easily to political figures.)

The League of Nations would not and could not tell the Nazi barbarians to cease, and it took inadequate steps to ameliorate the conditions of the refugees by setting up a League commission under the leadership of James McDonald, the former head of the American Foreign Policy Commission. Some fifteen countries served on the governing board. France, England, and the United States were represented by well-known statesmen. Despite his hopes, Samuel realized that this organization could never succeed. At that time, any additional Jews sent to lands that had already absorbed thousands of them would constitute too great a burden upon the resources of their co-religionists and also cause irritations and animosities in countries where unemployment was quite high.

Obliquely referring to Palestine, Samuel proclaimed that new places must be found and colossal funds obtained. Tens of thousands had already emigrated. The exodus had just begun. McDonald, a few days after his return from the commission's session at Lausanne, appealed to "the Christians of America":

I wish I had the power to give the Christian people of this country a realization of their responsibilities. Crimes against the Jew are committed in the name of Christianity and "Aryanism." . . . the result is that tens of hundreds of thousands of men, women, and innocent children are suffering because of certain theories about race and religion.

Samuel hoped that American non-Jews would show the world that they were not parties to such persecution. He considered the McDonald commission an important event that could arouse the conscience of humanity. He and almost everyone else viewed the League of Nations as hopelessly inadequate and much less an instrument for world peace than had been envisioned by its founder, Woodrow Wilson.

As a supplement to the League commission, the 1934 Jewish Economic Conference, held in London, marked the beginning of worldwide Jewry's ability to carry their many burdens more effec-

tively. Samuel wondered if, for this one cause, "we can agree to
work together." He feared that the notoriously disunited efforts and
manifest animosities between rival Jewish organizations and leaders would display glaring weaknesses before the world.

> The time has come that in self-defense and for the protec-
> tion of our honor, we must erect and maintain a united
> front. At this hour our energies must be directed toward a
> speedy rebuilding of the Jewish homeland; a home for the
> homeless. This is a test that cannot wait and if delayed, will
> add to our misfortunes. This is no longer a job for Zionists
> who seek no credit and wish no monopoly, but this is a call
> for all of those in whom the Jewish spark is still aglow, who
> must come and share in the labor.

The year 1933 was a banner year for immigration into
Palestine. By then-current estimates, 400,000 Jews had settled
there, and the country could have absorbed 200,000 more were it
not for restrictions placed by the British mandatory government.
Samuel knew that much more could be accomplished if large
resources could be obtained for Palestine settlement.

> Never in our history have the Jews in a critical hour, when
> hundreds of thousands are homeless, had the opportunity of
> restoring the Holy Land to its people. History will sit in
> judgment, whether Jewish refugees settled elsewhere, let us
> say in European countries or South America, may, within a
> few decades, suffer the same fate as under darkest Germany.
> A Jew saved and settled in Palestine now will in time bring
> in three more Jews into the land. By the end of 1933, that
> tiny strip along the eastern Mediterranean by the strength
> of its national will have accomplished the building of cities,
> planting of orange groves, draining of swamps, harnessing
> the Jordan for the electrification of the land, and trans-
> forming the Dead Sea into a reservoir of chemical wealth.
> These monumental achievements are taken for granted by

modern generations who view Israel as an independent and self-reliant entity, *not* dependent on private philanthropy and alms.

In 1941, Samuel Wohl understood that everything was at stake in the outcome of World War II. The vindication of his pronouncements surely places Samuel in the prophetic mold.

When we review the murder, degradation, torture, and destruction—moral and physical—which the [Nazi] barbarians have visited upon the earth, when we contemplate the utter fragmentation of the foundations of civilization, the dissolution of boundaries between good and evil, we see that more evil has been inflicted in these terrible years than in the long darkness of the Middle Ages, with their persecutions and cruelties. It is the time of the agonies the Messiah foretold in the convulsive visions of the prophets and in the Apocrypha. "God's lore will be wiped out from the heart of man. Samael will become the sole lord and ruler; the heavens will rain down stones and blazing arrows; the field will bring forth abominable beasts, such as the human eye has not yet beheld; the sea will spit forth dreadful creatures, which the imagination cannot conceive. There will be no hiding place." . . . for this period the Kabbalah and Jewish mysticism coined the phrase "the twilight." "The twilight has descended because corrupt, vicious, stupid rulers, greedy imperialists, and venal politicians have betrayed the humanity of man and the divinity of God. However, this is not the end. It is a scourge. It plagueth man, but the world needs to be cleansed, and needs to be awakened to a new faith."

At this time, officials of the Joint Distribution Committee and the Jewish Telegraphic Agency began publishing regular and accurate reports of German massacres and imprisonment of Jews. A pall had fallen over world Jewry with the knowledge that Nazi extermination camps were in operation. Samuel urged his congregation to partake of the divine spirit and divine power. On Rosh Hashanah, he urged them to "take the Shofar [ram's horn] of faith and drive out the demons within that are devouring your soul and you will transform every punishment from a curse into a blessing, —every degradation into a victory."

Then, four years later at the High Holy Day services in 1945, just after World War II had ended, he said:

> The long bitter years have come to an end. There is quiet joy in our hearts. Unlike the days of yesteryear, the mouth of the cannon is stilled, fear and terror cannot seize our hearts. We may take the hand of our neighbor and confidently hope for a happy new year.

In the flush of victory, Samuel nonetheless thanked his God for the vindication of justice and truth, and for what he termed the stouthearted and unfaltering faith of the Jewish people. He credited the United States with "the liberating word to raise up tortured and wounded nations, to snatch away big lands and small, white, black and yellow people from the maw of the ravenous tyrant." He visualized a covenant sealed in the blood of peoples: "Chinese blood is red, Russian blood is red, African blood is red. It is all one blood poured out on every land, not to dominate, not to enslave, but to bring liberty and justice." He called on mankind "not to betray us, not to cause the blood to have been spilled in vain." Speaking for the millions of dead, he cried out,

> Do not make deals for oil, for mines, for trade at the expense of the dead. Not for that did we die. . . . We the dead are young in years, but eternal in spirit. We summon you on the threshold of a new triumphant era. Keep the ennobled banner; do not let the demagogues, the haters, the rabble rousers, the despots ever take it from you. Remember Dachau and Buchenwald. Remember every land to which marauders brought misery and shame.

Remember the millions of your martyred brethren who were the innocent victims of a Germany poisoned and corrupted. . . . It was the negation of mercy and love and brotherhood which fired the inferno. When man went forth to rob and lie and undermine the foundation of his house, he brought down the ruin upon himself. Write it down that peace is not something to be won and then forgotten. It is to be kept in a garden. It must be renewed like the soil after it has yielded good crops. Write it down—no more overlords among nations, among classes, among races or religions. No more hunger in the midst of plenty. No more insecurity, unemployment or other man-made inequities. All of these should go. This is really why we are alive today. If not for that, all would be mockery. No more anti-Semitism. Tell this to our friends. We are sick to death of it. We abominate the rascalities of the hate mongers. If I were a Christian, I would be utterly ashamed of the profanation of a faith, the besmirchment of its escutcheon, with inquisitions, expulsions, pogroms, and exterminations of Jews.

Samuel always seemed to have words to match the power of the occasion. His sermons and addresses hammered relentlessly on the desperate situation of the Jewish people who he believed faced extermination in Europe. But these pronouncements and warnings often seemed to fall on deaf ears and were muted by the indifference and hostility of the free world and the massive denial of the Jews themselves, who apparently could not face the monstrous reality of a modern Western nation that purposely and systematically stripped them of their legal protections and human rights, and then even more methodically engaged in their destruction.

Samuel was a member of a worldwide united Jewish delegation that presented the distilled essence of hundreds of cables to President Franklin Roosevelt. This information was confirmed by the State Department and several governments in exile. Samuel noted that he could not systematically review or even conceptualize the horrible details and factual materials that constituted limit-less crimes of such staggering proportions that it was almost impos-sible to place them on paper. In 1942, he stated, the closed shut-ters of the gentile world had opened slightly upon the horror of horrors. He estimated that more than 2,000,000 Jews had been put to death and that other millions "are prostrate before the sadism of murderers." He commented that the president had received the united delegation and reiterated strong warnings to the Axis pow-ers. The press had at long last started to uncover the frightening details captured in the memorandum placed before the president. The president "promised to consider with sympathy the proposals of the delegation. The United States and the United Nations will establish a special commission to investigate all the terrible deeds and to place on record the names of all the guilty criminals."

Highly tentative discussions between Washington, London, and Moscow were occurring on how to stay or reduce the slaugh-ter. But Samuel wondered,

> Is this all we can do? Should we merely ask for an investi-gating commission? —The commission is intended only to recommend punishment for the mountains of dead, who no longer can be helped. Consider those who are still living. How can they be saved? Is there no plan, no way to save a large portion of them from the marauding beast?

He was to suggest again and again a ceaseless campaign to save as many victims as possible. He spoke many times of plans involv-ing the exchange of Jews in Nazi-occupied territories for German prisoners in the free countries. Also, the paying of ransoms, as done with other kidnappers and bandits, had seemed successful. He immediately raised the question that if we succeeded in some mea-sure in ransoming lives, the problem remained: who would admit the victims?

In tones of strained emotional control, he pleaded in order to stir the conscience of all democratic peoples. Why could not Russia

declare, for instance, that she would admit Jews from Poland whom
the Nazis would permit to cross the border, and why should not the
other Allies at least establish some places of refuge for those who
might escape from the slaughter, even if they were placed tem-
porarily on a reservation where they could be cared for by their fellow Jews? Why should not Palestine serve as a principal refuge?
Why could not tens of thousands of victims be brought there?

He wrote time and again in favor of establishing a permanent
life-saving general staff, not one that met on occasion, but one that
was constantly working, planning, and utilizing every opportunity.
One that would be always alert and would not rest. He knew that
public opinion had not yet been roused to action. Nothing had
been heard from Congress, from every state legislature, from governors, from labor leaders, from most editors. He pleaded in the
name of "our common God" and humanity to make this a preemi-
nent cause, a cause of mercy. He described the Jews as the first victims of this war.

> We more than any people have suffered. Not all the armies
> in the western world have suffered casualties as we have.
> None are doomed to total extermination as our martyred
> brethren. Surely we ought *not* to come begging. An aroused
> America, worthy of its heritage and its name, should rise up
> and offer help. It should tell its congressmen to permit
> every boat on its return voyage to bring back lives.

In the thirties and early forties, President Franklin Roosevelt
was much admired and idealized by the Jews of America. Samuel,
for example, was greatly impressed by Roosevelt's economic policy,
the New Deal, which he saw as basically restoring the country's
economic health and leading to a plethora of social and governmental reforms. And yet he knew that the State Department had
long been influenced by Britain's Foreign Ministry, and that both
were insensitive, if not hostile, to the plight of the Jewish people.
Very clearly, by 1944, the State Department was responsible for a

wall of silence and denial regarding what was happening to Jews abroad and was obstructive and resistive to belated attempts at a rescue.

Samuel realized that President Roosevelt could not be regarded as "different from the Congress and the State Department." He wondered how we can "ever raise our heads without humiliation, when the common enemy who would destroy our land and our children and whom we now fight all over the globe can point his finger in derision at our Congress. He might say 'You see, even if I would release some miserable thousands, you would not let them enter.' Is this true? I am afraid we have many in Congress so blind and callous that even disaster has not changed them." In private conversations with us, our father admitted that we should hold the president to the same standards as other public figures.

Despite all this, Samuel continued to hope that the great American nation would be awakened. He suggested that it should be part of her public and proclaimed war aims to save from the enemy, lives doomed to extermination. He challenged Winston Churchill and the British Parliament to say, "We shall be true to our pledged word; this is our answer to the enemy. Let people who can save themselves be admitted to Palestine. Let America, Britain and Russia proclaim 'We will not be partners by our passivity to these monstrous crimes of extermination.' " He pleaded with his "brothers of the Protestant and Catholic faith. Send your urgent plea to the President and Congress to stop the slaughter of the innocents. They should save all persons that can be saved."

This American rabbi had the vocabulary and terminology to present the Jewish view in the most cogent manner. His musings to his congregation and other groups in the late forties were from his heart and keenly analytical at the same time. The Holocaust unleashed by Hitler and the German people destroyed a third of the Jews throughout the world and caused survivors to undergo frightful hardships until they reached a haven of refuge.

Now we are confronted with the fact which cannot be overlooked or removed from the agenda of our consciousness; that no Jews are being murdered in the Soviet Union but *Judaism* is being murdered. Soviet internal propaganda defamed and disgraced the Jewish people within their country, over saturating them with fear and stressing a pro-Arab policy. They defamed Israel as "neo-colonists," imperialists and a culture that is being used to conspire against the so-called "popular" democracies in the Soviet Union.

Samuel's hands were thrown up in literal disgust and despair as he wondered aloud why Roosevelt, Churchill, and other statesmen sat by and did not aid the people who were haunted and hunted? Why was so great a burden placed upon the Jewish people? The American State Department, in a manner of excuse and explanation, implausibly emphasized that all energies and all consideration were directed toward winning the war. Concurrently, the president could tolerate a situation with boats crammed with refugees, roaming the seas and finding no country that would admit them. It was only toward the end of the war, when the obstructionism of the U.S. State Department had been revealed and the media at long last had begun to report the full depth and extent of the Axis atrocities, that Roosevelt, in a pitiful gesture, delegated Ira Hirschmann to deal with the Romanian Nazis in order to buy the lives of several thousand men who were doomed to extermination in Transnistria.

As we have already recounted, Samuel had the opportunity to learn about German Jewry in the pre-Hitler era. Through reading and avid attention to newsreels and news sources, he fully appreciated how Germany's relatively small community of some 600,000 Jews had achieved magnificently in all fields of the arts and science. When he actually visited that country, he was immediately engulfed in the tensions which the Hitler movement had created. He met with the leaders of the Hilfsverein der Deutschen Juden and found them remarkably slow in recognizing what appeared to him to be an impending catastrophe. German Jewry left a great legacy to world Jewry. However, after the war, it no longer existed as a community. In the late thirties, it was still uncertain whether any number would remain or find homes else-where in the world.

Samuel referred to Austria, whose people had welcomed Hitler with open arms and seemed to outdo other Nazi groups with their devotion to fascism. There had been intense Jewish life in the for-mer Austro-Hungarian Empire. The Jewish population was consid-ered relatively emancipated. Theodor Herzl did his great writing in Vienna, and that capital was the center of creativity for such men as Freud, Schnitzler, and Hugo von Hofmannsthal.

Continuing his historical perspective, Samuel described France as "quite unfortunate" during the period preceding Hitler. Her economy was stagnant, and her politicians were changing govern-ments several times a year. Léon Blum, who was premier of France at the time of the Spanish Civil War, declared his country's neu-trality, thus effectively preventing the channeling of aid to the anti-fascist Spanish loyalists. Samuel regarded Blum as "among the finest [leaders] of this age, a man of culture and genuine greatness." Blum was victimized by the Nazis when they conquered France. Fortunately, he escaped from a prison camp in Germany and was later remembered by the French as a leader who had brought not only glory but also integrity to the office of premier. It was a tragedy that the man who had signed the document that established the Jewish Agency for Palestine was later practically destroyed by his own party. Apparently, France was sensitized by the ongoing con-flict in Spain and reacted as if it were a rehearsal for another world war. Thus every leader was subjected to unnatural constraints, and France, like Britain, seemed to perform an endless gavotte of appeasement and futility.

As Czechoslovakia emerged in freedom from the Communist yoke, Samuel found himself intrigued and fascinated by this small country established by the Allies after the First World War and the dissolution of the Austro-Hungarian Empire through the efforts of Thomas Masaryk and Edward Benes. Masaryk proclaimed the founding of the republic from the steps of Independence Hall in Philadelphia. After World War II, under the auspices of the Joint Distribution Committee, Samuel journeyed behind the Iron

Always a teacher

First Hebrew class, 1915 (Cleveland, Ohio)

Age 22, Rabbi Wohl, Cleveland

Consecration class, Isaac M. Wise Temple, 1932

Consecration class, 1935

The joys of the pulpit of the historic
Isaac M. Wise Temple in Cincinnati

Rabbi Wohl receives the congregation at the foot of the altar at the Plum Street Temple

Distinguished faculty of Hebrew Union College, left to right, Dr. Samuel Cohon, Dr. Julian Morgenstern, Rabbi Wohl, Rabbi Solomon Freehof, Dr. Nelson Glueck, Dr. Israel Bettan

Samuel Wohl and beloved wife, Belle Wohl

*Perennial President of Isaac M. Wise Temple
Sidney Weil and his wife Florence pictured with Rabbi Wohl*

Always a world traveler representing
Histadruth and JDC and exploring Jewish life

Leipzig, Germany, last Jewish Maccabiad with Joachim Prinz

French Jewish orphans after the Holocaust

Spain, 1948, arriving for an important mission

Buenos Aires, 1956, with the leaders of Argentinian Jewry

Gregarious, friendly, sought-after – A man about town,
a man of wisdom, a man of vintage, a man of the people

1945

With High School graduation class, 1943

1965

With Dr. Nelson Glueck, President of HUC-JIR
as he celebrates his 70th birthday, 1965

In Israel in 1932 with the intellectual leadership of the Yishuv featuring Shmarya Levin

In 1948, Jerusalem with soon to be Prime Minister Golda Meir

In 1950, arriving at Lod Airport

With President Yitzhak Ben Zvi of Israel, 1959

With his beloved family

With beloved wife Belle

Three generations –
Rabbi Samuel Wohl, son Amiel Wohl and grandson Dewey Wohl

Three generations – Rabbi Samuel Wohl, son Ted Wohl and grandson Dan Wohl

In 1965 on his 70th birthday, flanked by his sons, the authors, left, Rabbi Amiel Wohl, right, Dr. Theodore H. Wohl

*In 1974, Rabbi Albert Goldman, Mrs. Samuel Wohl and sons participate in the
dedication of the Rabbi Samuel Wohl Chapel at the temple in Cincinnati*

*Sons Amiel and Ted Wohl at the final resting place,
United Jewish Cemetery, Cincinnati, 1995*

Curtain to Prague in order to evaluate and describe the country and its people, and particularly its Jewish population.

In connection with this mission, he recalled the time long before when Thomas Masaryk had visited Cleveland to address and win support from the city's Czechs and Slovaks. It had been Samuel's privilege to greet him as a member of the Jewish community delegation. Jews, even at that early stage of the existence of Czechoslovakia, knew Masaryk as a champion of their cause and existence. He was also received with great enthusiasm and affection in Israel, which he visited a few years before his death. There is now a small village named Kefar Masaryk in his memory.

Czechoslovakia became the best-governed and most prosperous country in Central Europe. At times there were flarings of animosity between the Czechs and Slovaks, aided and abetted by reactionary forces in Germany, Austria, and Hungary. Yet the country survived and prospered, utilizing its fine agriculture and excellent industrial economy to resist the European tides of inflation and depression. Shamefully, with the connivance of England and France, Czechoslovakia was dismembered and turned over to the tender mercies of the German Nazis. The murders at Lidice and Theresienstadt were direct consequences of this high-thuggery diplomacy. With the exception of the ethnic Germans of the Sudetenland, the Czech population could not forgive this betrayal by the Western Allies, and one must remember that it was the Red Army that liberated them.

The democratic leaders of Czechoslovakia, Edward Benes, and Jan Masaryk, were not friends of Communism, but they felt obliged to conclude an alliance with the Soviet Union. The Czechs, immediately after the war, were intensely friendly toward the United States but very wary of Britain and France, which they perceived as no longer to be trusted. The fear of a resurrected Germany drove all political parties to acquiesce to the seizure of power by the Communists and their political allies.

Despite the turning toward Russia, Samuel perceived that the new government had no objection to the return of political émigrés of any stripe, particularly when they were supported by British and American funds. From Professor Ventura of the Ministry of Information, Samuel was able to gain valuable insights into the mind of this small country. Before the war, while anti-Semitism was rising all over Europe, Ventura, a gentile, was president of the League Against Anti-Semitism, a role that earned him a long stay in the concentration camps of Dachau and Buchenwald.

Ventura told him that the lesson of Munich was too serious to be forgotten, and that the people of Czechoslovakia were hypersensitive to the reconstruction of Germany. Although they sympathized with the West and hoped for a two-way traffic in trade, the Czech people believed that their country must be intimately associated with the Soviet Union. The official opinion of the regime, which waxed and waned with the peaks and valleys of the Cold War, was that American foreign policy was imperialistic. There were official pronouncements, not believed by most Czechs, that the Marshall Plan would lead to later political and economic pressure and control. Despite the Communists, there was little friction between church and state. No church lands were confiscated, and the dominant Roman Catholic Church was not then engaged in oppositional acts toward the regime.

Samuel enjoyed Prague more than almost any other city in Europe. He viewed it as beautiful, quaint, historic, and yet contemporary. It retained much of its medieval atmosphere and was quite livable and intimate. As usual, he noticed the book shops ("more on one street than in the entirety of most of our larger cities"). He noted its glorious Jewish history. It was, after all, the city of Rabbi Judah Loew, the great sage known as the Maharal of Prague, who according to legend had created the famous Golem. In the earliest moments of freedom following World War II, the monuments of Rabbi Loew and the Golem were restored to the two front corners of the city hall of the Jewish district. The Old-New Synagogue, 800 years old in 1948, proudly presented its unique Gothic architecture with ornate iron railings, bronzes, ancient inscriptions, and a treasure trove of documents. The Jewish city hall still has a clock in its tower giving the correct time in Hebrew characters.

In the 1920s, the Jewish population of Prague was around 60,000, and the city was a great center of Jewish religion, learning, literature, and music. Throbbing with vitality, it was the city of Max Brod, Franz Kafka, and a score of novelists and poets. Samuel pensively regarded the city in which the native Jewish population had departed, first to the ghetto of Theresienstadt, then to Auschwitz and the gas chambers. Only 3 percent of the city's original Jewish population survived the war. After the war, Jews migrated to Prague from the small towns, from Hungary and from Carpatho-Russia, and became Czech citizens rather than live in the Soviet Ukraine.

Samuel noted that Czechoslovakia had taken a new path. It had made its choice, and as he observed, one might well remember that the great powers, having been guilty of betrayal, really had no right to sit in judgment. He advocated aid and understanding rather than isolation or force. The Czech people would never forget that the United States had played a major role in the restoration of their country. In view of their difficulties, he felt, and despite the unfriendly regime, we could help greatly in the rehabilitation of their trade.

Interestingly, at that time Jews were free to engage in any work or profession in the country, but most of them expressed a wish to emigrate to Israel, and only Jews were permitted to emigrate legally. Furthermore, at that time, the government furnished aid to Israel. Although Samuel was privy to the details of this exchange, he could not at that time disclose any details about it, but he did observe that "Czechoslovakia is to Israel now what France was to the United States in 1776."

Chapter 16
Denazification, DP Camps, Mexico, South America, and Japan

Continuing his series of journeys to Europe and Israel, Samuel visited Germany several times during the postwar period. He went there some two years after the war to view and evaluate the denazification process in the still glowing ashes of the charnel house that was the European continent. He found new growth beginning to appear, much like the aftermath of a raging forest fire when verdant plants poke their heads through the gray-black forest floor. Most of Europe was rebuilding at an almost frenzied rate, a frenzy fueled by American aid. Nevertheless, as Samuel lamented, European and even American propagandists of every stripe were still accusing the United States of all manner of crimes.

Samuel felt that it should be clear to any decent person with no axe to grind that the United States, although demanding unconditional surrender from Germany, took nothing for itself—no territories, no reparations. On the contrary, the United States immediately saw to it that relief was given to the Germans as well as their victims. This Herculean task was carried through under the leadership of Senator Herbert Lehman and New York's mayor, Fiorello LaGuardia. Even during Samuel's last visit to Germany in 1948, it was the USO, still functioning in Germany and Italy, that gave aid and reunited families, thereby helping to mend the fabric of their lives.

The so-called denazification process was another story entirely. The rabbi called it, quite bluntly, a farce. He perceived, correctly, that the few sensational trials of leading Nazis made little impact on the thinking German masses. The *Spruchkammers*, or denazification courts, neatly whitewashed and fragrantly anointed with purity most of the savage S.S. guards, storm troopers, and predatory industrialists.

Wherever he turned, Samuel found these "freshly born 'democrats' in key positions of influence." The editor of an important German newspaper informed Samuel that most of the *Spruchkammer* judges had little desire to carry out the denazification procedures. The accused were often the most politically influential people, who wielded social and economic power by which they threatened retaliation against harsh judges.

The editor continued, saying that for a short time after liberation, those who had genuinely suffered from the Nazi terror, former inmates of Buchenwald, Dachau, and other infamous places, were given priority in employment or services. For an even briefer time, he said, it was a mark of distinction to have been a sincere opponent of the Nazis. Passports contained entries identifying the bearer as a former victim of Buchenwald or Auschwitz. But in only a few years, there were numerous instances of men being refused employment because such annotations made them less desirable. Few would now publicly claim that they had been anti-Nazi.

Although the press was licensed by the occupying power, Samuel found, it seldom deplored the recent Nazi crimes. The party line of German superiority was noticeable in many articles about Russia and its satellites. They contained the familiar spicing of anti-Semitism. Although Jews were almost nonexistent in Germany, they were said to be quite actively manipulating the black market. Responsible German observers soberly prophesied that as soon as American authority was withdrawn, no "liberal" newspaper in Germany would survive and the nationalist press would certainly take over.

When Samuel landed on German soil, he found that the Germans were ignoring the many displaced persons in the American zone. Furthermore, they had not publicly admitted their own guilt nor, at that time, had they returned their loot. Wherever

American political or military advisers tried to assist in the birth of democracy, it was stillborn, or so weak one could not feel its pulse.

Although Samuel praised the Allied military forces, he questioned the wisdom of inducting tens of thousands of teenage boys into an army of occupation. The army command referred to this policy as "morale enhancing," but Samuel considered the omnipresent German frauleins as not only winning undue sympathy for Germany but enabling legions of friends and parents to receive economic support from the boy soldiers.

Samuel concluded that these liaisons were "bringing into the United States, thousands of German wives" with a "variety of Nazi-colored viewpoints." He cynically wondered what the House Un-American Activities Committee would "do about this." He knew that the adolescents and young men who arrived in Germany after the war did not even know what the Germans had done—how they had killed and tortured Americans and what they inflicted on other peoples throughout Europe. They viewed only the wrecked German cities and, of course, the pleasing frauleins. He wryly observed that Goebbels, Hitler's propaganda minister, had remarked as the end of the war loomed, "The German frauleins will yet win the war for Germany."

During this period, East and West were competitively courting the Germans, each wishing to attract the former Nazis into its own controlled German parties. In the British, American, and Soviet zones, there were no scruples wasted about welcoming ex–storm troopers, protecting and plying them with all sorts of inducements. Samuel heard an alumnus of five years in Dachau say with a sigh, "Oh, how nice it is to be a Nazi. Both sides are so eager to befriend you." Samuel observed that the Cold War delineated only the blunders that diplomats were committing. "To our great sorrow, Western diplomacy is once again proving inept and is losing the peace for which millions have died." The German problem must be firmly settled, he lectured sternly, and not be permitted to serve as "an apple of discord between East and West."

Meanwhile, three years after liberation, thousands of Jewish refugees and survivors were living in scores of displaced-persons camps. Samuel was not at all shocked by their condition. Thanks to the American Army, the Joint Distribution Committee, and the Jewish Agency, a magnificent job had been accomplished and was continuing.

As he sat with the Central Committee of Liberated Jews in Munich, Samuel experienced a feeling of deep admiration for these men and women who were engaged in planning for the education and cultural activities of tens of thousands of displaced children and adults. And he continually asked himself, "Why?" Why were *they* victims of so much horror, and why do *I* merit this role as benefactor?

> I asked myself many questions and had many heartaches. Their spirit, that flame of faith imbibing strength, made them live with a life of dignity and hope with their minds and hearts. They rose from the crematoria and gas chambers and created Jewish culture. I felt surging within me not pity, not merely the desire to help, but pride that I was their brother and (prophetically) that this remnant will yet become a great blessing for Israel.

Samuel considered it a privilege to speak in several DP camps. At one point, he addressed hundreds, perhaps thousands, gathered in the central square in Munich. He spent a morning observing a Jewish kindergarten and gymnasium (high school) in that city. He was stirred by the feeling that these children and young people were already, in a manner of speaking, in the cities and villages of Israel. The doors to Israel were partially ajar; thousands of Jews from the camps were already there. Every day the exodus continued. The remaining thousands knew, with hopefulness and faith, that their turn would come soon. Samuel predicted, with prescience, that soon the "accursed chapter of D.P. living will come to a close and that new citizens will join the ranks of pioneers and fighters in Israel."

Samuel made the obligatory visit to Dachau with its gas chambers and ovens and remarked, "Empty it was but the air will ever be polluted by its infamy." Nuremberg was the next stop. There, Samuel visited the court chambers where Hermann Goering, chief of the Luftwaffe and Hitler's designated successor; Rudolf Hess, deputy fuhrer; Hjalmar Schacht, minister of economics and president of the Reichsbank; and other major Nazi criminals had been tried. During the session he attended, three American judges were presiding over the war crimes trials of the second-echelon group of Nazi criminals; among them were Otto Dietrich, chief of the press office of the Propaganda Ministry; Otto Lebrecht Meissner, Staatsminister and judicial official; Ernst von Bohle, of the Foreign Ministry and the Nazi Party's foreign bureau; and a group of cabinet ministers who had served under Hitler.

Samuel read the charges and indictments. Each of the defendants was accused of instituting slave labor, all were acknowledged to have instituted torture all over Europe. Like other contemporary observers of the Nuremberg trials, Samuel observed no sadness or shame in the faces or demeanor of the accused.

To see Berchtesgarten and the Berghoff, the homes of Goering, Bormann, and other Nazi chieftains, as well as even the S.S. barracks, turned into rubble, drove home with force the enormity of the crimes committed there. Samuel found himself praying that never again should any people have to face the misery of war.

Leaving Germany, he confessed that he had little hope that the country was moving toward democracy. The thousand-year chapter of Jewish life in Germany, with its glory, triumphs, and achievements, was finished. He hoped that within the next eighteen months, all of the DPs would be out of Germany and that the land would remain "an anathema for Jews for many ages."

Samuel crisscrossed the oceans with regularity, in the years of rebuilding in postwar Europe. He was sent on most of these trips by the Jewish Agency, the Joint Distribution Committee, and Histadruth. The local and national Jewish press as well as the general media requested and eagerly received Samuel's findings and opinions garnered from these journeys.

Both the Jewish Telegraph Agency and the International News Service published the same picture of Samuel standing behind a group of Jewish war orphans. The photo was taken to highlight the joyful news in 1948 that the Jewish DP problem could be liquidated within eighteen months. Resettlement was only one project of the Joint Distribution Committee, a major Jewish welfare organization, which still today assists Jews in multitudinous ways.

Samuel managed to spend what he termed "quality time" in Israel. Thus, he was able to witness the all-consuming desire of the displaced persons to emigrate to Israel and its government's eagerness to absorb and quickly utilize their new strength and resources in building the country. During these many journeys Samuel visited DP camps located in Belgium, France, Czechoslovakia, Italy, and Switzerland.

After returning from a subsequent five-month, seven-country tour of Europe and the Middle East, Samuel was queried extensively by Joseph Sagmaster, executive editor of the *Cincinnati Times Star*, who then published a lengthy article addressed to a major question: Were the American people, in contrast to the United States government, very popular in the countries which Samuel had visited? Samuel stated his surprising opinion that the American tourist was frequently perceived as generous and sympathetic, an ambassador of goodwill. On the other hand, he criticized the government's policies in the conduct of foreign affairs. He cited, for example, the practice of forming alliances with regimes that had nothing in common with American principles of freedom, justice, and democracy. He felt that we were wrong in our policy of reacting almost automatically to steps taken by the Soviet Union. He noted, with regret, that Franco and the Falangists were still in power in Spain. Millions of Spaniards lived in bitter poverty and despair, utterly powerless in a country where the Fascist government held all of the weapons.

A question was asked about British policy in Cyprus. Had it destroyed the value of Greece and Turkey as Western allies? Greece, attempting rather unsuccessfully to strengthen itself after years of Nazi occupation, was focusing all of its hate on Great Britain. The way the British were dealing with the Cyprus issue only succeeded in increasing hostility among the British, Turks, and Greeks. A political deal in the recent elections in Greece had almost led to an anti-Western coalition. In Samuel's opinion, time was running out and the value of Greece as a British ally had been weakened considerably.

Turkey, in contrast, had a reasonably stable government, a tough army, and little sympathy for the Communists. If inflation could be checked and the economy bolstered, Turkey would stand firmly with the West.

Samuel then dealt with the inevitable questions regarding the status of the people and government of Israel. Egypt's General Nasser had been occupying center stage in the Middle East with a gamut of threatening gestures. His behavior reflected Soviet military support. Apparently, he was reenacting the role of the former Nazi dictator, directing his aggression against Israel. In a book reminiscent of Hitler's *Mein Kampf*, Nasser stated that he would (1) obtain dominant power over all the Arab nations in the Middle East and North Africa, (2) crush Israel, (3) drive the British and French out of Africa, and (4) with the help of the Russians, drive them from Asia as well.

Nonetheless, the Israeli people and their government characteristically showed no fear. Samuel emphasized his belief that they would defend their lives and homeland with all their means and with all their hearts. The United States, Britain, and France were attempting to placate Israel with formal pledges and pointed to the machinery of the United Nations as a sufficient guarantee against attack by Egypt and her Arab allies. Samuel pointed out the previously proven inadequacy of such pledges and noted that the United Nations machinery was slow and cumbersome to the point of being totally ineffectual for problems of this nature. He stressed his opinion that Israel needed defensive weapons, not only to protect itself and deter aggression but also to stand as a bulwark against Communist inroads in the Middle East.

The last country Samuel visited on his tour was England. He was asked by Sagmaster to rate Prime Minister Anthony Eden's chances of surviving his present domestic and foreign problems. He spoke wryly of the British system of "blundering through" and felt, therefore, that the Eden government would probably survive.

"It is sad," he said, "that in a time of crisis there is little enthusiasm among the people for the present Prime Minister. The British peoples, essentially civilized and better informed, deserve a government with greater vision and capacity for leadership."

The question was asked in conclusion, "Rabbi Wohl, did you come back from your long journey more hopeful or more apprehensive for the democratic future?" The answer was predictable.

I am a man of faith and despite setbacks, I *believe* in a democratic future. We may be late or we may be blocked for a time. Bad policies may deter us from going forward and, unfortunately, sometimes evil wins. Our faith and our integrity certainly will help democracy triumph. I want to believe an actual accommodation between Russia and the West will be a first step to sustain freedom and check the despotism of the present time.

During the war, as the miasma of horror engulfed Europe, and after the war, when the United States became concerned with the Communist menace, the Monroe Doctrine and the status of the people of Latin America increasingly engaged American attention. Samuel Wohl embarked on several journeys there, for the most part under the auspices of the Joint Distribution Committee. Commencing in Mexico in 1944 and culminating in a 30,000-mile journey in the early 1950s, his travels took him to almost all of the Central and South American countries.

Returning from his first trip, he announced that the Germans were losing influence in Mexico and declared, "Mexico is most friendly toward the United States and is making continued progress in lifting its people from peonage and illiteracy." This reversal in public opinion, he posited, was aided by a surge of more than 200,000 American tourists to Mexico and total American expenditures there of some $50 million.

Samuel credited Mexico's president with making determined efforts to destroy the vise in which the Axis powers had held his country until recently. Newspapers no longer published Nazi propaganda, and German-Mexicans who had held key positions in Mexico's businesses were being eased out wherever possible.

Samuel cautioned that the Mexican people had little in their background to ready them for democracy. Women had been denied the vote, a vast number of Mexicans were illiterate, and many lived in grinding poverty. For these reasons, Samuel suggested, they could not know democracy as it is experienced by the average American citizen. Nevertheless, he credited the government, which admittedly was dominated by the military, with building thousands of schools, giving token land grants to the landless, and even allowing opposition parties to voice their opinions. Churches, he noted, were open and often crowded.

The absence of large industry surely was a problem. Mexico depended almost entirely on the importation of manufactured goods from the United States. The native population heavily relied on handicrafts, such as weaving, silver working, and pottery. Samuel hypothesized that creative outpourings from Mexican artists heralded a decade that would influence art in the United States and Europe. Lengthy observations, as well as talks with Mexican natives and with Americans residing there, convinced Samuel that the nation's salvation lay in the development of a planned economy and a disciplined labor force.

Samuel advanced a concept that he would later suggest to the government of Israel. There needed to be a cadre of instructors who would show the Mexican people the most efficient ways to accomplish their tasks. Parenthetically, he suggested that a lack of capital was a reason that Mexico and her Latin American neighbors had done very little about arming themselves against foreign aggression. Because of this, they must rely on the United States for protection.

Before leaving Mexico, Samuel conferred with the country's foreign minister, an official who formally acknowledged the steadily developing friendship between the United States and Mexico.

He expressed his deep appreciation for the increase in the interchange of ideas among scholars, teachers, artists, and scientists.

Samuel considered President Harry Truman's then current plan for hemispheric defense quite desirable and felt that it would lead not only to hemispheric unity but to world peace as well. He found that thoughtful Mexicans were emphatic in their belief that it was no longer right for any country to create conditions that would negatively affect other countries. He was convinced that the United Nations must be concerned with every act that threatens the peace, not only between nations but also within each nation.

It was quite apparent to Samuel that under the conditions existing in Mexico, small Jewish communities could not survive and would have to migrate into three or four larger Jewish enclaves where they could experience a sense of security and maximize economic opportunities. He talked about a common faith in Zionism, which seemed to be "cementing the Jewish communities" together. It seemed to him that despite the favorable economic conditions for most Jews in Mexico, many would desire to live in Palestine.

The stated reason for Samuel's subsequent three-month, 30,000-mile odyssey to Latin America was to study Jewish life there. He was viewed by the local print media and the adolescent television industry as a burgeoning expert on Latin America. They understood his sensitivity to all forms of social process. Moreover, he had a remarkable propensity for cross-cultural comparisons and gifts for discussing harsh realistic factors and their potential for idealistic change. Samuel conferred not only with the dignitaries of the Jewish organizations but also with the ministers and ambassadors of all of the countries he visited. Very early, he became convinced that America's southern neighbors were in a state of change and would ultimately assume an important place in the shaping of world events. He felt that Latin American countries should not be looked upon as "wards" but as "full-fledged family members who deserve the concern of all other members." The United States and indeed the world should forcefully support the progressive and democratic forces in these countries.

"For the good of the world and for our sakes we must be the best neighbors possible," the rabbi said, "for with these countries we cannot only accomplish a perfect hemispheric defense but can find in them homes for tens of millions of people who would remain friendly toward this country." The study, he said, further convinced him that the United States must help bring into these countries, particularly Brazil, some millions of settlers. There were abundant resources there, he noted, and the welcoming country would be able to benefit economically and socially from American friendship. He suggested that if 50 million people from Europe were "siphoned off," not only would prosperity in the destination countries increase but tensions in the countries of origin would decrease also.

When Samuel arrived in Buenos Aires, the capital of Argentina, he was greeted by a reception committee representing the huge Jewish community of some 300,000. He immediately discovered that there was no contact between that community and the dictatorial regime of President Juan Perón. Perhaps this was because, at the very beginning of Jewish immigration into the Argentine, there had been fear of disturbances, boycotts, and confiscations directed toward the Jews.

Community leaders asked Samuel to arrange a conference with Perón or his representatives. He was confronted with a two-fold dilemma. First, direct contact with Perón's government would call attention to the fact that a United States citizen was talking with or negotiating with an "obnoxious" regime. Second, this contact could affect the policies of the Jewish organizations elsewhere in the world that were protesting the misdeeds of Perón. This would be especially true in the case of the Jewish community in the United States.

Because of these considerations, Samuel phoned officials in the United States and was given the necessary approval to undertake such conversations. A few days later, he was received by the foreign minister, who assured him that the regime was not interested in persecuting Jews and, in fact, would not tolerate anti-Semitic excesses or disturbances.

It should be noted that sometime later Israeli officials were assured that Perón would take a pro-Israel stance. In fact, it was due to Perón and his country's effectively affirmative position that, during the first years of the United Nations, Argentina was followed by several other South American countries in voting in favor of a Jewish state.

Samuel found that Buenos Aires, like Rio de Janeiro, the capital of Brazil, was a remarkable city, "a combination of Paris and Chicago." He was fascinated by the fact that each day, around noon, one of the beautiful streets was closed to traffic, permitting people to stroll in a newly created mall.

The Jews of Buenos Aires had little contact with the non-Jewish world. Even Jewish men and women who were native born did not enjoy full citizenship. Nevertheless, they were free to conduct their Jewish communal life without interference. The community had its own self-governing apparatus, or Kehilla, as well as other significant cultural and social bodies. Hebrew and Yiddish, respectively, were taught in the day schools of the Bialik and Peretz school systems.

An interesting aside: A certain rabbi became affiliated with the Perón regime when he went publicly to the grave of Eva Perón, the president's late wife, and recited the traditional Kaddish prayer for the dead. Because of this, he became a favorite of the Perón regime, which saw him as a spokesman for the country's Jews. In truth, however, he was detested and was suspected of misdeeds by his co-religionists.

Samuel noted that the religious situation in the city of Buenos Aires, as well as in the country at large, was most distressing. Very few rabbinic leaders were to be found in a city of more than 300,000 Jews. Only one somewhat liberal Conservative congregation existed. The few Orthodox synagogues were cold, unheated, and unattended. This might have been due to the fact that Jewish settlement in South America differed dramatically from the settlement of Jews in North America, where Sephardic, German, and East European Jews immediately founded small prayer houses. There were several hundred of them in the city of New York alone.

Later, many of these congregations built magnificent synagogue buildings. In Argentina, as in Chile and Peru, however, most of the immigrants, with the exception of those who fled from Germany in the twentieth century, did not organize synagogues. Religious institutions were few and far between.

Samuel was horrified to see what the Perónists had done to Argentina. Business and industries had been confiscated for the so-called welfare projects of Eva Perón. Samuel everywhere observed the deprivation the people suffered. Later on, when confronted with his just deserts, Perón escaped to Spain. It was common knowledge that he had confiscated millions of dollars from Argentina and deposited funds in banks in Switzerland and Spain. Samuel considered Perón, even in the autumn of his life, a menace to his country. Even in exile, Perón continued to conspire with the Perónists and with the country's many *descamisados* ("shirtless ones").

In Uruguay, Samuel found hidden treasure. At a time when there were few havens of refuge for Jews, that country, like many others, had little interest in Jewish affairs. Nevertheless, in prolonged discussions with the foreign minister, Samuel obtained a sympathetic reaction to his request that Jews somehow be permitted to enter the country. In fact, there were several Jewish communities in Uruguay at that time. While the number of Jews was not large, the amount of work they had accomplished was impressive. Samuel was moved by the lighting of six symbolic candles placed in a special menorah in the eastern wall of a new synagogue built in remembrance of the six million who had died in the hands of the barbaric Nazi regime.

Samuel came to regard Uruguay as the most democratic country in South America. For example, it had recently introduced the Swiss system of rotating the presidency among a group of elected leaders. The country played host to a very large meeting calling upon the British to cease their egregious activities in Palestine. British machinations in the Middle East had, in fact, sparked protests throughout the world. When in Buenos Aires, Samuel witnessed the outpouring of tens of thousands of Jews in Luna Park shouting angry slogans against the British. Samuel concluded that it was the will of Providence that while one section of Jewry in Europe had been systematically destroyed, millions of Jews living in the Americas in peace would give aid to their less fortunate brethren.

In Chile, Samuel found a thriving Jewish community. He was surprised at the number of people still speaking Yiddish, although he noted that the younger generation preferred Spanish. Intermarriage meant automatic conversion. Few Jews chose that path.

It was in Chile that Samuel met the famous American ambassador Claude Bowers, who had come there from Franco's Spain. Bowers had been given permission to publish his latest book as soon as he left the diplomatic service. He told Samuel much about the Franco Fascist regime and about his relationships with the generalissimo and other ambassadors. Samuel enjoyed many conversations with the ambassador, receiving many insights into diplomatic affairs as well as a view of the world as it appeared to this honest and forthright man. Years earlier, Claude Bowers had campaigned actively for Franklin Delano Roosevelt during the campaign for his first presidential term, but he had declined an invitation to make Roosevelt's nominating speech at the Democratic convention.

The future for Jews in South America seemed precarious in volatile countries where revolution followed revolution and one military junta followed another. Samuel recognized this instability as a way of life throughout Latin America. For example, while strolling peacefully in Guayaquil, Ecuador, he found himself suddenly in the midst of a demonstration. Thousands of people carrying placards seemed to appear instantly, ready to give battle against the police. Fortunately, the police exercised restraint and were able to keep the demonstrators away from the main arteries of the city. While nothing occurred, the government could easily have been seized by a new faction and a new regime installed.

On landing at the air field in La Paz, Bolivia, Samuel learned that only the day before, the president and some of his followers had been hung from the lamp posts. Unhappily, this, too, was the rule rather than the exception. The use of violence was, of course, a prevalent recourse for those who were constantly deprived of the means for a livelihood. On the other hand, Samuel mused, it was also a weapon of the ruling classes as a way to acquire a still larger slice of the pie.

Samuel drew many conclusions from his monumental trip. His insights were prophetic and profound. He made the point that our government was making few friends because of its paranoid attitude about the spread of Communism south of the border. Our alliances with dictatorial right-wing juntas were antagonizing the peoples of the continent, as well as causing precarious situations to become even more unstable. He made the simple and incisive observation that if only the governments of each country would do the decent thing for the common people, the threat of Communism would be something that need not be feared.

Samuel applauded the recent diplomatic journey by Milton Eisenhower, the brother of President Dwight Eisenhower, noting that he had been able to present the United States as a country sincerely interested in the welfare of the people. By the same token, he criticized McCarthyism as a blow to the prestige of the United States abroad. Eisenhower explained that the prominence of the activities of the Wisconsin senator in their newspapers led Latin Americans to believe that he was more powerful than the president. They wondered why Dwight Eisenhower, the leader of the Allied forces in the war, could not control McCarthy's activities. Samuel talked about the inaccurate impressions Latins received of American politics and life. Foreign vested interests focused on matters that were used to discredit the United States. Demagogues used such information to further their own ends.

After he returned home, Samuel did not bear easily the crown of South American analyst and sage. After all, it was not his predominant area of interest or expertise in the world arena. Perhaps he recalled with embarrassment his appointment to a committee consisting of Mayor Russell Wilson and Carl D. Groat, editor of the *Cincinnati Post*. The committee was charged with giving a farewell tribute to William H. Hessler, foreign editor of the *Enquirer*. The luncheon, to which a hundred persons representing diverse activities and interests in the Greater Cincinnati area were invited, was held at the Cincinnati Club.

Hessler was to be sent to South America by the Carnegie Endowment Foundation as part of a delegation made up of four other newspaper men, five university professors, and two representatives of the Foundation. Samuel presided at the luncheon and belatedly realized that this honor was primarily due to the esteem with which he was regarded by the local media and his home community.

Samuel continued his furious travel schedule, visiting Israel and making several European trips. In March of 1954, he confronted the almost limitless land mass of Canada, whose 12 million inhabitants almost all lived in the southern regions. The Jewish community of Canada was not large in number, although it formed a sizable enclave in some of the big cities. Many Jews had done rather well financially, but they felt isolated culturally. They were eager for news and wanted to participate more actively in world Jewish affairs.

On the occasion of the thirtieth annual Histadruth campaign for Israel, Samuel was asked to tour Canada for several months to promote the North American campaign. It was hoped that this would inspire Canadians to make generous contributions for the rehabilitation, health, training, and cultural needs of workers and new immigrants in Israel.

It should be stated that in spite of threats, infiltrations, and savage attacks, Israel had been able to create a democratic parliamentary government. Since 1948, the country had welcomed 1 million afflicted people from the pestholes of Europe, Africa, and Asia. At the same time, it had developed a military force that could be relied upon to defend and protect its inhabitants.

The Histadrut was a political organization whose membership claimed about half of the population of Israel. It had always provided the ideological justification for the life of the new Jewish state and continued to be the driving force sending the people of

Israel to reclaim the desert, to create a new land out of dust and sand. In the course of time, it prepared the way for millions of new inhabitants.

Samuel had been quite active at the highest levels of the Histadruth, participating in several international conferences regarding Palestine and later Israel. His first stop in Montreal was a stunning success by any measure. At a very large dinner where the city's annual goal was $250,000, pledges of more than $700,000 were obtained. The total Canadian annual goal was $850,000. Funds were to be spent within Canada on medical equipment, drugs, food, and building equipment that would then be sent to Israel. Listening as Metropolitan Opera tenor Jan Peerce thrilled the audience with several arias, Samuel realized that he was off to an auspicious beginning.

The momentum generated by the Montreal success carried throughout his more than 3,000-mile odyssey to the west coast city of Vancouver, spanning Ottawa, Toronto, Winnipeg, Regina, Saskatoon, and Edmonton. In all of these locales, the rabbi played to "sold-out houses." His message was one of inspiration and hope. Even so-called non-Zionists throughout the country were grateful for a message that included Israel's heroism and achievements in a view of future world Jewry. Some Zionist groups in Canada added new members and raised the level of their activities.

In the late 1950s, Samuel was an acknowledged expert on the Soviet Union, the countries of Europe, Latin America, and, of course, the State of Israel. He was surprised when editor Brady Black, speaking for both the *Cincinnati Times Star* and the *Post*, suggested that he go to Japan. Upon his return, the *Times Star* published a seven-part series titled "A Rabbi Looks at Japan." The newspaper introduced the series by posing a number of relevant questions for the decade: Is Japan our friend? How reliable is she in that part of the world? What is her danger of Communism? What part has American occupation there played? What influence has the United States had on her culture?

In this series, Samuel offered his "personal story," so to speak. He was not defensive about this; throughout his life he had not made an idol of "objectivity." He wondered, in fact, if anyone could be objective in dealing with the human drama, a subject that he often considered to be strange, varied, perverse, and yes, at times, exhilarating.

As usual, Samuel was exquisitely sensitive to the climate of opinion. The substance of his articles consisted of interesting narratives. He talked of his tandem interviews with Douglas Macarthur II, the diplomat nephew of the famous World War II commander, and members of his staff. He stated that he had learned "a great deal from working newspaper men" and commented not only that they were "very well informed" but that, moreover, their information exceeded what he had learned from diplomats. He told the American public that the Communist threat to Japan was quite small, and that, after analyzing Japan's current political status as well as the intricacies of her economic situation, he found the Communist Party in Japan quite insignificant.

Samuel noted that "economics is the breath of existence for Japan" and that America was continuing to play a "magnificent role." Even the American military establishment, by its consumption of goods and services valued at hundreds of millions of dollars, was a benefit to Japan's economy. He referred to Nippon as a land of sharp contrasts. Even topographically, Japan could overwhelm and charm the observer. It was both colorful and unique. One noted the deep green coming up from the water of the rice paddies and the steep, roughened mountain forests and covered hills. There were rushing river rapids and the quiet beauty of gardens. Almost insatiably, Samuel asked questions and was startled by the unanimity of opinion. He was convinced that the Japanese were friendly to America, perhaps its only friends in the Far East at that time. How remarkable it was, he observed:

> A people so utterly crushed in war with millions dead and crippled, with an empire lost, memories of atom bombs dropped on Hiroshima and Nagasaki, and with an army of occupation ordering its life, behaved so well towards its conquerors. It did not sabotage, did not resent, did not sulk,

but cooperated with the Americans to heal the wounds and restore life to the nation. The people work and toil ceaselessly to regain strength and stature.

Most of the series was a brilliant and sensitive exposition of the culture, religious, philosophical, and personal life of the nation and people of Japan. Samuel noted that there were certain elements of Japanese culture not altogether palatable to the Western mind. Despite the Japanese woman's institutionally subordinate position to her husband, she seldom complained. She was, in fact, the wife, not the mistress. She was the mother and she was within and not outside the family. She became stronger and more secure with age. Whomever her son or daughter married, she, the mother-in-law, was the one who commanded honor and obedience thereby increasing her power and status.

When asked what spiritual idea was prominent among the Japanese people, Samuel responded that it was loyalty. "There is no single deity to whom reverence is given above all else. In the land of a thousand spirits, the unifying idea is the family and the family of families is the nation." The Samurai and clans abruptly disappeared, and with the advice and concurrence of America, all titles and nobility were abolished. The emperor was retained as the continuing symbol of utmost loyalty. In fact, loyalty was the strongest bond within the family and reached up and down into the hierarchy of business and other areas of life.

It was explained to Samuel that the Japanese do not appreciate absolute virtues. There were no sancta derived from a god or a supernatural order. Freedom was not a goal. It was not a sacred principle derived from scripture and from a constitution, as in Western countries. The individual has no sacred rights which rise above the nation or loyalty to superior claims. In this context, the kamikaze suicide pilots were not unusual; they were *expected* to burst into flame when they attacked.

After fairly posing America's ethical-military dilemma in dropping the atomic bomb, Samuel was profoundly moved by his visit to the atom museum in Hiroshima. It was there that he copied a poem by Sankichi Toge:

> They dream: a workman dreams, lowering his pickaxe; his sweat turned into scars by the flash; . . . a match seller also dreams, with pieces of shattered glass sticking into his neck;
> They dream: that the rich craft of science may be conveyed in peace among people,
> Like bunches of abundant grapes, wet with dew,
> Gathered in, at dawn.

Samuel observed that the poet was dead. He had died from the after-effects of radiation. Samuel wondered whether someday men would direct their steps to Hiroshima, in reverence and contrition. For the present he concluded that American-Japanese relations were excellent. He felt that the American government had done "a superb job." He believed that the policy of kindness and helpfulness was the right one.

Samuel urged that our officials take a friendly approach to the ruling and opposition parties in Japan, particularly the latter, in order to draw them away from the "Communist fog." He urged Americans to keep in mind the fearful cataclysm that might result for the entire world if Japan, with its skilled and industrious population, were to become the workshop for the Communists.

If American forces were withdrawn, Japan would have to find a way to defend herself. Samuel felt, at that time, that Japan could not bear the costs of such defense. He knew that historical and current events had placed certain decisions about Japan before the American people. We may, he observed, still have time to save Asia from becoming a threat to America and her freedom. He concluded that if we used our opportunities wisely, Japan might become a dynamic partner in freedom and friendship for America and the West.

Chapter 17
Beloved Pastor:
Further Ideas of Consequence, Reform Jewish Practice, Congregational Personages, Educational Ferment, CCAR Manifesto, World Union for Progressive Judaism

We have already established the fact that Samuel's relationship with his congregation was consummately and reciprocally caring and tender. There is no question that his congregational status exceeded the effect of his frequent and prolonged absences. Indeed, we cannot discover that this was ever an issue. During the thirties, he was able to time his trips in accordance with the summer slowdown in congregational activities. The decade of the forties witnessed an increase in passenger air travel, enabling more frequent journeys for briefer periods. However, we are convinced, such was the congregation's love for their pastor that he seemed omnipresent, and other problems and considerations faded into the background.

Samuel inspired and lovingly led many others to significant goals over a period of four decades. Cincinnati and the nation were emerging from the deep trough of a debilitating economic depression, evolving and enduring through myriads of social and geopolitical patterns. His home and family life clearly formed a predictable schematic seldom interrupted by cataclysmic events. The authors' development and sense of stability as children flourished in an atmosphere of unconditional love and acceptance. When Samuel was at home, he was always available. Belle, our mother, also was always available and the actual implementer of our existence. Indeed, if we are characterized by a pervasive long-standing problem, it is (and was) the perceived impossibility of emulating our parental role models.

During the earlier years of his rabbinic tenure, Samuel maintained his slimness, conservative apparel, and russet pompadour. By the early 1940s, his fastidious appearance and impressive hair remained stable, while his body habitus softened and assumed a certain rotundity. As his metabolism slowly decreased with age, physical exertion subsided significantly. His at-home leisure periods were consumed by reading, study, and listening to the measured newscasting of Edward R. Murrow, H. V. Kaltenborn, Lowell Thomas, Raymond G. Swing, and other radio commentators.

One remembers that the era and locale of his Ukrainian childhood were pre–Industrial Revolution, marked by minimal technological inroads and the Jewish communities' centuries of denigration of physical labor. Well into young manhood, Samuel had never driven a wagon, rode a bicycle, or even seen a machine-powered object. He never played physically active games or grasped the conceptual roots of such activity. Driving a car was out of the question until the return of son Ted from military service knowingly presented his father with a marvelous opportunity to greatly increase his mobility. The task of teaching Samuel to drive was more than the family could reasonably endure and was assigned quickly to Cincinnati's Auto Club, which, in cowardly fashion, "passed" him after two full courses. There followed more than a decade of fender benders and (thankfully) minor mishaps embedded in a family atmosphere of tension and fearful expectations.

The congregation viewed all of this with tolerance and even renewed affection. Everyone, it seemed, had witnessed the rabbi trying to park and drive, or could relate a humorous anecdote. Son Amiel commemorated and memorialized his father's automotive prowess during the celebration of Samuel's twenty-fifth year in the rabbinate. Replete with a sports-car driving cap and attire, and wearing a reddish wig, he warbled:

In his merry Dodgemobile,
he was just a plain schlemiel.
Even Cincy's Auto Club
gave him up as a total dud.

Predictably, Samuel was helpless when confronted with mechanical challenge or sustained labor. Tasks involving the setting of screws, hammering of nails, painting, polishing, and housework of all varieties were the province of Belle and the boys. Lack of exercise and physical stamina inevitably led to painful low back problems and a host of other muscular-skeletal difficulties.

In view of all this, it is remarkable that Samuel was characterized by colleagues as a major proponent of "muscular Judaism." They were, of course, referring to gold-medal Olympic performances in behalf of the Jewish religion, culture, and nation/peoplehood. He was single-minded and indefatigable in pursuit of these goals. Much in the manner of a football breakaway backfield runner, he would choose his "holes" flexibly, and once in his opponent's backfield, he would slip, slide, and reverse field toward the opposite goal line. Carrying this rather improbable analogy further, he was somewhat assertive, but *never* aggressive or hurtful to an adversary.

We have mentioned already at least several times that Samuel's congregation regarded him primarily as a pastor.

Amiel, in satirical literary exuberance, published an article in the *Journal of the Central Conference of American Rabbis* entitled "How to Be a Successful Rabbi." Its sharp contrast with Samuel's understanding of the rabbinical role compelled a broad response of approving hilarity in the readership. Amiel chided the Hebrew Union College because it "gave us five years of esoteric material which, we found out later, could be discussed only with grizzled Orthodox Jews who were not in our congregation." Some of its other suggestions also "stand one in good stead," among them "how often and how far the rabbi travels are excellent prestige indicators."

On the other hand, there are some rabbis who feel erroneously that they must justify their wage or calling by keeping busy interminably. There is much to be done; even as Rabbi Tarfon said, "The day is short, the task is great, the workmen are lazy, the reward is great and the Master is insistent." He always used to say, "You are not called upon to complete the work, yet you are not free to evade it." The reader, overwhelmed by the profundity of it all, is enjoined that "deliberate ease is most appealing" to [the congregants]. . . . Of course, things must be accomplished somehow, but the same integration of admiration and envy pervades the scale of values which an admiring congregant applies to any person who can accomplish conspicuous leisure at the price of only an hour of so of honest daily work. Therefore, long vacations for the rabbi in summer and winter are to the congregation's innate liking and build up respect for the spiritual mentor. Many rabbis spend much time and show grave concern trying to build a genuine depth of Jewish programming, but neither parents nor youth actually care. The main thing is to have *rapport* with the teenagers. We might all go out swiping hubcaps together, and it wouldn't concern the parents at all. Of course, a bit of Midrashic homily occurring between parked cars might have some value.

The only solution, then, is to call on people when they are not at home. Drive around the block several times and be sure there are no cars parked anywhere. If there are also no cars within the garage, then, and only then you may stop. Have a note on the back of your card, place the card in the mail box, another in the door (always leave two, lest one blow away) expressing regret that they were not at home.

The son of the paragon role model for several thousand rabbis across the country concluded by noting that there were a few "postures" to be perfected: how to look sad at funerals, particularly those at which no one else seems to be sad; how to look devout during prayer, especially the silent prayer, and so on. The editor of the *Journal* apparently could not resist the footnoted counsel: "Let the reader decide for himself. If there are some who strongly disagree with what is here presented or dislike the article all together, then, obviously, they have no desires to be 'successful' rabbis."

We have alluded in some detail to Belle's personality—her supportive and loving presence, and her role in causing a doubtful, conflicted young man to become a leader, teacher, and "sage" in Israel. She was the stabilizer and architect of a home environment which permitted the rearing of two sons and a husband to inspire and create. Everyone who knew her perceived a "perfect rebbetzin" (a diminutive term for the rabbi's wife), modest, retiring, and sweetly concerned about the problems and misfortunes of others. However, we in her family could observe the strength and resolve forged in the stresses of her childhood and adolescence. She spoke quietly and confidently. She set consistent limits and did not easily change her mind. We are not objective observers in these matters.

Belle would seem to have long ago worked out her own personal doubts and conflicts regarding her life and chose her path with confidence. She would not or could not deviate, and in many ways was an anchoring point as life unfolded for all of us. It is interesting that she, along with Amy Blank, wife of HUC's Professor Sheldon Blank, served for at least two decades as adviser to an ever-changing group of HUC students' wives.

Our mother took a regular turn as hostess for the "sewing club," as this group was called. The two of us, lying in our beds, destined for slumber, pulled the covers over our heads as a protective shield against the spirally ascending decibels as a dozen women relaxed or simultaneously attempted to express their pent-up feelings of the day or week. Suddenly, the sound would subside, and Belle's clear and measured voice emerged magically, offering a rational observation.

As a clergyman's wife, she had all of the virtues, extolled (and criticized) by uncountable modern authors. She dressed plainly, totally abstained from strong drink and tobacco, and was an extraordinarily sympathetic listener. She stepped frequently beyond the limiting roles of wife and mother to champion the cause of early childhood (preschool) education in the Cincinnati area and was instrumental in obtaining the services of Mrs. Frank Bloom, who established an independent kindergarten affiliated with the University of Cincinnati.

Her interests turned toward creative Jewish arts and crafts. Belle and Thelma Tash co-chaired a sisterhood committee to produce the book *The Work of Our Hands*, which contained many interesting and novel ideas capturing the beauty of Jewish symbols in handwork of all kinds to be used on the Sabbath and holidays. The book is today playing a role in recreating the home arts of our grandmothers. It has, moreover, left a legacy in the arts and crafts groups of Jewish summer camps and centers.

Belle was also active in both Hadassah, the major Zionist organization for women, and the Wise Center Temple Sisterhood. She served on the boards of the local branches of these organizations. Her life assumed a predictable pattern until well after her sons left the nest. Then Belle permitted herself to accompany Samuel by plane or train and ultimately overseas and to Israel. Her travels culminated in an around-the-world three-month cruise with her husband on the *Rotterdam*. The trip, a gift from a grateful congregation, was quite enjoyable. Belle kept careful notes but was hampered by elements of a persisting upper respiratory infection. Indeed, following this magnificent odyssey, their traveling subsided markedly. When they alighted again in Cincinnati, it was only five years before Samuel's death.

Belle was not the only woman in Samuel's life, so to speak. Lee Rubenstein and Celia Singer were central elements in the temple's evolving role and prosperity and were also instrumental in enabling him to practice his style of rabbinics.

Young Lee returned to Cincinnati and became secretary to Rabbi James Heller just before the merger of the Reading Road and

Plum Street Temples. She then almost immediately assumed the role of office manager and de facto executive secretary of the institution. Her air of quiet confidence never failed to inspire trust. The various temple programs, its board and board officers, the religious school, and the rabbis found her indispensable in "understanding" their particular problems and, more important, in accomplishing the infrastructure that promoted the temple as a spiritual force within the community.

Mrs. Rubenstein served the congregation for more than thirty-eight years all told. One of the first full-time temple executives in the nation, she was a charter member and founder of the National Association of Temple Administrators. During the tenure of Rabbis James G. Heller, Samuel Wohl, and Albert Goldman, she witnessed the growth of the congregation from 600 to 1,500 families.

From the beginning, Lee Rubenstein realized that congregations consist of individuals striving in their own manner toward great ideals. She conceptualized the role of the temple executive in terms of four "D's": diplomacy, discretion, decision, and dedication. She was thoroughly familiar with every department and kept constant and careful watch over every detail of the temple's needs. She realized that rabbis were not only busy with many temple activities, but were active in communal and national affairs. She was, at once, both empathic and sensitive enough to anticipate the rabbis' wishes.

Lee also understood the immense value of a finely tuned relationship with the board of trustees. There was not a congregational president who did not leave office singing her praises. David W. Goldman, president of the congregation on the occasion of her retirement dinner, summarized it well: "I feel we never could express adequately all that Mrs. Rubenstein has done for the temple in these 38 years."

On the same occasion, Samuel remarked that Lee "knew the families of every member." She created much good will and friendship for the temple. Together with James Levy, board member and congregational treasurer for many years during the 1930s, she championed a dues structure based on the principle of "ability to pay." Dues, a vital fact of congregational life, became a matter of voluntary acceptance rather than arbitrary action of the board.

The temple congregation today strives to increase its income to meet the increased expenses that come from its vastly expanded activities. The temple continuously revitalizes itself by setting up fair and reachable budgets. Lee ventured an opinion only when necessary or when factual material was specifically requested. Several times during their long relationship, she remarked to Samuel that, through him, she could become animated by the spirit of the religious institution, and thus deeply enjoy her own accomplishments.

Before introducing Celia Singer, it will be useful to again reexamine Samuel's views on Jewish education. We have already noted his strong endorsement of contemporary methods and materials. Jewish education, indeed Judaism itself, could not properly exist without the replenishing founts of Hebraism, culturalism (including the Yiddish language), nationalism (peoplehood), and, of course, Zionism. From almost the very moment he arrived in the United States, Samuel was founding Hebrew language groups and Young Zionist groups, and he soon became the principal of Rabbi Solomon Goldman's Cleveland religious school. He was able to diffuse these concepts and activities throughout southwestern Ohio, where he almost immediately assumed leadership authority within already existing General Zionist, Labor Zionist, and other community groups. He worked closely with and supported close friends Azriel Eisenberg and Mordecai Halevy, both superb educators and administrative principals and directors of the Bureau of Jewish Education of Cincinnati. This may be regarded as a contrast to his early Cleveland experience, where he was, in a sense, cresting the renaissance wave of Jewish tradition and learning that accompanied the East European immigration to this country.

Later on, Samuel was to discover the ideological variance within and between Reform Jewish congregational ideology and self-perception. He was one of the few Reform leaders of that time who correctly foresaw the enrichments that would ensue when Zionism, the Hebrew language, enlightened "ethnicity," and meaningful traditional religious precepts were integrated into Reform Jewish ideology and practice. These enrichments came about as young people from Orthodox and Conservative backgrounds transformed what was earlier perceived as a lack of passionate idealism and sterility in the Reform movement.

Shortly after the merger of the two major Reform congregations, Rabbi James Heller agreed to consign a viable religious school program to Samuel, who would serve as principal and administrative director. Samuel undertook these responsibilities eagerly and without hesitation. He soon became uncomfortably aware that, due to his own investiture of great significance to education within the rubric of Judaism, he simply could not optimally accomplish his self-appointed mission. He reflected wryly on the delicate balance between laity and clergy in regard to pedagogy and theology. He was exquisitely sensitive to nuances of his congregation and realized that one cannot ardently lead far ahead of one's congregational followers. By the same token, an idea or concept seldom survives if it is introduced prematurely. Therefore Samuel was often content to introduce a concept and benevolently allow it to spring to life later in a more conducive atmosphere.

W. Gunther Plaut, the scholarly Toronto rabbi, provided American readers with two excellent source books on the rise and growth of Reform Judaism. Both of Plaut's books appeared in the sixties, and as Samuel perused the initial volume, *The Rise of Reform Judaism*, he noted Plaut's observation that current Reform leaders (which of course included Samuel himself) were still attending to the specific problems raised eloquently by the Reform leaders of Central Europe in the early and mid-part of the nineteenth century. For example, Should parochial schools be encouraged? How can a teacher in a community school deal honestly with questions pertaining to Reform, seeing that his teachings may run contrary to the cherished views held by his pupils and their families? How effectively can Hebrew be taught in religious school classes?

Samuel acknowledged the ambiguity of these early problems, but fervently observed:

Our forbearers knew the need for a Jewish education. . . .
They could not conceive how a Jew could live without
knowing the Torah, without understanding the wisdom of
the sages. Often the argument has been used that a Jewish
education compensates for the attacks of anti-Semitism. It
is beneath our dignity to belabor this point. An understanding of the genuine values of Jewish education should
make every Jew eager to participate, to learn. . . . It has
been said that many things can be inherited—homes,
money, materials, and possessions—but learning cannot be
inherited. Every person must initiate and accomplish the
learning himself. We are by now a mature community in
the United States. It is incomprehensible that we continue
to live with the low level of [Jewish] knowledge. . . . It
would prosper us and benefit relations with our fellow
Americans if we contribute something to the cultural reservoir of our country and became again the "Am Hasefer" [
People of the Book].

Colleague Victor Reichert concurred:

It is impossible to exaggerate the importance of Jewish religious education in the history of our people. The Bible
alone has been one of the fountain springs of idealism in
western civilization. It would be a profound tragedy if our
children were to grow up in ignorance of this rich treasury
of our heritage.

Samuel continually hammered the theme that Jewish education is a task for the entire community, in fact, the international
Jewish community. He noted that even the best of the organized
temple and synagogue religious schools were patently part-time
instruction. While ardently backing currently existing Cincinnati
programs like the Bureau of Jewish Education, he energized a
model Wise Center congregational religious school. In addition to
a tremendous increase in the number of children, his "junior con-

gregation" and two-day-a-week congregational school became an illustration for the nation. Many Hebrew Union College students, soon to be rabbis, taught at the Wise Center and applied much of what they learned within its walls later to their own schools.

Samuel agonized about the Jewish day school movement. From the beginning, we have considered Samuel a maximalist in the field of Jewish education. Anyone who knew him would agree, because learning and education in all of their forms are vital processes, permitting and nourishing the development of Jews and Judaism. Yet he could not offer unqualified support in this direction. A scholarly champion of the lawful need for church-state separation, he expressed his conflict as follows:

> It is generally recognized that even the best part time schools staffed with competent teachers are still unsatisfactory. The parents continue to demand very little. It is often the obligation of rabbis and educators to give more than the parents desire, sometimes even against the parents' wishes. Those who oppose day schools, or, as they are sometimes called, "parochial schools," base their opposition upon the fact that Jews live with people of other faiths and nationalities. Their children should rub shoulders with other non-Jewish children and have the opportunity and benefit from childhood to establish cordial and natural relationships. It is also true that Jews have been in the forefront of fighting for separation of church and state. . . . It is asked, "Could not a Jewish day school come under the category of a private school?" Is it not true when we desire to educate a physician, he or she is sent to a medical school?

Samuel at least supported the notion that the option of a full-time Jewish day school should exist, but seemed to feel that the greatest benefit would be derived from those in the community with the brightest intellectual endowment and highest motivation. He rationalized that the masses of the community were not as workable or as receptive to private school efforts. Historically, philosophers, poets, and sages have come from small segments of their parent population. He observed that it is truly miraculous that the Jews, scattered upon the face of the earth, martyred by merciless enemies, had given the world some of its most ethical teachers, the greatest of prophets, the greatest book in our litera-ture and, in contemporary life, had achieved such distinctions as Nobel Prize winners in fields that "only 50 years ago were closed to them." He eventually concluded that the community would bene-fit immeasurably if special schools were made available for Judaism, Jewish religion, and history, along with a curriculum of regular aca-demic subjects. Although many of these issues have since then evolved in positive directions, Samuel's conceptions were viewed, in the thirties and forties, as workable compromises in thought and practicality.

In 1934, early in his rabbinical career, Samuel sounded an alarm to the "now largest Jewish community in the world" by an address which was printed in all three Cincinnati dailies and rec-ognized by the regional and national press as well. He reminded us that the United States was on the road to economic recovery as a nation and posed the question as to why this could not be accom-panied by a spiritual/learning recovery for Jews. He indicated that knowledge, self-respect, and spiritual health were absolutely neces-sary for ourselves and "for the sake of our afflicted brethren else-where." He then proceeded to propose a "limited code for American Jews." Even before "mobilizing a force against ignorance of Judaism," he brought up a situation pervasive in the Cincinnati Jewish community—the practice of one Jew labeling his brother as inferior. Samuel argued that this kind of sectarianism, usually based upon country of birth and size of fortune, should be denounced with infinite sadness of heart. He was aware of the psychosocial insight that minority groups have a tendency to compare what they perceive as their worst traits with the noblest attributes of the majority. He explained "that this sectarianism has made us less potent in achievement and has sapped our strength. It has brought on heavy rivalries and stupid clashes. It has resulted in our inca-pacity to think about and grasp vital issues."

In the speech Samuel observed that a major achievement of the recently enacted National Recovery Act was its reasoned rebuttal of the laissez-faire philosophy and "rugged individualism," replacing them with "collective reasonable efforts of control and regulation." It was now essential, he declared, to destroy the "sectarian individualism in American Jewry and to build a communal responsibility and discipline which would form the essence of Jewish unity." This would be followed by the mobilization of "a force against ignorance of Judaism which must be waged with all the weapons at our command and we must forge new ones."

Samuel was genuinely disturbed by the tragedy of a generation of "Jewish illiterates," and in his view both Orthodoxy and Reform had sinned in this respect. He felt that there was no purpose, no goal, no plan behind the then-current systems of education. He continued to preach that in the country's era of recovery we must "save our children." He urged Jewish groups of all persuasions to strengthen their schools and to mold and create public opinion among their adherents that would make Jewish learning and Jewish information things to be sought eagerly. "The Jewish teacher should be equipped on a high plane and, in conjunction, we should encourage Jewish thinkers to give us ideals, Jewish authors to script books for us, and Jewish artists to create for us."

In short, Samuel was arguing for a Jewish culture that would strengthen and inspire the American Jew with pride, courage, and hope. He viewed Judaism as a deep reservoir serving as a source of strength that would enable Jews to meet hostile forces effectively and serve as a means of cultivating self-esteem. True to Reform's tradition of dynamic change, he stated without hesitation, current educational and religious institutions sadly needed an overhaul, and new ideas and methods must supplant those that had outlived their usefulness.

Samuel was by no means alone in this view of the current state of American Jewish education, nor was he the first to voice these concerns. Shortly after Samuel and Belle arrived in Cincinnati, Emanuel Gamoran obtained his doctoral degree in education from Columbia University and was appointed by the Union of

American Hebrew Congregations as head of its Department of Education and Joint Commission on Jewish Education. Samuel agreed enthusiastically with Rabbi Leon Fram's memory of "Manny" as a man (like Samuel) short in stature but of large vision. Fram called attention to the determined optimism and ever present wit that enabled Gamoran to overcome considerable barriers to his efforts and helped him to reorganize Reform education and religious schools throughout the country.

The Joint Commission on Jewish Education, a considerable proportion of the American rabbinate, and many powerful individuals in the Jewish community were determinedly anti-Zionist and strenuously resisted any imputations of Jewish peoplehood, even single words and concepts, embedded in texts. Despite their opposition, Dr. Gamoran succeeded brilliantly in every aspect of his projected program, including revision of old texts and creation of new ones for use in the schools of Reform Judaism. Understandably, Samuel and Emanuel became close personal friends. Emanuel could always provide the technical know-how and considerable support for Samuel in terms of his need to put education in perspective and to promote the larger message of its inseparability from Jewish belief and existence.

The third member of the aforementioned female triumvirate that significantly enabled Samuel to accomplish his mission and responsibilities was Celia Singer. She served the Isaac M. Wise Temple as a teacher and educator for more than forty years. Celia began as a third-grade teacher laden with a plethora of opinions and cogently reasoned educational approaches. Even before she attained national prominence in the professionalizing of Jewish education, she was active and committed to a wide variety of temple and civic activities. She organized the National Association of Temple Educators and became its first woman president, and served on the board of trustees of the Union of American Hebrew Congregations. She was, moreover, a president of the Ohio/Michigan/Indiana Jewish Religious Schoolteachers Association and served as president and editor of the newsletter of the Avondale School (Cincinnati Public Elementary) PTA.

Samuel recognized, along with the UAHC, that Celia Singer had made many significant contributions to Jewish education in the United States through her perennial deanship of teachers institutes, as an editor of textbooks, and as a friend and counselor, a maternal figure if you will, to several generations of Hebrew Union College students, who were to soon lead their own congregations throughout the country.

Ceil, in turn, acknowledged Samuel as a continuing supportive presence. In her State of the NATE (National Association of Temple Educators) address, she specifically thanked three previous directors of the Commission on Jewish Education: Emanuel Gamoran, "the architect who gave Reform Jewish education the design for its program"; Eugene Borowitz, who had once taught under Ceil and then became professor of theology at HUC-JIR; and Alex Schindler, vice-president of the UAHC, later to become president, and, as a scholar and a poet, "ever lift[ed] the sights of those toiling in the vineyards of Jewish education."

One may state confidently that Celia, even in her sixties, was championing efforts that only today approach successful accomplishment. It was resolved that NATE would establish, publish, and distribute standards and requirements to its members, and to the education committees and boards of temples. It was further resolved that these standards would include a program requiring active parental involvement in the school's activities and attendance, and study sessions in harmony with the studies perused by their children. Thus there would be a type of three-way sharing between child, parent, and teacher: the child's learning, the teacher's guidance, and the parent's involvement in the learning process.

Rabbi Jack Stern, Jr., now rabbi emeritus at Westchester Reform Temple of Scarsdale, New York, captured the persona and essence of Ceil Singer in his eulogy at her funeral. He called to mind all of the "children who grew up under her tutorage." In Rabbi Stern's case, this had begun more than sixty years ago. One of the authors (Amiel) taught under Ceil's direction. Jack quoted one of her disciples, Rabbi Lawrence Kushner, as stating: "What we learned from her was not simply to teach the subject but to teach the child." Jack added, "She taught us how to be teachers, even when she was criticizing us, even when her lips tightened and her eyes flashed, and we knew that the barrage was coming." Above all, "she taught us how to be rabbis, a role which she dearly cherished. We, her boys, were fiercely devoted to her, fiercely inspired by her—and loved to laugh with her."

The human quality that Ceil Singer prized the most was responsible personal independence. Jack explained that this applied to her own children, to the children in the religious school, to the teachers, to rabbis, to human beings in general, to herself. Perhaps most revealing of her personal philosophy was a letter to Rabbi Stern in 1972: "I long ago made up my mind that my children must live their own lives. Anne Morrow Lindbergh said it in a poem for me: 'Him whom I love, I wish to be free, even from me.' "

We have already explained how Samuel, at the very inception of his professional life, explained Judaism as the collective expression of the Jewish people. He stressed that we are "God-centered people," the sum total of Jewish life and Jewish experience. He saw nationalism and the resurgent Hebrew language as integral and dynamic facilitators of Jewish health and growth. Samuel felt the need to create a plethora of goals, many of which he understood would be unreachable during his lifetime. He always felt that the religious school deserved much more attention and commitment from the congregation. In Ceil Singer, he perceived a person who had the motivation and energy to take a leading role in molding the Wise Center's religious school into a high-quality, effective, thoroughly professional institution. As Roland Gittelsohn concluded, "A Jew who knows about his people's past, who feels that he really belongs to the Jewish group, and who knows all the noble contributions we have made and are still making to the world, such a Jew is the only one who can feel proud and be happy. The only way to reach that goal is through education."

Jacob Schwartz, in a scholarly discourse on Reform Jewish practice, noted the weakening and vitiation (we have called it sterilization) of worship and observance in the temple and the home.

Only the rabbi was still regarded as a "repository of Jewish religious truth." The pendulum of change began to swing back during the early twenties, and many rabbis and congregations activated a revival of Jewish practice and observance.

By the time Samuel entered the rabbinate in 1927, the Reading Road Temple and subsequently the two merged congregations were ready to examine and creatively modify their practices. Schwartz quotes the Central Conference of American Rabbis Committee on Responsa as locating the practices of the majority of Reform Jews in four categories:

1. Practices which are not prohibited in traditional law or viewed as inconsistent with the spirit of the times.
2. Cases where traditional practices are discarded from the viewpoint of changed conditions.
3. Cases where changes in traditional practices are held justifiable for the same reason.
4. Cases where Jewish law is held still applicable to present day conditions without change.

It is beyond the scope of this book to analyze and discuss these responsa. However, Samuel actively promoted change in all of these areas, bringing a noticeable increase in warmth, traditional ceremonial, and Jewish knowledge and lore. The religious school, starting with consecration and ending with graduation from the high school, became a means of reviving and continuing American Judaism. Samuel was able to lead and inspire by virtue of his own life examples and moral suasions. Yet, at his retirement in 1965, he would not admit that he had reached a "transition phase" in religious education. There had been much progress in areas of worship, holiday observance, and ceremonials taught and practiced. There continued to be room for great improvement in home observance and influencing the congregational family in their daily individual lives.

The early pioneers of Reform Judaism had opinions that permeated its early development and arguably served as a hindrance to education and practice. By the same token, these attitudes, the absence of established Jewish authority, and democratization reflected an antipathy toward observance and traditional practice. To its credit, Reform Judaism has never been static, and in recent times it has worked through many of the former barriers and "hang-ups." We see the fruits of new values and insights, which are becoming increasingly inseparable from aspects of daily life.

Schwartz, despite his finely drawn description of Reform Jewish practice and education almost fifty years ago, confessed to failure in reaching desired goals. However, he required us to look backward through history, pointing out that "with faith in God in their hearts and with unshakable loyalty to Jewish idealism, our people in every land and time have always found the opportunity and the means to create new observances and new practices to meet their changing and growing needs." He concluded, significantly, that "on the rabbis and lay leaders . . . devolves the task of creating proper and adequate standards for such indispensable observance."

Samuel accepted his personal obligation to draw copiously from the accumulated past. Through example, drama, innovation, and sheer persistence, he contributed strongly to an American Judaism based on ethical and religious conduct, inexplicably bound to and sustained by an idealistic nationalism of universal application.

Samuel was exquisitely aware of the grave and growing succession of crises that were confronting the Jewish people. Both at home and abroad there was confusion as to "Who speaks for us? Who acts for us? Who is in control of the purse strings and why?" Samuel regarded as deplorable the continuous struggles, recriminations, and battle for position among organizations for the support of the Jewish community of America. He wondered if such disunity might be responsible, at least in some measure, for a great many of the evils that crested over and submerged the Jewish people as a mighty wave. He acknowledged a mass of accumulated data drawn from authentic sources showing that the synagogue had for generations exercised authority and leadership, most often holding the central position in the direction of Jewish affairs. He consistently advanced this concept, urging the synagogue to find its way back to leadership. "It must do those things that will make the Jewish community aware that they [synagogues] have experience, knowledge, and necessary techniques to guide and act on behalf of and for the Jewish community."

Surprisingly, he de-emphasized the inspirational aspect of the synagogue. He even wondered about the worthiness of such an inspiration. He found no reason to preach "Judaism" in the same manner as "our sister religions speak of preaching the gospel." He wrote:

> Indeed, action comes first—work with the people, *then* you will obtain the ear of the people. Do the things which impinge upon the lives of the people; then you can speak to them of their ideals. . . . in this manner the synagogue is not and can never be patterned after a denominational church. The synagogue has the right to assume direction of Jewish affairs because it is a permanent democratically constituted Jewish institution. . . . A rabbi is *elected* to deal primarily with matters of ritual and ceremonial practice, *not* to conduct civil courts of justice which was the chief role of our predecessors. Ours is a separated task of leadership. We are to teach, to instruct, to guide, to build public relations, to establish comity within the community.

He then posed the question, "Shall the control of Jewish affairs be lodged completely in the hands of those who control the purse strings, or shall there be a rabbinic tribunal or some other method of expressing the judgment of the synagogue authoritatively?"

Samuel was concerned about the degree of control of Jewish affairs increasing vested in the executives of social agencies, the managers of fund-raising campaigns, and major philanthropic donors. He felt very keenly then—and if he were with us today, he would continue to warn—that it is dangerous to sanction such a state of affairs, which may reduce further the influence of the synagogue in the direction of Jewish affairs.

A rabbi has a right and a duty to know what is going on in Jewish life. He must lead and responsibly guide his community. He needs his own guidance, not the conflicting advocates of special interest. The authoritative voice of a rabbinic body should advise him on matters of fact and policy. The synagogue will be strong or weak in proportion to its effectiveness in meeting the needs of the Jewish community.

In a lecture entitled "The Synagogue and the Direction of Jewish Affairs," Samuel discussed anti-Semitism, the processes of normalization and stratification of Jewish economic life, and, of course, the ubiquitous crisis concerning the future of Palestine. For him, Judaism and Eretz Yisrael, the Land of Israel, could not be placed in separate compartments. At the 1937 annual meeting of the Central Conference of American Rabbis, he pleaded with the membership to "energize our constituencies and our communities by deeds." He conceptualized a series of synagogue agencies which could mitigate the daily life problems of congregants and enable them to see that their personal abilities, knowledge, and skills could be utilized for the advancement of Jewish life. He enumerated new methods and techniques that might strengthen the internal organization of the synagogue.

The Conference [CCAR], the Hebrew Union College, and the Union of American Hebrew Congregations could augment and implement their services. It would be valuable to have a national coordinator and international coordinating body dedicating themselves to such efforts. Rabbinic commissions or conclaves would not only utilize the pulpit but also the round table, the seminar, and youth conferences to inform, teach, inspire, and guide the optimal direction of Jewish affairs. This approach would lend itself to fellowship with the ministries of other faiths, with civic leaders, the press, and with academic groups. A special office for press releases would not furnish publicity, but would disseminate articles, essays, and columns of information regarding Jews and Judaism to existing newspapers and periodicals.

Samuel himself provided a stirring example of these "agency actions." While still a young rabbi, he put together a "pronounce- ment" and in 1935 steered it through the Central Conference of American Rabbis, the leading organization for Reform Judaism and Reform rabbis. The CCAR at that time was by no means a strong- hold of Zionist understanding and sympathy. Despite this, Samuel was able to obtain the signatures of 241 Reform rabbis, cementing a statement that accomplished a true meeting ground for liberal Judaism and Labor Zionism. The integration of liberal Judaism with Labor Zionism (as expressed by the Histadruth and its American arm, the League for Labor Palestine) assumed historic proportions. It was welcomed and reprinted in the Jewish, American, and international press. On a more basic level, the doc- ument permitted liberal Judaism for the first time to express agree- ment with the principles and ideals of the Jewish labor movement in Palestine. We will revisit this statement when we discuss Samuel's American Zionist leadership and his important role in the birthing of Israel and in its post-independence nurturing years.

In considering the Isaac M. Wise Temple congregation, one cannot omit mention of the eighteen congregational presidents who served it in the years since the 1931 merger of the Reading Road Temple and Isaac M. Wise congregations. They were, as already noted, canny and wise in congregational politics. Some represented the traditions and beliefs of the older, financially secure German-Jewish population. Some were self-made people who were able to impart a sense of energy and purpose to congre- gational affairs. As individuals and as committee leaders, they had the expertise and the capacity to negotiate the financial and legal barriers confronting the congregation. Many assumed active lead- ership roles in broader Jewish communal activities and institutions. At least three were honored along with Samuel himself by the Hebrew Union College Board of Governors for their efforts on behalf of that institution. They all viewed Samuel as "genuine, caring, and idealistic with roots in reality," and as "really caring." It is not surprising that, in addition to Sidney Weil, whom we have discussed thoroughly, Samuel had close personal friendships with most of the temple's leadership, and thus that rabbi and leaders were able to work in close harmony.

The organic life of the temple is probably best represented by the brotherhood and sisterhood organizations as well as by the individual congregants themselves. In addition to their stated religious goals, both organizations assumed subordinate labors which, in fact, were their major contributions to the congregation and the Jewish community. Early brotherhood achievements and activities included maintenance of buildings, erection of edifices, participation in study groups, and the continuing enrichment and facilitation of religious school activities. The sisterhood was the first identifiable congregational group, tracing its inception to 1914 when the names of its officers were first published. The brotherhood was convened by Rabbi James G. Heller in 1921. By the time of Samuel's tenure, both organizations were working smoothly with the rabbis and officers of the congregation.

The congregation maintained its forward and positive evolution as James G. Heller furnished historical perspective. He noted that the early congregants made a strong attempt to modernize and liberalize, and this "met with much actual weakening of conviction and custom." They were able to maintain the "Jewish cohesiveness, partially as a habitual instrument, partially as a result of a certain native self respect and dignity." They founded their institutions well and supported them generously, but the pressures of assimilation and basic weakening of Jewish ties took their toll. Heller felt that for "our concept of Jewish life, the heart is not dead." Samuel seized this theme eagerly, originating and stimulating a renewed consciousness of Jewish existence in a warmer and more conducive atmosphere of Jewish practice.

In a recent article, Marmur explains that Reform Judaism and Zionism are now "intertwined." He comments on the early universalism of classical Reform and the particularism of Zionism, and on the change in the Reform position on Zionism from the early nineteenth-century pronouncements to recently formulated theological statements concerning the "centrality of Israel in Jewish life."

Samuel was one who could flow from Reform Judaism into Zionism and simultaneously seek their integration and fusion. He felt it was to the credit of Reform Judaism that it never established itself as a separate denomination. He invoked the voice of Klal Yisroel (the totality of Israel), maintaining that Israel is one people though it may have various forms of worship.

It was, of course, true that the Pittsburgh Platform of 1887 was anti-Zionist, and that similarly Zionism cast jaundiced eyes on Reform Judaism. Samuel pointed out that there was no violation of Judaic principles in bringing the two together. He argued that this had already occurred among a few distinguished members of the Reform rabbinate in the early years of the century. Bernard Felsenthal of Chicago, Maximilian Heller of New Orleans, James Guttheil of New York City, and Judah L. Magnes of New York City all expressed their faith in Reform Judaism and Zionism with great eloquence and conviction.

Samuel alluded several times to Stephen S. Wise as perhaps the "great tribune of the first half of the century." By means of indomitable will, commanding voice and personality, Wise brought to bear his tremendous powers, first in the New York area and then throughout the country. His Reform Judaism compelled him to be a progressive Jew in every respect. His founding and development of the Jewish Institute of Religion (JIR) and its later integration with the Hebrew Union College ensured that in subsequent years the young men and women who graduated from Reform seminaries would not foster any kind of division among Jews, and, of course, a great many of them are giving great service in key positions throughout the land.

Samuel considered it a privilege to have been the first Reform rabbi to become a member of the Labor Zionist movement and the first president of the League for Labor Palestine in the United States. He enlisted the help of hundreds of rabbis, Reform and Conservative, for the ideas and ideals of the Histadruth. The "pronouncement" Samuel steered through the CCAR in 1935 was indeed a historic document; thanks to his importunings, 241 rabbis signed the manifesto, thereby declaring their solidarity with the Histadruth.

Samuel's purpose was to show that the ideas of Reform Judaism, social justice, and the lofty ideals of Labor Zionism were in harmony, and that they were being fulfilled in Palestine and later in Israel. Because of its firmly entrenched programs and institutions of cooperative living, no organization has served the morale of Palestine and later Israel in their hours of peril better than the Histadruth. Amid almost unbelievable difficulty, it inspired the pioneers to continue the process of building the land. When all other lands closed or were rapidly closing their doors, the Histadruth loudly and continuously demanded that more and still more harassed fellow-Jews be admitted to their welcoming homeland. Samuel credited the Histadruth-inspired cooperative way of life as the invaluable factor making it possible for the tiny area of Palestine/Israel to care for an impossible number of victims of persecution.

In addition to the 241 Reform rabbis, the aforementioned manifesto was adopted unanimously by the rabbinic association of the Conservative movement in the United States. Samuel went to Jerusalem and presented the document to the British high commissioner for Palestine, Sir Arthur G. Wauchope, well before Israel attained formal statehood. Wauchope was very much impressed and forwarded the statement to the Colonial Office in London, where it was published in the secular and religious press.

Levi Weiman-Kelman, citing Professor Eugene Borowitz, points to the ideological divide separating the liberal (Progressive) Jews in Israel and the Israeli Orthodox religious establishment. "Granting the self a substantive role in our faith makes us Reform Jews." Samuel anticipated this concept some fifty or sixty years ago, when he wrote, "At the very heart of liberal Judaism is freedom." He refused to be yoked to ideas, practices, and traditions that had lost their meaning, historical significance, or were no longer essential to living a Jewish life.

If a rite or ritual today seems inappropriate or inexpressive, we claim the right to modify or abolish it. . . . The scientific method can and should be applied to religion, and, indeed, the theory of evolution is a great service toward a better understanding of Judaism. We do not recognize the difference between folk lore and mythology, law, custom and inspired truth in the Bible. We need not explain away that which is not explainable and we need not take fancy for fact, poetry for history. The Bible, studied and interpreted by modern man in *this* age by means of rationality, i.e., scientific method, is infinitely more true and of finer value to our generation than the belief, ultimately unacceptable to the modern mind, that every word, every letter, and every vowel point was dictated by God and is the essence of all wisdom. It is much more inspiring for us to know that the noblest of all books was the product of the magnificent genius of our people who out of their lives and joys, their agonies and their victories, their myths and their fears, their courage and their love over the period of many generations, created a glorious literature which has become the divine source for many religions and for countless millions of men.

Samuel confessed that his view comforted him in times of stress and furnished courage in crises. The people of Israel, descendants of the prophets and sages, might again send a new message for all humanity. He felt that sober consideration of "our gains" would undoubtedly strengthen us in our convictions, and convince us that we had been on the right path. At least thirty years before Sally Priesand was ordained a rabbi in Israel by the Hebrew Union College–Jewish Institute of Religion, Samuel proclaimed that liberal Judaism had religiously emancipated women, which he felt was easily confirmable by observation and experience. No matter how imbued one may be with the qualities of traditional Judaism, it is true and cannot be denied that in Orthodoxy and even to some extent in the Conservative movement, the Jewish woman is still fettered by an inferior status linked to religious custom. It is consistent with the aims of justice and equality that mothers in Israel be acknowledged by liberal Judaism and take their honored place as equals in the synagogue and in all avenues of life. Reform Judaism had boldly and openly faced the new conclusions of history and sought to find new adjustments and new solutions to meet them.

Samuel posited that the liberal approach had attempted to fashion a Judaism that can look science in the face without flinching, freeing Judaism from obsolete ideas and superstitions. He concluded that we should seek to fashion a Judaism that will be broad enough and will make its own doctrines of richness and worth. We all, in fact, should hold on to our own truths, so that our liberal faith can be enriched in succeeding generations.

Samuel Wohl began campaigning very early for a renewed emphasis on Jewish peoplehood in Reform Judaism. Our faith, he maintained, need not take the idea of a Jewish mission as one of its cornerstones.

> We are told that it is the *mission* of the Jews to teach monotheism to mankind and therefore the dispersion or diaspora was a "blessing." . . . It was simply a *calamity*, the greatest of all misfortunes. More than two thousand years of martyrdom, and the perpetual and continuous tragedy of a people is a frightful continuous event, unparalleled among peoples of the earth. What *are* these phrases really? A unique people—a particular people. Why not simply a people, the Jewish people? . . .
>
> How long must the course of teaching [monotheism] take? One hundred years, a thousand years? Have we been obtaining results for our efforts? And if we have been successful, when are we going to cease this instruction? There ought to be a graduation eventually. I confess I am often embarrassed to make this the whole raison d'etre for my Judaism.

We have already alluded to Samuel's continual and successful efforts to reintroduce the best aspects of past tradition into Jewish life and Jewish observance. However, he ventured aggressively beyond that point, creating new ceremonials and instrumentation for religion and a religious life.

In this connection, we must observe that Samuel was a master at judging how far and how hard to push the Jewish community and its adherence to liberal Judaism. Many Jews, sensitive to the implicit threat posed by their gentile neighbors, resisted their Jewish identity for fear it would make them conspicuous and somehow cast doubt on their Americanism. Social scientists are quite familiar with the psychological paradigm of identification with the oppressor, wherein one incorporates the persona of the persecutor, thereby protecting oneself from perceived overwhelming threats. In line with this, the successful German-Jewish Americans of Cincinnati resisted, consciously and unconsciously, the "threat" of traditional Judaism and often viscerally responded with self-hatred to even slight reminders of what they perceived as the stereotypical ghettoized European Jew.

For example, our father considered the ceremony and ritual of Bar Mitzvah to be an important milestone and beautiful event in Jewish practice. However, the ceremony was unknown and probably had not occurred in the congregation for a hundred years. Therefore, he wisely enlisted the aid of an Orthodox zaddik (venerable wise man) to teach us to chant lengthy portions of the Torah and Haftorah. We each accomplished our Bar Mitzvah in a small Orthodox shul (synagogue) in Cleveland, thereby honoring our maternal and paternal grandparents.

Samuel viewed the Seder night as a poetic drama based on ancient ritual and ceremony hallowed by centuries of practice and very beautiful in its meaning and purpose. He decried the fragmentation of ceremonial practice that had taken place as a result of immigration to a new country. He feared an ongoing process of dissolution, which he felt would threaten the vitality of the Jew.

As we have noted several times, he acknowledged that through the ages many doctrinal weeds had grown and would have to be removed. Many practices had become oppressive, meaningless, a barrier to progress, and others had lost all of their value in modern life and in new surroundings, now serving no purpose whatever. He would not adhere to traditions *solely* because past generations considered them statutes and ordinances of God. But he was flexible enough to see that no purpose is served by destroying unless there is something that contributes value and adequately supplants it. He viewed ritual and ceremony as a "poetry of life" speaking to the heart and to the eye. He went on to say:

> It is not a matter of logic, it is not necessary to analyze that which feeds our hearts and sends a thrill through the veins of our body. This is holy in its own right. . . . Jewish life was sanctified, often living on a higher plane. . . . it united all peoples in a true brotherhood. When the Jews of Morocco, Baghdad, and of Rome, observe and practice the same mode of life, there are higher unities and finer understandings. The great scholar and teacher, Maimonides, speaking of dietary laws, did not state merely that they were archaic and useless, but he also said, "It cannot be denied that these laws actually disciplined the medieval Jew so that during centuries of wild dissipation he practiced sobriety and moderation." . . . they serve as lessons in self-mastery and . . . keep him clean in soul as well as in body.

Samuel correctly understood modern authorities as unified in the opinion that the best education for life is achieved not by mere accumulation of information, but by actually doing and living. It is the practice and the experience that is important—what in modern pedagogy we call the "project method." The practice of ritual, therefore, is vitally educational in helping to keep the memory of our past vividly alive.

> [Ritual keeps] fresh and green the loyalties and affections for the Torah, for God and for Israel. . . . in the Passover ritual, we live again the experiences of our people in ancient

Egypt. Through the Succoth ceremonials we feel again the trials of our people wandering in the desert. . . . the Hanukkah lights make us feel that we are battling to preserve our people and *to* delineate ideals of freedom at the side of the Maccabeans. . . . The child who sees his mother bless the Sabbath candles, set the Seder table with all of its symbols and partakes of traditional foods of the festivals, will sense the beauty and loveliness of the holiday and will consequently be strengthened in his love for family, home, and in devotion for his extended kin. A psychological factor should cause us to cling to a ritualized Jewish existence despite all the changes that modern life has brought about. Ceremonial rituals have but a single aim and *motive*, i.e., to keep the Jewish people alive, preserve them from annihilation and remove them from the danger of assimilation. Perhaps there are individuals who can do without them, but a people such as ours can ill afford to *discard them*. You will agree from your own observation [that] when rituals, attendance at synagogue/temple, home ceremonies and celebration of holy days have been abolished, Jewish loyalties have decidedly weakened.

Samuel then proceeded to focus on the Jewish child, depicting the vulnerable years of childhood as a strategic and necessary time in which to enrich the child's life with emotional content. He emphasized the almost universally accepted idea that we all need defenses against the slings and arrows of prejudice, disappointments, and "when malice and vilification reach your heart." In this situation, your ritualized and living faith will protect you. He perceived Jews who fled the faith as overly defensive or as "not gaining enough nourishment to promote religious health, who could not withstand the trials of Judaism because they had no fortress of pride, courage or appreciation."

It is false that Reform Judaism has abolished ritual and ceremonies. We have simply removed some and refashioned others. . . . The Sabbath evening [before the Sabbath day] can still be beautified and made radiant by the blessing of the candles, by special food, by the kiddush [sanctification and prayer over the wine], and the home service in which father, mother, and children can participate.

We will again mention that Samuel was able to take old customs and give them new forms, so-called new wings. The new consecration ritual and ceremony, originated by him only seven years earlier, had by 1927 had already penetrated fifty or more communities in the United States and had been installed successfully in Havana, Cuba, Melbourne, Australia, and Johannesburg, South Africa. "The holiday of Shabuoth has been saved by the confirmation service and given new form and new content." In view of the dynamic success of the Gesher program of child and family bridging in the Wise Center's religious school today, it is interesting to read how Samuel, in 1934, sermonized, "There has been a real awakening with our congregation much due to our religious school, but unless the home becomes our partner and carries out its share, we will have labored in vain."

Samuel's relationship with the World Union for Progressive Judaism and one of its founders, Lily Montagu, of London, England, is a pure example of his universal idealism and enthusiasm for a cause. The World Union was organized in 1926 in London. Two years later, it adopted three major objectives, as cited by Schwartzman: "(1) to preserve Judaism by enabling it to respond to modern conditions and stimulating all Jews to participate in religious life, (2) to encourage the growth of Reform everywhere in the world and (3) to promote cooperation among the existing Reform movements." Since that time the WUPJ has analyzed and attempted to cope with religious issues throughout the world. Numerous countries, such as South Africa, New Zealand, Australia, Central and South America, India, Israel, and Europe have benefited from the seminaries, training sessions, and educational techniques it established.

Lily Montagu first approached Samuel to obtain his advice and help in soliciting funds in the United States. Samuel proved helpful, making numerous suggestions regarding fund drives and successfully recommending Dr. Julian Morgenstern as a member of the World Union's advisory committee. In 1936 Samuel became convinced that the growing Jewish community in Palestine strongly needed a liberal movement. In his position as chairman of the League for Labor Palestine in America and Canada and through his association with the leaders of the Histadruth, he was certain that a liberal movement could capture the imagination and loyalty of the youth of the beleaguered little country. The work of establishing or creating this movement, Samuel felt, would necessarily take into consideration the "things which are indigenous and holy in the *modern* life of Palestine. . . . In short, the aims and ideals of a new Palestine as . . . expressed . . . in the new patterns of social and economic justice must play a dominant role in the forms which we are to give the liberal synagogue." Samuel counseled that the liturgy and organizational forms of this liberal movement would also have to take these values into consideration if it was to appeal to the thousands of young people outside of the organized synagogue.

Samuel proposed an initial conference of "leading spirits" in Palestine to plan the most important steps. Popular support throughout the world be centered on a campaign to build a "magnificent synagogue and center either in Jerusalem or Tel Aviv," an undertaking that would simultaneously be of great value to Reform temples and synagogues in the United States. He visualized a project that would have the support of the World Union and the Union of American Hebrew Congregations. He could enlist the support of other national bodies in the United States.

In the following months, Samuel accepted an appointment to the World Union's Palestine Advisory Committee and began to labor eagerly for the "Palestine Project." He noted that action had already been taken by the executive board of the Central Conference of American Rabbis through the manifesto of the 241 rabbis mentioned above. He launched a barrage of suggestions regarding the means, philosophy, and practical considerations of fund-raising in the United States. In a letter to Lily Montagu, for instance, he asked her to send him a letter, on behalf of the World Union, "expressing satisfaction with the action of the executive board of the Conference [CCAR] stating the opportunities confronting the World Union generally, encouraging Progressive Judaism in Palestine and urging strongly the boards of the congregations to appoint from their midst special committees for that purpose."

The World Union was apparently not yet ready for plans of the magnitude envisioned by Samuel. It proposed, instead, a plethora of investigations and practical assistance to numerous small causes. It tactfully explained that the building of the synagogue was surely a practical possibility, and at the appropriate time Samuel's "kind suggestions" would certainly be utilized.

Rabbi Samuel Cook, in a letter to Justin Friedman, chairman of the Samuel Wohl 70th Birthday Committee, reminisced that when he was a student at the Hebrew Union College, Rabbi Samuel Wohl, then the rabbi of the Reading Road Temple, was known to the students as the "idea rabbi." Not that all his ideas were successes when implemented, Cook said; lots of them floated like bubbles into the air. But the saying was, "Better ten Wohl successful projects out of a total of one hundred ideas than three successful ones out of a total of three ideas offered by a more cautious planner."

Samuel accepted a position on the World Union's advisory board and, despite his surging creative propensities, was subsequently content to offer counsel only when asked. The underfunded, understaffed World Union had accomplished surprising results in the brief years of its existence. Samuel correctly perceived that the significant potential of Reform Judaism would spur the international Jewish community to undertake the heroic venture of self-analysis and rejuvenation. He differed from many American Jewish leaders in viewing this process not as "the sacred burden of missionary leadership, but as a means of enablement and education, that is, in every Jew and in every Jewish group there exists the capacity for self realization and self actualization." During his entire adult life and many years of multivaried leadership, Samuel worked decisively toward this goal.

Despite the World Union's "intensification" of its "Israel program," we think that one can be deeply disappointed by the status of liberal Judaism in Israel today. The World Union actually applied for admittance to the World Zionist Organization in 1974 and was a full-fledged member by 1975. Three years later, as if powered by a pendulum, it formally transferred its international headquarters to Jerusalem, where it was guided by its then new director, Rabbi Richard Hirsch. A few years earlier, the Progressive cause seemed to gain authority when the Hebrew Union College opened its school in Jerusalem. Indeed, in 1970, it became the first Jewish seminary to require all students to spend their first year in Jerusalem.

From his vantage point in the mid-1970s, Rabbi David Polish enthusiastically described the Jerusalem school of HUC as the "spiritual center of the Progressive movement in Israel. . . . its influence radiated beyond the small progressive community and encompassed Israeli society and generated great moral strength within the Reform community in America." We think that Rabbi Polish may be excused for his stated enthusiasm, because there were undoubtedly positive consequences manifested in both Israel and the United States.

Chapter 18
Notable HUC Presidential Successor, Light of Reform Judaism Transplanted, Dissent from Respected Mentor's Opinions

Samuel consulted closely with Dr. Nelson Glueck, who succeeded Dr. Morgenstern as president of Hebrew Union College. Glueck was instrumental in establishing a branch of HUC in Jerusalem. Samuel further supported Glueck by facilitating contact between the new president and two close personal friends in Israel, David Ben-Gurion and Levi Eshkol. Samuel directly assisted Glueck in dealing with the opposition of the Orthodox religious establishment and helped him navigate the bureaucracy of the municipality of Jerusalem.

Professor Michael Meyers, in his history of Reform Judaism, details the attitude of the Hebrew Union College board about the presidential appointment of Dr. Glueck. It was common knowledge that Glueck intended to pursue two major roles, continuing his work as an internationally famous archaeologist in the Middle East while occupying the presidency of the steadily flourishing Hebrew Union College. Rabbi Floyd Fierman, a former student of Glueck's, considered him a "fascinating, private, but charismatic figure." He was a slender, impeccably dressed multilingual scholar. Often distant with his friends and colleagues, he became animated when discussing Palestine and later Israel. In the two decades before 1947, he spent months, even years, traversing the ancient

lands of the Middle East. He became an associate and then colleague of William F. Albright of John Hopkins University, world-
renowned archaeologist and founder of the American School of
Oriental Research in Jerusalem. Fluent in Arabic, he was quite at
home in a burnoose and other Arab garb. He knew the desert terrain as did few people. His scholarship was broad-based. His strategic digs, using the Bible as a guidebook, captured the imagination
of the American people. He added actual historical meaning and
support to biblical drama and narrative.

Later, Samuel was to laud Glueck as not merely an interpreter
of the past, but equally as a guide and molder of the future. Glueck
was not caught off guard by the Nazi juggernaut. During the thirties, Cincinnati welcomed German refugees, including a number
of scholars who horrified the Jewish community with tales of life
in Nazi Germany. Glueck perceived that German and East
European Jews were closing ranks due to the threat posed by Hitler.
He felt that Reform Judaism was an evolutionary process akin to
the "unfolding of the Jewish spirit." During the Second World War
he successfully petitioned the Office of Strategic Services, the predecessor of today's CIA, to utilize his knowledge of the countries
and terrain of the Middle East. Several days after Pearl Harbor, and
for at least three years thereafter, Glueck was intensively engaged
in his scientific work and espionage. Stan Sulkes, in a 1987 magazine article, quotes Helen Glueck, Nelson's wife, and renowned
physician in her own right, with a clear statement of Glueck's mission based on the contingency that the British forces might be
defeated in the decisive battle of El Alamein and be driven out of
North Africa and Egypt: "He was to plan a retreat, perhaps a road,
noting every spring, every unusual formation which would facilitate egress. Of course, the Allies won this major battle which
allowed access to oil fields and their own routes to India and
Australia."

Samuel was aware of what were then merely rumors well before
Fierman's published proof and revelations. Samuel, like Dr.
Glueck, petitioned the Honorable Herbert H. Lehman, director of
foreign relief and rehabilitation at the State Department, for a gov-

ernment military intelligence appointment. In a letter of recommendation, Julian Morgenstern described Samuel as

> a man of remarkable initiative, energy and resourcefulness, an able organizer and administrator. He has had a rich experience in organizational and public relations work of many aspects, both of communal and national character. . . . He has participated in conferences in most of the European lands and Palestine, and he knows intimately many of the key men in various countries and has participated in the leadership of a number of important movements.

Letters of reference were also obtained from Clarence Dykstra, chancellor of the University of Wisconsin, Charles P. Taft, normally of Cincinnati, but then located in Washington, Fred Hoehler, Joseph Heyman, secretary of the Joint Distribution Committee, and David Ben-Gurion, of the Jewish Agency. Samuel's efforts in these directions were rebuffed when, after some months, he received a tactfully worded letter from the State Department rejecting his applications, citing the anatomical fact of a malpositioned stomach.

Somewhat in contrast to the warm intimacy of his relationship with Dr. Morgenstern, Samuel Wohl and Nelson Glueck formed a friendship based on quiet mutual respect and admiration. Glueck perceived a man whose knowledge of Palestine/Israel and its people rivaled his own, but on much different planes and levels. There were also a fervency and idealism that Glueck could not help but admire. In his structuring of the HUC presidency, he was quick to delegate responsibility to the "right people." Samuel served as a major resource on American and Palestinian Zionism. In due course, Glueck gratefully appointed him to the Hebrew Union College board as a replacement for James G. Heller.

In addition to being a vital conduit to lay, national, and international Zionist groups, Samuel enabled Dr. Glueck and the college to work in harmony with the Union of American Hebrew

Congregations, the Central Conference of American Rabbis, and other important American and international Jewish organizations and congresses. He was awarded special honors and a "proclamation" for "being committee chairman and contributing immeasurably to the effective celebration of the Hebrew Union College's 70th anniversary and to the formulation and inauguration of the program for its foundation fund."

In later testament to Nelson Glueck, Samuel noted that during his presidency, like that of his predecessor, Morgenstern, new academic departments continued to be introduced, new buildings were erected, and the college continued to grow in status and quality. During the Nazi period, a dozen European scholars found a welcoming environment at HUC chiefly as a result of Dr. Morgenstern's efforts. However, it was Dr. Glueck, along with Samuel and Rabbi Stanley Brav, who formed the welcoming committee for Rabbi Dr. Leo Baeck, the great German-Jewish leader who is credited with keeping the flickering candle of hope alive for German Jewry during the stygian darkness of Nazi domination.

During Samuel's first visits to Germany, he met several times with Dr. Baeck and noted that for a time the Nazis recognized him as the only spokesman for German Jewry. Later, Baeck was sent to the Theresienstadt concentration camp. He gave up his mind and heart to hundreds of victims and managed to write his last book on slips of paper, which were somehow preserved to be published later. Differing from many of his predecessors and colleagues, he had a positive attitude toward the restoration of Israel. His eminence did not prevent him from believing that the Nazi menace would eventually ignite the world. However, paradoxically he speculated before the burning of the Reichstag that "these hooligans would never come to power in Germany." Amazingly, Dr. Baeck was saved from death by the fact that there was another Leo Baeck in the Theresienstadt camp. When this other Baeck died, the otherwise precise Nazi records pertaining to Rabbi Baeck were permanently muddled, thereby sparing him from execution. Dr. Baeck spent his later years in Cincinnati at the Hebrew Union College and in London with his beloved daughter.

When Julian Morgenstern retired, he and Samuel continued their close friendship, maintaining a copious correspondence. Morgenstern's letters clearly indicate that the venerable scholar was increasingly physically infirm but crystal-clear of mind until his death. One of Samuel's defining and excruciatingly painful life tasks occurred in the early forties. In the currents and eddies of local and international events, Samuel Wohl consistently struck the anvil of Zionism. Following a representative American Jewish Conference, Dr. Morgenstern felt compelled, in a highlighted address, to analyze and contest the major recommendation of the conference: a formal request to the international community for a Jewish commonwealth. Samuel was present at the conference and realized that the newspapers had highlighted the anti-Zionist utterances and, either by design or simple forgetfulness, not mentioned those portions that expressed friendliness toward the aspirations of the Jewish people for a homeland in Palestine.

In at least two major subsequent addresses and in a sermon to the congregation, Samuel dissented from his mentor and friend. We have already explained that Samuel deeply deplored controversy, particularly at a time when he knew that every ounce of energy should be devoted to the destruction of the enemy and the saving of lives of "our tortured and tormented brothers." Indeed, he regretted, more than he was able to express, that simple candor and duty compelled him to point out where Morgenstern's views were mistaken and potentially hurtful. Samuel, of course, had the advantage of knowing Dr. Morgenstern's actions over a period of more than fifteen years. Dr. Morgenstern had been associated with the United Palestine Appeal since its inception. He had given his wholehearted support for many years to the policies adopted by the Central Conference of American Rabbis and the Union of American Hebrew Congregations and he was friendly to the restoration of Palestine as a national Jewish home. He did not press anti-Zionist views on students or faculty, and it was quite evident that for many years the overwhelming majority of the Hebrew Union College student body had been Zionists or sympathetic to Zionism. These students, he observed, had recently condemned the American Council for Judaism, a self-appointed body that fed the flames of anti-Zionism.

Dr. Morgenstern, Samuel declared, had been one of the first to sign the great declaration that was made and signed by 241 Reform rabbis, which contained a ringing faith in the renaissance of the Jewish people and their ancient homeland by expressing solidarity with the ideals of the Histadruth, the Jewish Labor Federation of Palestine. Dr. Morgenstern had emphasized his long-held views that the Jews were merely a religious denomination and nothing else. Although this concept was popular in the early Reform literature, it had become increasingly untenable and was being discarded by thinking people. Samuel contended that Jews are not only co-religionists but also brothers. Samuel once again advanced his universalistic concept and, as we have already stated, his conviction that "we are one people, a unique people, a God centered people who have created ideas that have gone beyond the boundaries of Israel and have been accorded universal recognition."

Samuel elaborated that a major contribution has been "the magnificent vision of humanity and the quest of God," but he could not comprehend Morgenstern's point or distinction that "peoplehood" was all-important and a nation nothing. This seemed to confine nationhood to a mere governing function. He added that such a distinction had not been made between any people and its nationhood.

Despite the public nature of their disagreement, our memories, and accumulated correspondence from those years, do not even hint at an interruption in the deeply caring relationship between Samuel and Morgenstern. In time Morgenstern was to officially and privately adopt a syntonic view of Zionism corresponding with the official birth of the nation of Israel. He was to support Samuel fully in his association with Zionist causes and his attempts to utilize the universal teachings of prophetic Judaism and animate them into practice in Palestine. The people of the new state and future immigrants considered concepts of the brotherhood of man, non-exploitation, self-labor, and economic justice very seriously. The very actions of draining swamps and turning desolate land into blossoming fields and orchards thus formed a vital haven for Holocaust-seared refugees and was to Samuel the very paradigm of God worship.

Few people, even in the congregation, truly realized the scope of Samuel's interests and work. These were more varied and in many instances more intensely pursued than was characteristic of clergy throughout the country. Very simply, Samuel did not simply conduct the worship and preach the sermon, but felt obligated to deal with the education departments of the temple, administer its affairs, work with the various committees, agencies, and subsidiaries of the temple, maintain hundreds of pastoral contacts, labor on Jewish communal boards and institutions, participate in the religious work of the non-Jewish community, and cooperate in every civic endeavor in southwestern Ohio. He eagerly responded to calls for action in the larger Jewish national community in its various phases of reconstruction and relief, and the many movements for revitalization of Jewish life in America.

A calendar month in Rabbi Samuel Wohl's work typically contained an almost impossible count of religious functions, addresses, lectures, board meetings, all accomplished locally, statewide, and even nationally. We have, in the course of our narrative, referred to a spectrum of many religious and lay organizations and groups within which he was both participant and frequently a leader. However, we are compelled to admit the omission of a wide panoply of affiliations and memberships in organizations such as the International Rotary Club, the Cincinnati Club, the Jewish Community Relations Council, the Cincinnati Community Chest, and the board of the American Cancer Society, to name but a few. The authors found it manifestly difficult to describe the intangibles. These are best conceptualized by the stress and scope of the effort and even better by the numerous testimonials contained in milestone celebrations for Samuel's tenure and service to the congregation. The common content of letters from almost four decades of congregants concerns a person who "never forgot a face" and was unfailingly kind, compassionate and, despite the universalistic and international scope of his interests and activities, exquisitely sensitive to the problems and achievements of his individual congregants.

From his kindly family practitioner, Ely Miller, M.D., to the internist David Graller, M.D., Samuel admired the acumen and work ethic of the practicing physician. He viewed the medical profession as indispensable to his personal health and family. He was quite uninformed regarding bodily states and physiological processes. He was on a first-name basis with many prominent physicians and surgical specialists, and he had a childlike faith that, by virtue of their skills and mysterious knowledge, they could dispel pain and misery. By the same token, he was unaware of the esteem tinged with awe characterizing their feelings toward him. He lamented that physicians typically did not participate strongly in congregational affairs or assume leadership positions. He harked back to his earlier years in Cincinnati, when he had met and formed strong personal ties with Morris Schulzinger, M.D. A veritable dynamo of positive Judaism, Dr. Schulzinger seemed indefatigable and adept at reaching stated goals. He founded and led numerous Jewish movements and organizations in Cincinnati, and was peripatetically involved with Jewish leaders throughout the United States, Israel, and Europe. Somehow, he was also able to pursue a medical career and accomplish scientific research. He and Samuel collaborated eagerly in Zionistic and educative areas. Of course, both men shared their origins in the fermenting environment of the East European shtetl. Their friendship was secured firmly when it was discovered that Belle's parents and Mrs. Schulzinger (Pupi) were from the same Lithuanian locale.

Morris, at the age of eighty, wrote a chatty, colorful, and quite authoritative autobiography. The book, *The Tale of a Litvak*, chronicles Jewish events and personalities in Cincinnati at least as well as any publication we have read from the early twenties to the mid-eighties. Samuel is characterized in the book as a man of "achievement" and "stature," one who was a "dynamic leader and great innovator, and made himself greatly felt in the community." All of this only deepened Samuel's need to discover a physician within his own congregation who would approach the standards set by Dr. Schulzinger.

Part V
The Land of Israel:
Culmination of a Dream

Chapter 19
Angry Dismay
at Israeli Clerical Privileges

We have already portrayed how Zionism, its political ideals, philosophy, and religious-cultural perspectives, became the early structure and driving force in Samuel's life. The polemics of East European thinkers like Pinsker and Ahad Ha-am, the generative actions and writings of Theodor Herzl, and the very rush and crush of world events engulfed him. Earlier in this narrative we have also noted that Samuel, as a fledgling rabbi, defined Judaism through nationalism and its finest manifestation, Zionism. Our earlier discussion succinctly reflects his views in this respect, namely,

> that Judaism is the collective expression of the Jewish people, not of any other people; that twenty centuries in the life of the diaspora have not stunted the Jewish creative spirit. Even the prophets of old were first and foremost Jewish nationalists. Their noble and matchless utterances are results of an exalted love and fervor for their people and for their national verities . . . that Eretz Yisrael is the land where creative spirits blossomed and bore to fruition our greatest and noblest cultural heritage.

As the weary overnight traveler approaches and sights the radiant coast of Israel, it is still, we think, the practice of Israel's national airline, El Al, to broadcast peals of triumphant music over the plane's public address system. The weary traveler almost always experiences a sense of expectancy and an adrenaline-driven urge to disembark into the "homeland."

Samuel seemed to have these feelings *perpetually*. Well before the existence of Israel as a state, and shortly after his arrival in this country, he began to innovate, conceptualize, and integrate Zionism and the Zionist movement into his personal life and the scope of his work in the United States and the international community. In his adolescent years, the Zionist Organization of America (ZOA) offered him positions of leadership. Over the years, he monitored the status of Jewish groups throughout the world and was active in movements and causes to alleviate their suffering.

Perceptive analyses and self-evident truths were embodied in Samuel's numerous written communications designed to further his views and his goals. He continually wrote to radio stations and the print media, and composed sermons and addresses that were delivered to innumerable groups in the city and during tours of the state, the nation, and the world. Members of his own congregation, over a period of many years, were recipients of copies of his published letters concerning Zionistic, Jewish, and international matters. He wrote lengthy "memoranda" addressed to the world's politically powerful, both friend and foe. Whether there was a response or not, Samuel then reprinted the missive, often utilizing the content in part or in whole for sermons or communications with other important people. The sheer volume of these communications is mind-boggling, and the number of recipients probably totaled as many as 500 individuals and groups. Quite typical was Samuel's letter to Secretary of State George Marshall before the establishment of the State of Israel:

> There is shock and embitterment in our hearts at the failure of our government to put an end to the murderous attack upon Jewish Palestine by the Nazi Mufti and his marauders, aided and abetted by British sabotage and vindictiveness. . . . Who is responsible for "law and order" in

Palestine? What kind of law prevails there now and what kind of order? . . . Mr. Secretary, there is deep appreciation of all our citizens for the great leadership you gave us in time of war. You led us in a good cause to rid the world of the unspeakable Nazi juggernaut. Now you have been entrusted with the great and more difficult task of winning the peace.

Subsequent to a very long visit to Israel, the Soviet Union, Hungary, and Romania, Samuel searched for a commentary based on many interviews of people, officials, and a thorough digestion of the press and radio. President Lyndon B. Johnson, Premier Alexei Kosygin, Minister for Foreign Affairs Andrei Gromyko, First Secretary of the Soviet Communist Party Leonid Brezhnev, United Arab Republic President Gamal Abdul Nasser, His Holiness Pope Paul VI, and Secretary of State Dean Rusk all were recipients of letters following the 1966 trip.

In light of the current controversy regarding such questions as "Who is a Jew?" in Israel, it is instructive to examine Samuel's simmering vexation with these matters over forty years ago. At that time, he dashed off letters to Golda Meir, David Ben-Gurion, Abba Eban, Ambassador Abraham Harman, Prime Minister Levi Eshkol, and President Zalman Shazar. His message to his close friend Golda Meir is still pertinent in regard to today's problems.

I do not want to comment on many of the things which I could view from within, and I certainly do not want to have American Jewish public opinion know of these hurtful matters. For instance, I am offended by the fact that the clericals, who call themselves religious Jews, have imposed themselves and are exacting a type of blackmail from the government. The longer it lasts, the worse it will become. . . . as a Jew within the United States, I cannot prepare myself to be free and equal and strive for the separation of church and state or resist the intrusion of church in matters of state and, at the same time, permit the kind of coercion that goes on within Israel and which is proudly proclaimed from the house tops. It might require a Hearst journalist to make shambles out of this situation, and paint Israel as bigoted and as a place where it is difficult to breathe. They [the clericals] should know what they are entitled to receive, that they have no right to declare that you or I, members of the Kibbutz, or other Jewish Conservative or Reform adherents, are not religious. This, should it become more permanent, would cause great resentment here and the image of Israel will be blighted and blackened. . . . I am sending this to a friend as a friend, and you know that I will certainly do all I can here in the United States to mitigate the rising anger of the American rabbinate who will be meeting soon in Toronto, Canada.

In a parallel letter to President Shazar, Samuel included a letter he had circulated to the members of the Central Conference of American Rabbis whom he discerned as "demanding action." He had received an enormous response prior to the conference and in several conference addresses, Samuel advised, and had even pleaded with the membership to restrain themselves "at the present time" and thus not hurt the United Jewish Appeal, the Histadruth campaign, and Israel Bonds. He had proposed that no formal resolution of protest be forwarded to Israel and that steps be taken in the immediate future to ameliorate the conditions. His circulated letter passionately stated, "We cannot fight for freedom of religion in the United States and then turn around and support the so-called clerical institutions and clerical movements of Israel." Samuel, in addition, reminded President Shazar of two problems that he had brought to the attention of Levi Eshkol, Golda Meir, and the Labor Zionist leader Berl Locker as early as 1950, namely, that "more native Israelis are leaving the country than new immigrants coming in and that every effort must be made to encourage [Jewish] immigration to Israel from the west."

The negative immigration problem has only recently been assuaged by the massive immigration of Russian Jews to Israel, but emigration remains a fact and is perhaps an inevitable trend. Samuel's sense of urgency regarding this matter was tempered considerably by the knowledge that the Israeli government had to juggle a delicate coalition of political organizations. The price of stability and effective government was associated with granting clerical factions certain privileges and monopolies on marriage, conversion, and personal status. At the time and for the foreseeable future, it was increasingly difficult to resolve important domestic issues because of the seemingly perpetual crises in Israel and in the world.

Samuel was somewhat mollified by conversations and written correspondence with Avraham Harman, Israel's ambassador to the United States. Both men were unenthusiastic about "agitational efforts." Both agreed that there was a "broad public in Israel," especially among the youth, who were searching for new religious experiences and who would respond positively to varieties of religious expression. In a 1969 newsletter sent to congregational members, Samuel displayed enthusiasm over the "considerable progress of our movement within Israel." Recognizing the institution of the Hebrew Union College in Jerusalem, he was quite impressed by the peaceful and productive work of the young rabbis and HUC graduates then living and working in Israel. The number of Israelis forming Progressive congregations was increasing, and the number of attractive places for worship was multiplying.

Chapter 20
The Religion of Labor, Israel and the United States, Developments and Personages in Palestine/Israel

W hy did Samuel believe in the "religion of labor" and the revolution it was effecting in the spiritual transformation of the Jewish people in Israel and the diaspora? Basically, the Jewish religion without the dynamic power of Israel was unthinkable to him. He simply could not differentiate his religious feelings from the energy of Zionism. He sought to authenticate the faith of his people and its accomplishments in times when it had been loudly proclaimed that religion no longer bore any potency. He asserted that it was faith that made possible the beginnings of the reestablishment of the Jewish commonwealth in Palestine.

As Samuel saw it, the initial progress of the Jews in establishing and developing a land seemed to portend the possibility of the "revolution without violence," which is a central and fundamental concept of most of the major religious faiths of the world. He employed the word "conquest" in two different ways. Thus, for instance, when he spoke of "the two greatest needs in and for Palestine," he stated that "one is the conquest of the soil, the redemption of land transforming desert and swamps into fields and orchards. The second is—the conquest by labor to transform every human into a productive member of society and make self-labor a significant principle of love." And in this connection he certainly held that exploitation of the labor of others was not to be tolerated.

These major principles necessitated, first, a creative instrument for land redemption, which would substitute for or enhance the private ownership of land and effectively mitigate speculation in land. Such an instrument was the Jewish National Fund, known as the Keren Kayemet, which bought and owned the land on which the early settlements were built. By the 1940s, several hundred such settlements existed.

The second conquest, or self-labor, created the most important experiment, known as the communal settlements, or *kvutzoth*. These were and are today cooperative and collective settlements. Samuel pointed out that Jews of many lands had created the Zionist movement, which, particularly in the formative years, guided and maintained the political, economic, and spiritual impetus necessary for the advancement of the cause and the restoration of landless people to their land. It is important to stress that Samuel did not advocate socialist labor as a political movement. Rather, he felt sincerely that this emphasis was needed to accomplish the early aim of establishing a Jewish communal movement, which he fully expected to fuse with enlightened capitalism, and, as we will see, the formation of the Histadruth soon evolved exactly in that direction. Once again, we can gain better insight into Samuel's work and principles by briefly alluding to the decisive impact of Labor Zionist ideas in Palestine and ultimately the State of Israel.

The League for Labor Palestine was born in Berlin in 1930, when an international conference met for what its conveners termed their "pioneer mission." Widening channels of influence in new directions were debated and discussed. The League achieved formal life in 1933, and by 1935, under the leadership of Rabbis Wohl and Edward Israel, a bridge was established between the American and Jewish labor movements as well as between the labor idealists in Palestine and in the United States. Samuel was instrumental in founding the *Jewish Frontier*, the monthly English-language journal, which reciprocally strengthened the League and helped elicit interest and support from Jewish intellectual circles in this country. Chaim Greenberg was the nominal editor. Samuel was an associate editor and helped to support the magazine for several years, securing the financial aid of Justice Louis Brandeis. A high point was achieved in 1935–36 when the Palestinian and North American labor movements were accorded recognition and financial aid by the Jewish governing body in Palestine.

A special meeting centering around the problems of American Zionism was held in the home of David Ben-Gurion and was attended by Ben-Gurion, Berl Katznelson, Golda Meir, Edward Israel, Herman Zeidel, and Samuel Wohl. They decided that the League had potential to become a truly creative instrument with the necessary help. Pinchas Cruso was elected executive secretary. Golda Meir agreed to embark on a tour of the United States to assist in the recruitment of new members and to help strengthen the various chapters. Samuel, as elected president, projected the mobilization of a large membership. He decided to unite the League with the Histadruth fund-raising campaign. Each potential contributor would add an automatic two dollars to the Histadruth membership dues or otherwise indicate the wish to make a League campaign donation. This worked well in some of the larger U.S. and Canadian cities. Unfortunately, the leaders of many of the other parties viewed the fledgling League as a competitor and did not grant it the necessary cooperation.

In addition to his presidency of the League for Labor Palestine, Samuel served for many years as vice president of the Histadruth and as a member of its board of directors. Investing his heart in the mobilization of forces to spread the seminal ideas of Labor Israel, he criss-crossed the country, attending and addressing mass meetings in many cities. As noted several times, in 1937 he was the architect of a written changeover in the ideology of the Reform rabbinate which subsequently influenced the liturgy and Hebrew orientation of Reform Judaism. As much as anybody in this country, he stirred the fires of idealism among America's youth and enabled the channeling of young strength and support to Israel.

Meanwhile, despite these achievements, the League for Labor Palestine worried about its financial existence and had to make do with relatively meager resources to support its cultural activities and publications. Cruso complained bitterly that if organized Zionism had granted only 1 percent of its usable funds, this would have removed the need for the League to stand "with hat in hand to beg for small budgets." Samuel fully understood that world-wide Zionism gratefully accepted the help of the League but, in fact, often demonstrated a disproportionate lack of regard for its basic needs in order to sustain the vigor of the American movement. Samuel's giving was, as always, unreserved. It seemed that there was little or no quid pro quo in his makeup.

The distinguished historian and newspaper columnist Walter Laqueur has detailed how the growth of political Zionism witnessed the spread of socialist ideas among the Jews of Eastern Europe. Nachman Syrkin and Ber Borochov were Labor Zionist idealists from different sides of the spectrum. Both men, through their writings, and despite basic disagreements, attempted to identify means of integrating mass immigration, settlement, and worker primacy.

Laqueur explains how the mentality of the Jewish worker differed from that of the rank-and-file working men of other nations. In fact, the young immigrants who began arriving in Palestine from Eastern Europe between 1904 and 1906, the group known as the Second Aliyah (immigration wave), possessed a "strong mystical element" that provided an identification with the land and work ethic. They foundered quickly when they encountered the harshest reality. Those who remained were eventually to provide the leadership of political parties, the Zionist movement, and the State of Israel. David Ben-Gurion and Yitzhak Ben-Zvi shaped the Poale Zion program along activist lines. They predictably emphasized manual labor, but focused most of their energy on such undertakings as the establishment of an organization of Jewish watchmen (Hashomer).

As the "old guard" of the Second Aliyah gradually passed, the settlers of the Third Aliyah, less ideological and academically learned, pragmatically devoted their attention to the economic and administrative issues confronting the evolving Jewish society.

Eliezer Kaplan, Golda Meir, and Abba Khoushi were dynamic leaders who, together with the Second Aliyah's Moshe Sharret, Yitzhak Ben-Zvi, Yosef Sprinzak, David Ben-Gurion, Berl Locker, Berl Katznelson, and Levi Eshkol, became close friends with Samuel—all toiled intensively for the Jewish state and the Zionist dream.

The Fourth Aliyah may be considered properly the growth of the middle class, populating the area around Tel Aviv and Haifa. The settlers of this wave of immigration demonstrated as early as the mid-twenties that the economic health of the country could be sustained without constant help from the government and foreign supporters. It was finally decided in 1926 that the Palestinian economy was to be administered strictly on a business basis.

At the same time, Labor Zionism rose triumphantly and became a dominant factor in Palestine and in the diaspora. Membership in the Histadruth, the General Federation of Jewish Labor, grew rapidly, and many new and creative economic and cultural enterprises were sponsored during this period. The chalutzim, young Jewish pioneers primarily in the diaspora, nursed the ideals of Labor Zionism and prepared themselves for a life of manual work in Palestine. They added strength and vitality to the kibbutzim (communal agricultural communities) and eventually formed support structures of paramilitary and military forces along the outer perimeter of settlements to serve as defense outposts.

In contrast, the last of the early waves of immigration, the Fifth Aliyah, stemmed from Central and Western Europe. These immigrants were less interested in pioneering than in production. Some, in fact, were budding entrepreneurs and business-oriented farmers.

Samuel's frequent and lengthy visits to Palestine and Israel occurred during the transition from the fourth immigration wave to the fifth. His early and subsequent visits coincided with the rapid development of the Histadruth as it assumed the posture of the largest employer in the country and advocated for the rights and interests of employees. The Histadruth was the ultimate entrepreneur, furthering marketing, industrial, and agricultural products, building roads, houses, factories, and setting up retail companies large and small. At this same time, the Mapai political party and its leaders, with Samuel as confidant, placed Labor Zionism in the center of Palestinian and later Israeli Jewish existence.

The Haganah Jewish defense organization was founded shortly after the First World War in response to sporadic Arab attacks. It gained effectiveness and organization following the Arab Revolt of 1936. It was, perforce, the military evolution of the Histadruth through its youth organizations and kibbutzim. As "illegal" immigrants streamed toward the Palestine coastline before the ominous scudding clouds of war, the Haganah played a vital role in their reception and absorption. During these years, the Haganah and the kibbutzim fused and became strategic strong points for weapons storing and bases for military training.

Despite his identification with the mainstream elements of the Zionist movement, Samuel was fascinated as much as repelled by the colorful, powerful, and perpetual activist Vladimir Jabotinsky. Jabotinsky headed and brought to a focus the dissatisfaction with official Zionist policies during the thirties. Samuel wondered that this aggressive militarist and disseminator of internal strife was at the same time an accomplished essayist and brilliant speaker. Jabotinsky was a Russian poet and lover of literature. Once infused with Zionist ideals, he attempted to further the cause in many foreign groups and countries. He was a continual thorn in the side of Labor Zionism. His opinions and oratory were dramatic and pervaded with gross oversimplifications. The leaders of Palestinian Jewry could not tolerate an individual who would not abide by the will of the majority and was constantly and destructively criticizing without offering well-developed alternatives.

As Samuel entered the stage of international Zionism, the Revisionist Party was giving Jabotinsky an unlimited mandate while he basically assumed authoritarian methods and behavior. Jabotinsky was an admitted "liberal anarchist." Under his leadership, the Revisionist movement separated from the Zionist main body and became an effective force working for the establishment of a Jewish state, mass colonization, and emphasizing strength and militarism. The Revisionist movement, in turn, generated the Irgun and later the Stern party. These radical fighters (some would call them terrorists) contributed significantly to Britain's surrender of her mandatory restrictive powers and to the subsequent establishment of the Jewish state, whose first task was military self-defense against invading Arab armies.

The Irgun was more or less a continuation of the Jabotinsky tradition. After a four-year interruption, Menachem Begin took command of its small but potent forces and resumed attacks on the British. As was also true of the supreme leader, Jabotinsky, Begin's goals were congruent with those of the Haganah and mainstream Zionism. However, his methods caused horror and revulsion in Samuel and in the hearts of thinking Jews in many nations. It was not long before the Irgun split acrimoniously from the Haganah, and during World War II it ceased operations entirely, only to resume in 1944 under the leadership of Menachem Begin. The veteran warrior was at first reactive and pugnacious, but steadily developed the attributes of a statesman and, as prime minister of the country, he seemed truly interested in the welfare of the totality of Israel. When the flamboyant Jabotinsky died in 1940, the Revisionist movement seemed to wither and die. Its components reintegrated into a political party, Herut, which later, under Begin's leadership, became a conservative force reshaping popular roles and offering alternative goals and philosophies to the evolving Israeli society.

Samuel, of course, was involved in this panoply of events on both sides of the Atlantic. He propelled himself into active committee work, personally buttonholed members of the CCAR, assumed leadership positions in the Zionist Organization of America and the Histadruth, and attended all the meetings of the American Jewish Congress and the World Jewish Congress. Not a power broker himself, he was intimately involved as a behind-the-scenes activist in Abba Hillel Silver's roiling relationship with the State Department. Rabbi Stephen Wise, frequently perceived as the titular head of the Zionist movement in the United States, studied the reaction of American Jewry to the burning questions of immigration, DP camps, Cold War flashpoints, and the survival and development of Israel under continuous military pressure from her Arab neighbors. Samuel was often summoned to participate in national and international delegations and convocations to present the Jewish or Zionistic case.

Rabbi David Polish includes Samuel in what he calls the humanist wing of the Reform rabbinate, the group of rabbis who sought to imbue their fellow clergy and American Jewry with the social ideals of Labor Zionism, "a synthesis of Jewish and humanitarian concern." Despite his recognition of Jabotinsky as one of the architects of the movement that led to the establishment of the State of Israel, Samuel, as an ideologue and as an accepted member of the Labor Zionist leadership, had little direct contact with him. However, he appreciated and respected Jabotinsky's charisma and enormous leadership qualities and his impact on the Zionist movement.

Samuel soon found himself unable to condone or tolerate oversimplified solutions and the end-justifies-the-means mentality of militaristic Palestine/Israel groups and their American supporters. He felt personally injured by the writing and speeches of Ben Hecht and other American Irgunists as they irresponsibly attacked the leaders, political machinery, and the defense forces (Haganah) of the Jewish community in Palestine, soon to be an independent nation.

In several respects, the tumultuous birth of the State of Israel and the bleak postpartum period when five invading Arab armies proclaimed their "holy" intentions to drive the Jews into the sea, signaled a new focus for Samuel's efforts. He now provided counsel to Israel's leaders and administrators, and gave practical direction assisting in growth and development. By the same token, he became one of the important liaisons from North America to the infant country. He was a valued observer of the international scene as Soviet Russia engulfed the Middle East in Cold War machinations.

The authors have several times alluded to their father as an "ideologue." The appellation is, at once, both accurate and misrepresentative. Samuel undeniably was a product of his East European childhood, but simultaneously identified with American

and world affairs. Goldberg, in describing the great Hebrew national poet Chaim Nachman Bialik, noted, "It is not enough [merely]
to know his country; one must attune one's ear to the melody of his
era." In attempting to cope with the despairing stress and transition of his times, Samuel attempted to understand and modify his
ethos. Goldberg opines that Bialik was "a witness to the desolation
of the Jewish scene, he lacked belief, and as a result his heart was
consumed by profound sadness and despair." Samuel did not permit
himself to be consumed by bitterness and despair. Rather, he strode
forth, repeatedly empowered by motivating idealism in search of
positive solutions.

Samuel recalled a great physician and linguistic scholar, a contemporary of Bialik's—Saul Tchernichowsky. Tchernichowsky
responded to the cauldron of his East European background and
the current ubiquitous problems of the Jewish people with a joie de
vivre and a positivistic lust for life. Samuel concurred, agreeing
with the "essences of Labor Zionism," as noted by Jacob Katzman
in a personal memoir: "people and nations, while they must live
together in mutual respect and international harmony—must each
also enjoy the right—to develop their national ethos and make
their own contribution . . . to man's culture and the advancement
of human civilization."

Samuel resonated to the kaleidoscopic images emanating from
Israel. One example is the image of the pioneering early settlers
withstanding heat, privation, and disease—the healthy bronzed
chalutz (pioneer) draining the malarial swamps, living in an ideal
communal settlement and epitomizing the role of labor and manual work in providing the foundations of a just society, the social
miracle of the successful diversification and integration of multi-
ethnic groups and societies fleeing from Europe's holocaustic
killing fields, the progress in Israel toward an ideal society serving
as a beacon and symbol of fulfillment for the remaining millions of
world Jewry.

However, Samuel could not accept this as sufficient. He viewed
such progress as "motivationally nourishing" but masking the
essential needs of the developing Jewish state. Basically, he

attempted to utilize his leadership positions in the World Jewish Congresses, his major status in the ranks of Labor Zionism, and his close relationships with Israel's leadership and government to accomplish pragmatic goals and educate the American Jew regarding Israel's needs. Later, in his tour across Canada to promote a Histadruth campaign, he cited Israel as proof that free enterprise and socialism can work side by side in harmony and achieve top economic efficiency. He detailed the partnership between the two ways of life and frequently opposing philosophies, stressing that the Histadruth (Labor Zionist organization), the acknowledged backbone of the communal settlements in Israel, was also partner to several of the country's foremost capitalist institutions. It was not a question of one attempting to overthrow the other, he explained, but rather a fusion of the best of free enterprise and socialism.

That same year, 1950, Samuel advanced a far-reaching plan which was widely covered by the general and Jewish press in this country. He had just arrived in London from Israel, where he conferred with cabinet ministers and the leaders of the Jewish Agency. He had discussed with them a plan that came to be conceptualized as "skilled manpower for Israel." Some viewed it as a "plan for mobilization in the Diaspora." The original plan was designed to ease Israel's acute shortage of skilled manpower. Samuel called for the mobilization of resources in all the English-speaking countries. The salaries of the skilled workers would be paid by the local communities in their native countries and not by the Israeli authorities, although the people concerned would work under the direction of the government and the Jewish Agency. The local communities of origin would also be responsible for maintenance in Israel. The appeal for skilled manpower was to be conducted along the same lines as fund-raising campaigns. The Israeli government must visit the various communities in the Diaspora and request "not only hundreds of millions of dollars, but also a finite number of men and women skilled in a given useful field."

Samuel freely admitted the potential snags, but the plan nevertheless aroused great interest among Israel's leaders. He assured them that the participating communities paying the salaries for the needed skilled workers would not necessarily decrease their monetary contributions to fund-raising campaigns. On the contrary, Samuel posited, the plan might help to increase the total amount collected for Israel. It would place the fund-raising campaign on a different level, helping to provide a concrete link between the peoples of Israel and those of the Diaspora. The *New York Times* further quoted Samuel:

> This plan would serve Israel more tangibly than money serves her. . . . the arrangement would establish a two-way passage for the interchange of culture and ability. . . . [It] would also lift United Jewish Appeal contributions from the level of mere money giving to something more durable and more valuable.

In answer to a question concerning the possible sacrifice of income by some 5,000 persons while they were in Israel, Samuel proposed that the United Jewish Appeal reimburse them by paying the difference between what they earned normally in the United States and what they would receive in Israel.

Samuel's idea was widely circulated in the United States and Israel. A great many replies to the "Lend Lease" statement were received. They were of varying lengths, ranging from cautiously critical and complimentary to enthusiastic praise. A few responses from prominent organizations and individuals may be cited.

Columnist Max Lerner of the *New York Post* wrote, "I think your idea of a 'Lend Lease' of personnel to help build up Israel is a brilliant one. It's one of the few really creative ideas about Israel that has come from the American side recently."

Samuel's very good friend, Rabbi Solomon Freehof of Pittsburgh's Rodef Shalom Temple, described the plan as "your very fine proposal for human resources for Israel," and went on to say: "I believe its fine vision and worthy suggestions will win a response in many hearts. [But] Why awaken hostility by . . . envisaging a vast immigration of Jews from America? You do not mean that. That was just to satisfy certain theoreticians."

The Jewish Telegraphic Agency's Boris Smolar stated, "I think that the recommendations are excellent. I have my doubts however in regard to your point six. I wonder whether American Jewish communities will be inclined to assume the financial obligations which you indicate."

Benjamin G. Browdy, president of the Zionist Organization of America wrote, "I am enclosing herewith a copy of my report to the last Zionist Organization of America Convention. The items dealing with chalutziot [pioneer matters] should be of interest to you. Our economic department has already been working along similar lines. It is my suggestion that this work be undertaken by the combined Zionist organizations."

Moses A. Leavitt of the American Jewish Joint Distribution Committee conservatively observed, "If the thought is to mobilize young men and women, I think you will be up against the matter of the draft and the inability of many of these people to get permission to leave the country for extended periods of time. . . . If a new campaign is to be undertaken for this purpose, there would be considerable reluctance on the part of many to a new fundraising effort."

There was a further flurry of discussion and consideration of Samuel's proposal and even efforts to shape it up into a formal plan that could be introduced into the machinery of the United Nations. The plan eventually faded as a viable entity, but at the same time it fused with many of the existent policies of committees and governmental agencies in Israel and the United States. There was, indeed, an increase in the number of Americans going to Israel with technological contributions. Such contributions strengthened the efficiency of Israeli production methods and embodied the concept that Israel at that time had more need for technologists than for ideologues.

One need not have been anti-Zionist to perceive that at certain points in the development of a nation, the achievement of concrete results can be of equal importance to the introduction of social and economic systems. In 1962 Gabriel Cohen, editor and publisher of the *National Jewish Post*, asked Samuel directly, "What

would happen if you were to rise in your pulpit and seek to per-
suade 50 young people from your congregation to emigrate to
Israel?"

Of course, the question was rhetorical, but not entirely frivo-
lous. No answer was really required. However, Samuel responded
that in the 1930s, the only development toward aliyah (settlement
in Israel from abroad) was the establishment of training camps dot-
ting the eastern United States, where young American Jews went
through months of preparation for farming in Israel. Samuel was
advocating what in 1962 was becoming a principal hope for emigration: the training of Jewish youth in industrial and scientific,
rather than farming, pursuits, so as to fill the needs of Israel's
expanding industrial economy.

Chapter 21
Eyewitnesss to History: Summary and Musings about Zion

As we have already observed, the events of an era, the history of nations, and transcendent developments of every kind may be best understood through the interaction of instrumental personalities with the Zeitgeist. Samuel Wohl's style and manner of personal recollection were particularly engaging and revealing. Garnered from newsletters, sermons, and golden conversations with his son Amiel, dry history became alive and vital. Israel's founders and great men and women held him in high regard because they knew that he understood and identified with their values. In his own words:

Henrietta Szold was born to Rabbi Benjamin Szold in Baltimore, Maryland. She became interested in Jewish life by teaching night school English to recent Jewish immigrants. She was one of relatively few American women of splendid Jewish scholarship. The American Jewish Publication Society elected her as the chief editor of its books. Several ensuing translations were regarded as great contributions and brought exceptional honor to American Jewry. She emigrated to Palestine immediately after the first world war. She organized the first Hadassah medical unit and developed a beneficial national health program. Hospitals and clinics were built and nurses were trained. Ms. Szold was appointed head of the Department of

Welfare. She proceeded to achieve the great and memorable goal of enlisting Hadassah and other organizations for Youth Aliyah. I have heard from her successors that more than 100,000 Jewish boys and girls were literally snatched out of the flames and brought to live in Israel. At first, many of the youngsters were placed in kibbutzim [communal farms]. More recently, Youth Aliyah gives considerable attention to the young people who come from Oriental lands, and those whose needs require cultural and social adjustment.

I was present at the World Zionist Congress and experienced a touching moment when Dr. Weizmann presented 60 roses to Ms. Szold on her 60th birthday. It was a great privilege to have spent a few weeks in Jerusalem at the same table with her during mealtimes. If we do not use the word "great" loosely, but know that it represents vision, courage, and a magnificent pride and building of people, then Henrietta Szold is certainly among the great and will take her rightful place among the immortals of the Jewish people.

Golda Meir, whom I have known since 1935, might have remained in Milwaukee U.S.A. as a teacher and librarian had she not been consumed by the flames of Jewish renaissance. She journeyed to Palestine in the early 1920's and worked on a communal farm. She was compelled by circumstances to accomplish a fusion of two strong political parties. However, she was always more than a leader of a party or a country. After she turned over the Ministry of Foreign Affairs post to Abba Eban who completed ten years in that capacity, she became a spokesperson for the State of Israel at all sessions of the United Nations. She dealt with foreign ambassadors and discussed many incidents of incitement transgressing the Israeli borders. She became a world renowned individual. . . . I recognized and appreciated her greatness when I invited her to spend a year lecturing for the League of Labor Palestine when I was its national chairman. Golda was always indis-

pensable to the leadership of Israel and to the people of
Israel before and after the state was formed. Unlike many
great women, she wasn't primarily interested in social or
welfare work, but her keen intellect perceived the great
political and international issues of our time.

It was in 1948 that Golda first arrived in Moscow in the
Soviet Union as a minister of the new state of Israel. She
attended a synagogue and was not aware her visit brought
to the Russian Jews the realization that a Jewish state was
born and that its first diplomatic envoy was a woman.
When she emerged from the synagogue, tens of thousands
of people filled all the neighboring streets. There is a picture, which appeared in the *New York Times*, of Golda
entering her car to be driven back to the embassy. She told
me later that all she could hear were voices of people saying, "Don't forget us, don't forget us." Additionally, when
one considers her prime ministership, it is amazing to think
of the load, burdens, and responsibilities she bore stolidly
for so many years. She was always most cordial and interested in my visits and supplied me with rich information
about her country's foreign and domestic situations.

"The third president of Israel was Zalman Shazar, whom
I call a "chaver" [friend], and who is a uniquely endowed
man with the richest gifts of heaven. From my first visit to
the editor's office of the *Davar* [daily paper of the
Histadruth] to my last visit three decades later at the house
of the president of Israel, his eyes remained clear and
undaunted by world tornadic winds. He did not realize that
the Knesset [parliament] would elect him to the presidency.
He had a unique gift for translating great Hebrew into
Yiddish and Yiddish poetry into Hebrew. Some months ago
during my visit in Israel, I was invited to Shazar's home for
Kiddush [blessing-sanctification] on a Saturday afternoon.
We sat, some thirty people, men and women, not subject to
any protocol, but as friends of the president. It was interesting to follow the discussion of Hazaz, one of the foremost

Hebrew novelists, and with Mordechai Halevi, the founder of the Ohel Theater, who had dramatized Chayim Hazaz's story concerning Jewish Yemenite life. The president was very animated in his conversation, and a number of us who did not feel any constraint also contributed some observations. This is the way a Kiddush on Shabbat [the Sabbath] was celebrated in Israel.

Moshe Sharett was a man of magnificent stature, compelling the love of the entire country irrespective of party, and, through him, spoke the conscience of Israel. From the days of my first visit to Israel in 1932 to my last visit in 1966, he was to me as he was to many others, —one of the blessed sons of our people. He suffered much in political struggles. Before the formation of the state, he was a foreign minister for Israel and after the establishment of the state, he continued in that role. He became prime minister, and later was the chairman of the Jewish Agency. There is still great sorrow within me at his passing, and, while I placed a wreath at his grave in Tel Aviv, I recalled vividly some of the remarkable achievements of this well-beloved son and leader of Israel.

I can speak with great emotion of the second president of Israel, Yitzhak Ben-Tsvi, whom I first met after his exile from Palestine by the despotic Turkish leader Gemal Pasha. Ben-Tsvi was a scholar chiefly concerned and interested in many of the lost and forgotten tribes of Israel. Today, there is a Ben-Tsvi Institute on the campus of the Hebrew University in Jerusalem for scholars who are working in the same field. In the pre-state days I met him several times. He was not one to indulge in pretensions or seek honor for himself. He was the head of the Va'ad L'umi, which was the representative body of the Jewish settlement during the mandatory period. It was this simple humble man who became the second president of the state of Israel. During his presidency, he lived in a very small apartment in Jerusalem. Soon however, there was a reconstruction of more spacious living quarters which he preserved for many years. It was in the newer building that he received the ambassadors and the great of other nations. It was here too, where, on a windowsill, stood a very small replica of a matzevah [gravestone] with the name of his son lost in the War of Liberation.

As we have indicated already, Samuel reiterated that America had contributed many great leaders to Israel.

Immediately after the Balfour Declaration and the establishment of the [British] mandate, Dr. Judah L. Magnes became the first chancellor of the Hebrew University. He was a great spirit brooding on the destiny of his people. He was subjected to many political ordeals. Standing alone as a pacifist during the first world war, he was a formidable opponent of the division of Palestine into two states, part Arab and part Jewish. Magnes was not only a handsome man, but he assumed heroic stature, and it was due to him in great measure that the University survived the first two decades. His experienced controversies were sharp and very difficult for him to bear. He appeared ready to resign frequently. Influential people wished to see him depart as University head. I vividly recall one morning when I came into his study to say a departing word before I returned home. He silently handed me a statement in Hebrew and in English which he was to issue to the press within the next half hour. People who remember the living Magnes will recall his fine facial color. At that moment he was pale and drained; indeed, he was visibly shaken. I could not respond to him for several moments as we sat silently—just stunned. I finally gathered some composure and said to him, "This is what your enemies have wanted. It would be a great misfortune for the University and for all of Israel for you to depart under fire." He answered simply: "I can no longer endure it." Whereupon, in response to almost

instinctive defiance, I tore the statement to shreds and said:
"Now place all the mimeographed copies in the safe and
wait until the next board of governors meeting in Lucerne,
Switzerland." He came back from Lucerne still the president of the Hebrew University and, despite ensuing activities which were interpreted (unfairly) as pro-Arab, was held
in continued great esteem by friends and foes.

Samuel's perceptions and recollections of David Ben-Gurion,
best known to the world as a founder and first prime minister of the
State of Israel, are particularly interesting and thoughtful. Samuel
had met and heard Robert St. John, a guest speaker at the Wise
Center forum. As a foreign correspondent, St. John penetrated the
substratum of international events. Samuel assimilated St. John's
book *Shalom Means Peace*, which is infused with the life of a man,
David Ben-Gurion, "who assures us that an ancient people such as
ours, which has seen so much brutality and recently came through
an epoch of stygian darkness, is *not* accelerating to oblivion. On
the contrary, something fresh, vibrant, heroic and far-visioned has
come into the life of our people." Samuel mused,

> If you think of the centuries of prayer, of longing, of exile
> and dispersion, the new redemption has come now in our
> time—It is preface to a miracle. . . . Think of the struggles
> of empires, of the dissolution during the last fifty years of
> the Ottoman Empire, the Czarist Empire, the German
> Empire interacting within the arena of new states; the
> transformation of some into oligarchies and dictatorships;
> the rise of the Communist octopus with its crushing weight
> in the power struggle for the hegemony of the world; the
> birth and survival of Israel: All of these remain truly mirac-
> ulous. . . . I can confirm as much as a participant in the
> World Zionist Congresses. I can see the fires stemming from
> the ideological clashes between Ben-Gurion and Berl
> Katzenelson, who in some respects was Ben-Gurion's
> teacher. I can see Ben-Gurion during the first armistice ris-

ing as head of the provisional government. I saw him in conference with the first generals at Ramat Gan, planning the battles for the Negev [southern desert]. I have seen and heard Ben-Gurion in times of grave crises. . . . It was on the 20th of Tamuz 1948—the anniversary of Herzl's death when the new armed forces marched before Ben-Gurion in the Taarucha grounds in Tel Aviv and the prime minister took the salutes. I was invited by Paula Ben-Gurion to sit at her side. At the moment when the flag was rising slowly to its full height, she whispered to me, "He is a great man. I knew it all the time." Well, I believed it ten years ago and I believe it now.

And a quieter, no less impassioned remembrance:

The time I spent in the home of Ben-Gurion seemed to me quite significant. The great man was sitting at his desk in a warm jacket writing. Now that his 80th birthday had been celebrated, he is completely correct when he says that even having two times 40 years, his tasks have not been achieved until he can put down on paper what he knows and what he thinks. He estimates that he has enough material for another decade. He wants, above all, the younger generations to understand how it all came about. How the events among the various powers of the world somehow ran parallel to the dreams, yearnings and determinations of the Yishuv [the Jewish community of Palestine] to achieve independence. I [Samuel] am still stirred and baffled by how these events could have transpired as they did. Many drawings and pictures, as well as interviews and telecasts have taken place depicting Ben-Gurion in various roles but there is something unique and real in talking quietly, not of political ambitions but of the days yet to come. Ben-Gurion is certainly a realist; he knows that the countries that were friends yesterday may become opponents tomorrow. He knows that the remarkable strength of the young people in

Israel and devotion and dedication count more than any
political utterance. He knows that the Jews of the friendly
world are not flocking to Israel to settle, and there are
"Yordim" who emigrate from Israel to seek their fortune
elsewhere. The problems are many and there is no single
solution for them except to stay with all one's willpower
and tenacity continuing to build and develop the land.
There will be many who will decry some of the political
machinations of Ben-Gurion, but history will inscribe for
all generations and will faithfully depict what this man has
accomplished. For example, he was able to stand up to the
mighty forces of chaos and destruction, welding and creating the armed forces, maintaining the nation which con-
sists of a variety of people from all corners of the earth,
keen and determined not to go under.

Chaim Weizmann was a renowned scientist, Israel's first president, and one of the founders of the Zionist movement.

He physically resembles Lenin, but with a more aristocratic and gentler spirit emanating from him. In our time he
was one of the great master builders not only of the Zionist
movement but also of the state of Israel. It was unfortunate
that he was not well when he assumed the mantle of the
president of Israel and had to curtail his work. Today, his
tomb is a place of pilgrimage in Rehovot and one usually
visits the Weizmann Institute.

Samuel admired greatly the mayors of two of Israel's major
cities.

Haifa retained its mayor, Abba Khoushi, for a long, productive administration. He was a man of such dynamism
and vision that he commanded the acclaim not only of his
own party, but of the entire population. I still remember
when Abba Khoushi was the secretary of the Trade Union

Council during my first visit in 1932. I have seen him many times and, as the saying goes, he gets younger and younger with the passing of years. There are many aspects to Haifa. There is the Panorama Road and harbor, which is perhaps one of the great sights of the world. There is a Japanese museum in Haifa which Abba Khoushi obtained from a Dutch-Jewish donor who gave all his Japanese art and total collection to the city of Haifa. In Israel you can expect many things to happen, and to have a complete Japanese museum on Mt. Carmel is accepted as a natural occurrence. The mayor was responsible for the building of a municipal theater where actors were paid by the city and had full-time employment. It would be right to say that this man who now begins again to build a college, and eventually a liberal arts university will succeed in this effort also.

During the [British] mandatory period, Jews were not permitted to hold the position of mayor of Jerusalem. Jerusalem began to elect its mayors only with the formation of the state of Israel. Gershon Agron was a distinguished man of whom we can be proud. A former newspaper man in Philadelphia, he founded the *Palestine Post*, later renamed the *Jerusalem Post*. The *Post* simply was an outstanding English newspaper, performing a vital function in Israel and the United States. It made it possible for the thousands of English personnel within the country and English-speaking Jews to know the problems and difficulties as well as the challenges and daring of the men and women of Israel. Gershon later became the popular mayor of Jerusalem, and it was my great joy to have been present at his home for the first Seder several years ago. Unfortunately, Gershon died while he still possessed activity, vigor, and vision. Indeed, he was a key figure spanning the years of the British mandate.

. . . The War of Liberation had begun, and I was then in Prague. I beheld the first diplomatic representative of Israel; the Israeli minister Ehud Avriel. I expressed to him my eagerness to see the week-old Israel, but considered it impossible to arrive there in the midst of battle. On the next day Avriel informed me that an air ticket was ready, and I may fly with a certain assignment. I landed on the airstrip in Haifa. The city of Lydda, where the modern national airfield now exists, had not yet been taken by the Israeli forces. I emerged from the plane and was escorted to the customs shed. I opened my bags to the first Jewish customs officer in 2000 years and said to him, "I'm glad to pay any fee for this experience. I was rather disappointed he seemed content with only a few dollars."

In Tel Aviv I witnessed a session of the Knesset. The walls were still covered with pictures of the last [museum] exhibit, and I witnessed the first provisional government and its cabinet in action. I knew most of them from earlier days and World Zionist congresses. A pen or speech can scarcely echo what I saw and felt. I was taken by a military convoy over a new road, later known as the "Burma Road" and which was built under fire breaking the siege of Jerusalem. I entered the city pockmarked by mortars and bullets and viewed the ruins wrought by the British and their endless barbed wire. I heard the rattle of guns and the explosions from munition dumps. In walking the streets I bent down while in open spaces, because the Arab legionnaires were on high posts behind the walls of the Old City.

I stayed in a pension [small commercial residence] and was rationed two glasses of water for all uses. The people of Jerusalem were still hungry and had little water. The Old City was evacuated and the Haganah and the Palmach [elite striking force] were not yet merged. They had to collaborate and contend with military units that were still under Irgun guerrilla fighters command. From a gun emplacement within the French Notre Dame monastery, I could see across the Old City and Mount Scopus, where the old campus of the Hebrew University and the new Hadassah hospital were orphaned and inaccessible. . . . I was given the privilege of a noon luncheon visit to Ben-Gurion's military headquarters at Ramat-Gan. During the meal I met and conversed with the chief of staff—General Yaacov Dori, Yigal Allon, and other high-ranking military figures who had distinguished themselves in the War of Liberation. . . . The Arabs already were disrupting the first armistice agreement. During this meal, Ben-Gurion asked questions and discussed the strategy for the forthcoming campaign ultimately compelling victory in the Negev. The generals perhaps were suspicious of me, this stranger at their table, and I had the feeling that what was said was not intended for my ears, but I shall be ever grateful and never forget that moment when Ben-Gurion, with a smile and glint in his eyes said to them (in Hebrew), "You may speak. He is one of us." Thus, what later eventuated in the conquest of the Negev, was decided in my presence.

Shall I say that I was the eyewitness of a great hour in Jewish history? It is so. A few weeks later I stood with the president of the Knesset, —Yosef Sprinzak on a balcony of the old Histadruth building and saw the first parade of the forces of Israel's liberation.

. . . I met the great novelist, Sholem Asch, at a convocation of the Jewish Agency in Switzerland. He was among the first signers of the declaration prepared by Dr. Chaim Weizmann and Louis Marshall in 1929 creating the Jewish Agency. During the last years of his life, he was bitterly resentful of what he termed his "defamity." The attacks upon him for having written several Christologic novels were unfairly harsh. He apparently suffered so much from his critics' accusation that he was ready to convert to Christianity. As I sat with him on the balcony of the Dan Hotel in Tel Aviv, he exclaimed several times, "Vas villen sie frum mir?" [What do they want from me?] He furnished a glimpse into his tormented soul. Later, he moved to Bat Yam, a suburb of Tel Aviv, and after his death, his residence became a museum, which he bequeathed to the city.

In 1950, while attending the United Nations, Samuel monitored sessions and understood the complexities of the new Israel.

> Discussion of the Jerusalem issue in political convention. Here again there was tremendous drama. . . . A year ago the United Nations passed a resolution to internationalize Jerusalem. The unfortunate alliance of the Communist nations, the Catholic Church, and the Arabs made possible a decision which would have torn Jerusalem from the State of Israel. Strenuous opposition from Trans-Jordan and Israel prevented the resolution from implementation. There was much soul-searching and considerable change of view on the part of many important nations, however, the Catholic Church and the Arabs were still insisting upon internationalization of the city and its environs as a whole, rather than upon the supervision of holy places by United Nations administration. . . .
>
> It was exhilarating to hear the address of the British statesman, Lord MacDonald. His was the most important plan offered on the side of Israel. Recognition should be given to the fact that the United States, despite the pressure of the Catholic hierarchy, was in favor of the Swedish resolution with an amendment which would have been acceptable to Israel and to Jordan. It is a pity that the last resolution, sponsored by Britain, the United States and Uruguay was not adopted and the Jerusalem issue settled.

Samuel's reminiscences during and shortly after the establishment of the state convey a rare insight and flavor into the origins and patterns of the developing Israel. They may also be regarded as a statement of faith.

> Israel never yielded the hope of restoration of land and redemption of faith. In my view, this is a testimony to the in-dwelling spirit of God. It was this faith that enabled the light and fire to prevail in our sanctuaries everywhere.

Of course, history may teach us of the causes and effects of events and conditions upon people. For example, we may learn that a given movement had originated due to a quarrel between men who were rivals for power or because of economic and social conditions prevalent at a certain time and place. Without negating the rationale of history, I am inclined to see in acts such as a reborn Israel: the guiding hand of God, the voice of the prophet, the unquenched spirit of a people that, with all realities against them, kept alive their faith and will. . . . I can still recall the first glow of exhilaration that came with the Balfour Declaration in 1917, and I am grateful to God for the privilege that was mine in participating in the hopes and dreams of our people during these recent decades. My first pilgrimage to the land was two decades ago. It was already apparent to me [in 1932] that the few hundred thousand inhabitants had already set a new course in the life of our people.

. . . Two years ago, I saw the first ship of liberated immigrants released from Cyprus arriving in Haifa. The great port was opened to receive the shiploads of Jews who streamed from the barbed-wire concentration camps. I was escorted to the "Pan-Crescent." The ship was commanded by a young Jewish captain, who, under cover of dark night, brought in precious cargos of survivors. I should mention that during the last months of the mandate, all captured ships and their passengers were routinely sent back to point of origin or regulated to concentration camps on Cyprus.

I beheld a thousand or more humans, whose only possessions in addition to wounds, illnesses, and hunger, were their radiant joy, their awareness of their release, and their redemption. I saw those people who came from darkness into the light. Abba Khoushi [the mayor of Haifa] escorted me on board the ship which was decorated with flags and blue-and-white steamers surrounding Hebrew words of joy and welcome. From the top deck of the ship I looked down on men and women with handkerchiefs and flags waving, some calling out names of people they recognized on the dock. Some days later and for several successive days I witnessed the arrival and departure of boats and planes to Haifa and Lydda. These men, women and children had come because they were wanted here. Within this short space of time the first Parliament was elected, and the first independent Israel government in two thousand years took the helm of state. . . .

Now there are deepening economic crises. There is inflation and austerity more severe than the English had to endure during the Second World War. There is need for more housing, bread, food, shelter, clothing, farms, factories, trees, and goods—there is a gigantic and pervasive deficit of everything.

And why? Israel is in a race with time. Emigration is restricted behind the Iron Curtain. The Communist regimes of Hungary, Poland and Romania shut the doors on the remnants of Jewry in these lands. If you ask Jewish Moroccans, the Tunisians, and Yemenites to stop emigrating, they may be doomed to murder, riot and ultimate extinction. Kibbutz Galuyot [the gathering of the exiles] cannot be improved. These people are indeed exiles. It is more security for them but also for the State of Israel. They are needed to populate the wasteland, to redeem the Negev and the Upper Galilee.

To have brought in and cared for half a million people in two years is staggering. For a moment, consider the mix of people. I have observed the Yemenites in many settlements, in the hills around Jerusalem and in the immigration camps. They have had no contact with what we term civilization for centuries. They are out of the stream of Jewish events as we know them, but they have faith, piety, and endurance that seems to transfigure them. Their standard greeting is, "Blessed be God." Last Passover, the foreign minister, Moshe Sharret, and his wife, flew to Aden, where several thousand [Yemenites] were still waiting in a camp. A beautiful and particularly meaningful Seder [Passover] service was held with these brethren. Some weeks ago Mrs. Sharret said to me, "There was more elation, more faith in the hearts of our brethren in Yemen than among those of our forefathers who went forth from Egypt."

Samuel understood the miracle of Israel as it was unfolding.

In Israel it is the dangerous life that becomes the good life. The impelling call is to come and witness how cities grow where there were no cities. Factories hum, farms produce. Now, where there was no grass, grass grows. Where there were no people, people live. Where there was no water, there is water beginning to flow. I was in the Negev, that awesome desert that cost the lives of thousands of our youth . . . and now, it too, is beginning to live. Beer Sheba is no longer the terminus. We now say from "Dan to Eilat," and it is most significant that the first craft arriving at that port on the Red Sea carried the Torahs and holy utensils of the Yemenites. . . . I heard the voice of the prime minister when he announced that irrigation water is now flowing on the land near Eilat. It is being poured into the soil and that soil will live again. It may well feed thousands, and we shall build cities and towns, farms and factories.

Samuel perceived himself as a major player in the worldwide mobilization of Jews for Israel.

It is a living democracy surrounded by perfidious despotism. A lighthouse for Jews who are homeless. It speaks in the voice of the prophet. We hear it say to each afflicted heart—"Comfort ye, my people." We call out to the Jewish people of the world to rally to our side in the task of immigration and development and to stand by us in the great struggle for the fulfillment of the dreams of generations: the redemption of Israel.

The immortal modern prophet Theodor Herzl, called the first Zionist Congress into being. This congress took the dreams, hopes and prayers of the ages, incorporated them into living institutions, and began the process of the re-establishment of Israel. This movement is infinitely more than the restoration of a land to the people. It has achieved a transformation in the short space of one generation. The new flesh and muscles have enveloped the bodies of the bent, darkened, and grief-stricken. It gave them the moral fiber to withstand the cataclysms of two world wars.

In 1962, after returning from Israel, Samuel expressed his feel-ings to a reporter from the *National Jewish Post*.

I stand in awe before this old-young nation. . . . It is a home standing on a precipice of risk and danger, but secure in its heart—that redemption is coming. . . . I stand in awe before my people who have risen Phoenix-like from the ashes of the Holocaust. They have made a dynamic life for millions who seek a homeland. . . . I bear witness to men and women who transform themselves from the past horrors to the pre-sent builders of a good and just life. . . . They walk forward in the midst of strife and danger, speaking of tomorrow. . . . A day will come when terror and fear will cease and the whirlwinds of rocket and bomb will be made dumb. The sons and daughters of this sacred land will walk with digni-ty. . . . They will seek to ease the suffering of the powerless. They will irrigate parched land and parched hearts. They will live in this land amidst the social and political storms of the age and peacefully bring together divergent economies and clashing national systems. . . . It shall be this "little land," holy of age and depth, that shall lead mankind to an era of concord. . . . Israel loves America for what she has done, aiding millions of the poor and oppressed and nourishing humanitarian ideals which will confirm peace and freedom for all.

Samuel inspired but continued to transmit events and ideas continually and consummately. We allude to his "opinions and observations" regularly circulated to his congregation in the late 1950s and through the 1960s.

I have seen much with my limited vision, and heard more from friends who were with me in the ranks some decades ago.

Now they are in the high echelons of governments and in the embassies around the world. The nations of the world watch carefully because of *what these people did and how they did it*. When I ask numerous people, "What did you do during the great days?" the answers were limited to a few words. "'I was at Sinai," "in Jerusalem," "the Syrian Heights." No one claimed heroism. From the highest chief of staff, Itzchak Rabin, the brilliant strategist and supreme commander, to the soldier who only yesterday taught a chapter in the Bible to his class or worked with a tractor in the field . . . *modesty and humility* were the chief characteristics of the citizens' army.

Only a year ago, the people in civil life were troubled by inadequacy of employment and housing that affected large numbers of the population from Libya, Kurdistan, Morocco, Egypt, and the Atlas Mountains, and many from the mellahs [Muslim ghettos] of the Orient. It was feared that the "have-nots" would outnumber the "haves," resulting in moral, political, and social ferment. There were fears for the future of Israeli justice, equality, and humanitarianism as a way of life. *It did not happen.* The amazing and yet to be understood fact was that the Oriental youth began to equal the sabras [native-born Israelis] in achievement. They lifted themselves by their own bootstraps to great heights. How did it happen? In less than a generation the men and women of the concentration camps (I saw a quarter of a million in 1948), the exiled and the hurt, and others driven from their native Oriental countries, —"the Avak Adam" [dust of humanity] rose to such stature. . . . It was beyond the rational and miraculous. We still wonder, "How did we do it?" . . . Jerusalem was always *one* city. It was due to the "cease-fire" in 1956 [the Sinai Campaign] that the Arab Legion remained in the Old City. King Abdullah from Amir (a Bedouin chieftain made king by the British) annexed the Western Bank. The ancient cities of Hebron, Bethlehem, Nablus (Shechem in the Bible), and the larger part of Palestine were taken by Abdullah since the Arab leaders did not permit the Palestinian Arabs to form a separate state as decided by the UN. In view of all prevailing circumstances, and King Abdullah's feelers for peace, Israel thought it better to support Abdullah's rule of the Palestinians over the interests of other Arabs. It is told that Golda Meir (in Arab garb) visited him several times for peace talks. Later, you may know that king Abdullah was assassinated by his own people when he emerged from the mosque. Jews lived in Old Jerusalem for many centuries. The Mount of Olives was a Jewish burial ground from time immemorial. There was a large living quarter in Old Jerusalem where Jews dwelled for centuries. During the War of Liberation the Jews were compelled to leave the Old City, and the Trans-Jordanians moved in. The armistice provision of 1948 stated that Jews were to have access to the holy places. However, Jews were not permitted to enter the Old City. Walls, cement blocks, and barbed wire constituted a border and the Old City was effectively sealed off. Indeed, they could not go to the Western Wall (Wailing Wall) to pray. I have seen the rubble of desecrated old synagogues. More than 20 yeshivot (talmudic schools) were destroyed. They built a hotel and a road on the Mount of Olives looking down on hundreds of desecrated graves, among them the grave of the immortal Henrietta Szold

. . . Following his father's removal to a chronic mental hospital, son Hussein became Jordan's ruler. Apparently he aroused sympathy by his appearance at the UN and his visit with President Johnson. I ask why he severed relations with us and still receives subsidies from our government. From my sources I know that this little king was always in danger from the hired assassins of Nasser and the Syrians. The ghoul Shukairi, organizer of the "liberation army" was a gangster who delivered unspeakable hate to Israel and also tried to liquidate Hussein. The same Shukairi actually flew with Hussein to Cairo to sign a war pact against Israel. Israel considered that Hussein might merely show a token participation. He was given six hours time to sit it out and Israel would not attack him. However, Hussein gave the order to bombard Jerusalem. Israel mobilized in epic fashion. Every person was at his designated post within a few hours. The two weeks preceding the war were more trying than the war itself. The civilian population did not panic, children and adults went to the shelters. Sandbags by the thousands were everywhere, and there were blackouts every night. Three days before the order was given to march, Moshe Dayan was called to become Minister of Defense with a consequent elevation of the country's morale. Dayan was not sworn in until the day after the war began and the members of the Knesset (parliament) came out of the shelters to witness the ceremony.

We have mentioned already that Samuel was angry and mortified by the Israeli political culture that necessitated undue secular and religious domination by Orthodoxy. After "calming down a bit" he wrote to Rabbi Jay Kaufman, American executive vice president of B'nai B'rith. He felt that the B'nai B'rith ought to take the leadership in creating a conducive atmosphere for freedom of religion in Israel.

We cannot continue striving for freedom of religion and the separation of church and state in this country and then proceed to defame Reform Judaism in Israel. . . . I resent the fact that 14 percent of the Israeli voters elected a number of political *clericals* as our representatives. They in turn use coercion to force the rest of the Jewish community in Israel to consider themselves "non-religious." I consider these aberrations of a religious movement which ought not continue. We have missed the boat for the last 30 years and we should begin earnestly to think of what might happen to the growing generations in Israel. That I, and others like me, should be classed as non-religious; that members of the kibbutzim and others who have dedicated their lives to the upbuilding of the land and the people should be characterized as non-religious is an insult to all of us here *and* there.

We also have alluded to Samuel's letter, widely circulated within the Central Conference of American Rabbis, urging colleagues *not* to use financial pressure, United Jewish Appeal, or bonds for Israel as a means of expressing displeasure over Israel's religious situation. In a letter to Rabbi Jacob K. Shankman, then president of the World Union for Progressive Judaism, Samuel firmly stated:

Much can be done now if we have the means to do it. Israel will not respond to "peanuts." If the Reform movement is to have stature and recognition it must be done on an impressive scale. The three outstanding young men that we have in Israel are doing a good job. They ought to be encouraged. They should be given the means to expand their work. A home for progressive or liberal Judaism in Israel must be of the kind resembling the Hebrew Union College branch in Jerusalem. Even now, as you know, there are several outstanding institutions in Tel Aviv, such as the Hamlin House, the Sokolov House for Journalists, the Tchernichowsky House for Writers, and the Shalom

Aleichem Home, recently completed. The Zionist
Organization of America (Z.O.A.) House, for instance, is
humming with various cultural and educational activities
and is known from one end of the country to the other. You
will see serious problems when you arrive in Israel. We cannot wait for the native population to do things themselves
for they are harried every day and they do not have the necessary means. We have the opportunity now to give the
Israeli community something which they desperately need.
The younger people and many of the older generation are
not going to the Orthodox synagogues. The synagogue is
associated with something archaic and with past suffering.
We must change that image. We must have people and
means. The means could be made available if we are serious
enough to undertake a project that is in keeping with the
importance of the cause. During my recent three month
visit I've had the opportunity to observe the services which
we have now. I have had the opportunity of presenting our
needs to people in the higher echelons of government.
Things are not done in Israel by asking questions or by
telling other people to do it. You establish what you wish to
establish in the manner you wish it done. Then, if they like
it, they come, and I am absolutely certain that they *will
come*. We can achieve all the recognition we want once we
have several congregations that have large constituencies. I
am not speaking of separation of church and state today,
which of course is something looming importantly for the
future. There are many people even among observant Jews
who would like to see it accomplished. Even under the present circumstances it is possible to move ahead. We need to
create the climate and a favorable image for Reform
Judaism in Israel.

As noted previously and as an ultimate goal, Samuel visualized
an impressive building or buildings from which would emit great

waves of Reform suasion. However, his "preliminary steps," conveyed to Rabbi Shankman and others, seemed more useful and had current topical application:

A. Annual symposia concerning Reform Judaism held in several of the important cities of the country; accomplished by sending outstanding speakers for a few weeks to address various forums.

B. Convene representatives of the Kibbutzim [communal farms]. Discuss with them general measures and methods of work.

C. Once a month if not more often, place in two or three of the Hebrew newspapers and perhaps also in the *Jerusalem Post*, a written statement by outstanding American rabbis. These could be published as advertisements, if you will, for which we should pay.

D. A few of our most accomplished speakers might address the various Rotary Clubs and the Friday night forums which are named in Hebrew as "Eton Haeetonoeem." These are in fact oral newspapers. Large gatherings often attend these functions and provide an opportunity to present all aspects of Reform Judaism to the public. This could be supplemented by media (radio) support. All of these preliminary activities should create a very positive atmosphere.

Samuel went on to say:

Certainly the meeting ought to attract a great deal of attention in the country and I hope it will be carefully handled. Interviews to newspapermen should be given only by authorized persons because otherwise, we risk that journalists will have a field day recounting how a great many *outsiders* have gathered to introduce Judaism to Israel.

A later letter to Rabbi Shankman in 1967 seemed to conclude Samuel's thinking on the subject.

My reaction to the ploy of waiting until some indigenous groups become interested in the [Reform] movement is negative. I believe that I have a fairly good picture of Israel as it was yesterday and as it is today. I have recently received letters from Ben-Gurion, Eshkol, Golda, and President Shazar who would like to discuss the matter with me during my next visit to Israel. Despite the (ever-present) critical situation and all kinds of crises that may burst forth at any time, there is and there must be work done for our movement in Israel. Every institution that wishes to have a foothold in the country must build something of importance. Our [Hebrew Union] College has done just that. So has Hadassah with its hospital. So has Bar-Ilan with its university. I enumerate these to point out that unless we have something visible, something of importance in one of the communities in Israel, we shall be considered what we are—very insignificant.

Chapter 22
Epilogue

The ideas of Samuel Wohl have reached the point of denouement. Employing a straightforward narrative style, the authors have summarized and resummarized them through the evolution of the book. Modest and self-effacing, Samuel nonetheless maintained an enormous warmth and care manifested in his scholarship, public relations, the dynamic flow of international events, and of course the ideals of Zionism. He accomplished remarkable results in disbursing and reducing American Jewry's apathy, Jewish illiteracy, and lack of self-respect. His unreserved love for the Isaac M. Wise Temple congregation resulted in innovations in Reform liturgical practice, avoiding or discarding rigidified traditions and sustaining the pervasive beauty of observance. Interactions with the important personages and great thinkers of the newly formed state of Israel cannot be isolated from his leadership in the world milieu.

It is appropriate now to examine an analogy drawn from impressionist painting. Samuel not only perceived the external or apparent meaning of events and presented ideas, but also was able to convey reality, subtly and emotionally, by thousands of irregular strokes eventuating in details that were readily understandable. Each of the thousands of "little dancing strokes" are in vital competition for the whole impression. Samuel somehow was able to distinguish life's most sensitive interactions and gradations.

The authors willingly join the reader in musing and asking the question: How shall this man be viewed within his context and the continuing stream of historical events?

Robert M. Seltzer has contributed a foreword to Professor Ellis Rivkin's book, *The Unity Principal*. Dr. Rivkin emphasizes the larger background of Jewish history and the diverse string of civilizations containing Jewish participation within the knowable history of the world. Without looking for "deeper meanings," for this would introduce intellectual distortions, one must utilize an empirically honed microtone enabling the sweep of the ages to be studied in exceedingly fine slices. At any given moment it may be impossible for any of us, in our own time slice, to fully understand the nature and meaning of interactive social and political events. However, we may attempt to analyze the current world and the national and local communities of the United States and to understand the broad scope of Samuel Wohl's influence on congregational development and leadership. His memory was eidetic when it pertained to the welfare and whereabouts of his friends and congregants. He absolutely reveled in their achievements and accomplishments. He personified the true sense of a pastoral calling: remembering the lives of his people. His life was intertwined with the epic happenings of the last eight decades of a climactic period of Jewish and world history. Rabbinic colleagues and other important friends and authorities wrote that he served as a model, an example of integrity and idealism, and of human and Jewish concern.

Thoughtful thematic analysis of testimonial, personal, and informational letters over sixty years depicts an emotional and intellectual bond unceasing and uninterrupted. We have already noted Samuel's extension of the past in order to achieve Reform's optimal direction. Whether touching on liturgical expression, human relations, civil rights, or the security of American and world Jewry, Rabbi Wohl framed his actions to the needs of a creative and vibrant Jewish community. He offered instruction and enlightenment, as well, to the surrounding gentile and secular community. He would not settle for simple and rigid traditions. He gave himself enthusiastically and imaginatively to the goal of developing Judaism along aesthetic and artistic lines. Some of his finest achievements were expressed in the sphere of communal activity. As Professor Jacob Rader Marcus observed, he was not oriented to splashy spectacles or hackneyed apologetics, rather, he attempted to quietly teach and inspire while underscoring the values of our spiritual heritage.

We know that Samuel devoted himself tirelessly to the beleaguered Jewish communities abroad. He became one of the most distinguished Zionist spokesmen and activists in the United States. In this regard he recognized the need to establish a beneficial relationship between our State Department, the American Jewish community, and the growing Jewish communities of Latin America.

The authors, in their zeal to propound and understand the schemata of Samuel's ideas, perhaps have fragmented the underlying continuity of his personality and family life. Immediately, a sentence from the plaque inscribed on the wall of the Samuel Wohl Chapel of the Isaac M. Wise Temple presents for our reflection: ". . . he cherished others as his own family and will remain ever in our hearts."

In this sense and as a benevolent parent, Samuel consistently stressed the value of a positive self-image and the crucial experiences of pride and expression, of love and respect, rather than fear of punishment or a sense of violating one's values. Perhaps in infancy and young childhood there are many things to fear and a set of "laws" that demand our acquiescence, but as individuals and societies develop value systems, habits of obedience give way to generic self-guidance that impels conduct in certain directions. Samuel, for example, felt an obligation to maintain involvement with his congregation while supporting Israel and various peace initiatives. We may regard this as simply a posture forming the context of his behavior.

During his lifetime, Samuel worked for many goals even though he knew that he could never attain all of them. Since he was very clear in his own mind about his value orientation, he could discern major pathways and make decisions on specific issues. As we have explained, Belle's role and loving presence strongly enabled him to choose his career. She provided a stable and well-organized home environment that facilitated the rearing of two sons and made it possible for a husband to lead his congregation, study, achieve, and create. Daughters-in-law followed by grandchildren appeared in the fifties and early sixties. Collectively and individually the family loved and identified with Samuel.

By the early sixties, Samuel's reserve of energy, high levels of motivation, and physical sense of well-being subsided, occasioning a widely attended seventieth birthday celebration and de facto retirement from the position of senior rabbi of the congregation. He consumed the next seven years gladly and reflectively, his life ending in the pain (mercifully brief) of a cardiac (aortal) aneurysm.

Colleagues, friends, congregants, and his children had many personal recollections and examples of how Rabbi Wohl had influenced their lives. He did not present religion to his family and the congregation as a matter of dependency or of reliving family or cultural configurations. He warned against perceiving it as a prophylaxis against fear. He taught that one need not account rationally for every detail of the system. He wanted to facilitate individual attitudes that could form a dynamically interacting totality. He sincerely believed that the intellect must continue to exert itself, but that the intellect alone will almost certainly fail. Perhaps the individual (and the group) *needs* faith and love. Religion can provide fortification against the inroads of anxiety, doubt, and despair, but perhaps more important it provides a forward intention where we may locate ourselves in relation to our perception of reality.

Samuel taught us that religion and religious thinking are influenced by our temperament and training and may be subject to destructive influences as well as growth. The psychologist Gordon Allport contends that the religious form of appropriate striving is common in the world. Samuel utilized his freely offered love and acceptance to help us form a perspective of our self-image as compared to our ideal self-image, thus providing a raison d'etre for our conscious value systems.

Judaism offers organized sets of meanings within which individuals may provide mutual support for purposes of communication and common worship. Samuel may be viewed as a kindred spirit— a passionate companion and witness to the revolutionary chapter of Jewish existence that began with the end of the tsarist regime. He participated in the anguish and the survivalist strength stemming from the chaotic Holocaust to the continuing success of the Jewish presence in Israel.

Perhaps the immediacy of these events has decreased here in the United States as we grind closer to the cultural norm. Samuel championed all aspects of culture and civilization. There was, in fact, no greater expert on contemporary Jewish life and history than he. He willingly carried within himself the pathos of Jewish and human existence. He was immersed in the language and literature of the Jewish people and Western civilization. He knew intimately the poet Bialik, the prophet Judah Magnes, the writers Sholem Asch and Maurice Samuel, the ideologists Katznelson and Zuckerman. He associated personally with Moshe Sharret, David Ben-Gurion, and Golda Meir. His expertise in contemporary Jewish life filled the lines between generations and epochs. Samuel urgently knew that as events worsened on the tortured European continent, people must be alerted to the shrouding doom. At the same time, rebirth was occurring in the Mid-East. On a practical plane, funds had to be obtained, people had to be redeemed by building and rebuilding the land. Vital communication had to be established between America and Israel. American Jewry must somehow remedy its Jewish illiteracy and reduce its passivity and self-image as enduring a body of persecuted wraiths buffeted over the earth. As Samuel walked the way of Reform Judaism in the twentieth century, he continually visualized success in infusing congregations with needed warmth. He led the way in cherishing and propelling the ideals of Israel, civil rights, and brotherhood long before they became common coin.

Samuel Wohl was outraged by international immorality, selfishness, and gross materialism—by Jewish life as a professionally managed enterprise instead of a moral and spiritual force led by enlightened, educated, and cultured Jews. Today a modern, emancipated American Jew is beginning to emerge from the confusion of ethnic and anachronistic ritual. It is certainly no accident that the fair and generous American and the pioneering and enlightened Israeli emerged from the intense interaction of these two countries. Rabbi Wohl was an unabashed idealist—and a demanding one at that. There was so much to accomplish. His ideas, plans, analyses, and projects were sound and needed completion; they still do. His most profound pride and gratification came when children in the congregation attained adulthood and made their mark in the world.

We opine that Samuel would have been content enthusiastically with the continued dynamic development of Reform Judaism. Holding the factor of dedicated leadership constant, there seems to be a renewed sense of purpose for evolving debate and discussion. Leaders such as Eric Yoffie and Richard Levy have made passionate statements covering the continua of traditionalism, codification, definitions, goals, and principles. Mere verbalisms are not enough. Samuel would concur strongly with Yoffie that a platform must emerge that will unite and promote coherence. Long ago he gave up on the idea of an ultimate goal, writing "Let us settle for what can be achieved now." The world of books and ideas shaped his leadership and translated into a paradigm for his congregation and the Reform movement. He always told people to be worthy of their past experiences, to flexibly discuss and change their approach to issues, and to take responsibility for the propagation of the highest qualities of the Jewish people.

Bibliography

Letters and Correspondence

Atwater, George P. Letter to Samuel Wohl. Collected papers, 1919.

Baker, Newton D. Letter to Samuel Wohl. American Jewish Archives, Collected papers, 1930.

Brandeis, Louis D. Letter to Samuel Wohl. American Jewish Archives, Jan. 10, 1919.

Brav, Stanley R. Letter to Justin Friedman, 70th birthday observance. Collected papers, Cincinnati, March 1965.

Brown, Sally. Letter to Samuel Wohl, 70th birthday observance. Collected papers, Cincinnati, March 1965.

Cleveland Plain Dealer. Article "Harding Letter." Collected papers, ca. 1920.

Cleveland Press. Photo and article, "Zionism Discussed at Weekly gatherings." Cleveland, 1933.

Cook, Samuel. Letter to Justin Friedman, chairman, Samuel Wohl 70th birthday committee. Collected papers, 1965.

Daniels, Josephus. Letter to Samuel Wohl. Collected papers, 1919.
———. Naval dispatch to Samuel Wohl. Collected papers, 1919.

Ferger, Roger H., Letter to Samuel Wohl, 70th birthday observance. Collected papers, Cincinnati, April 1965.

Gittelsohn, Roland B., Letter to Samuel Wohl. Collected papers, Boston, 1965.

Goldman, Nachum. Computerized summary, "Novaya Ushitza," Dec. 29, 1981.

Harrison, R.G. Letter to Samuel Wohl, War Dept., Army Service Forces. Collected papers, 1943.

Immigration and Naturalization Services. Letter of information, U.S. Dept. of Justice. Washington, D.C., January 1993.

Lodge, Henry Cabot. Letter to Samuel Wohl. American Jewish Archives, Collected papers, 1919.

Montagu, Lily H. Letters to Samuel Wohl. American Jewish Archives, July 16, 1936–Dec. 24, 1936.

Morgenstern, Julian. Letter to Samuel Wohl. American Jewish Archives, Collected papers, 1946.

Polish, David. Letter to Samuel Wohl. American Jewish Archives, Collected papers, ca. 1929.

Stern, Jr., Joseph. Letter to Ted Wohl. Collected papers, 1992.

Straus, Nathan, Letter to Samuel Wohl, H.U.C., American Jewish Archives, Collected papers, 1919.

Weil, Irwin. Letter to Samuel Wohl. Collected papers, March 1965.

Wohl, Samuel. Letter to Rita Brody. Collected papers, Cleveland, June 1936.

———. Letter to Lily H. Montagu. Collected papers, London, December 1936.

Books and Articles

Allport, Gordon W. *Becoming*. New Haven: Yale University Press, 1955.

Asch, Sholem. *The Prophet*. Translated by Arthur Saul Super. New York: Putnam, 1955.

———. *The Nazarene*. Translated by Maurice Samuel. New York: Putnam, 1939.

Ariel, Yaakov. "Kaufmann Kohler and His Attitudes Toward Zionism: A Re-examination." *American Jewish Archives* 48, no. 2 (1991).

Ausubel, Nathan (ed.). *A Treasury of Jewish Folklore*. New York: Crown, 1978.

Baron, Salo W. *The Russian Jew under Tsars and Soviets*. New York: Macmillan, 1964.

Birmingham, Stephen. *The Rest of Us*. New York: Berkley Books, 1985.

Black, Maury. *Beyond the Golden Door*. Tel Aviv: Beth Hatefutsoth and New York: Bank Leumi Trust, 1978.

Blackman, Murray, *A Guide to Jewish Themes in American Fiction, 1940–1980*. Metuchen, N.J.: Scarecrow Press, 1981.

Brav, Stanley R. *Dawn of Reckoning*, Cincinnati: Shalom Press, 1971.

Bush, Lawrence. "Abba Hillel Silver: A Profile in American Judaism." *Reform Judaism*, Winter 1990.

Campbell, Thomas T., and Edward M. Miggins (eds.). *The Birth of Modern Cleveland, 1865–1930*. Cranbury, N.J.: Associated Universities Press, 1988.

Charofsky, Michael, *Jewish Life in the Ukraine: A Family Saga*. New York: Exposition Press, 1965.

Cohon, Baruch J. "The Structure of the Synagogue Prayer Chant." *Journal of the American Musicology Society* 3 (Nov. 1, 1950).

Cohon, Beryl D. *Judaism in Theory and in Practice*. New York: Bloch, 1948.

Cohon, Samuel. *Essays in Jewish Theology*. Cincinnati: Hebrew Union College Press, 1987.

Dubnow, Simon. *History of the Jews in Russia and Poland*. Translated by I. Friedlaender. 3 vols. Philadelphia: Jewish Publication Society, 1916–20.

Encyclopaedia Judaica (1971), s.v. "Russia," "Russian Literature." Jerusalem: Keter.

Essays by Alumni of the Hebrew Union College. Cincinnati: Hebrew Union College Press 1949.

Feinberg, Louis. *The Spiritual Foundations of Judaism*. With an appreciation by Emanuel Gamoran. Cincinnati: Congregation Adath Israel, 1951.

Fram, Leon, *Reform Judaism and Zionism: A Zionist Interpretation*. Cincinnati: Hebrew Union College Press, 1949.

Friesel, Evyatar, "The Last Great Rabbi: Review Essay." *American Jewish Archives* 43, no. 2 (1991).

Freeze, Gregory L. *Russia: A History*. New York: Oxford University Press, 1997.

Gamoran, Emanuel. Introduction to *The Spiritual Foundations of Judaism*, by Louis Feinberg. Cincinnati: Congregation Adath Israel, 1951.

Garber, Suggs, Collected Papers, 1920–1978, Jewish Archives, Western Reserve Historical Sources, 1983.

Gartner, Floyd, *History of the Jews in Cleveland*. 2d ed. Cranbury, N.J.: Associated Universities Presses, 1978.

Gitelman, Zvi, *Assimilation, Acculturation and National Consciousness Among Soviet Jews*. New York: Synagogue Council of America, 1973.

Gittelsohn, Roland B. *Modern Jewish Problems*. Cincinnati: Union of American Hebrew Congregations, 1943.

Glueck, Nelson. *Dateline: Jerusalem*. Cincinnati: Hebrew Union College Press, 1968.

Goldberg, Abraham. *Pioneers & Builders*. New York: Abraham Goldberg Publication Committee, 1943.

Goldman, Nachum. Novaya Ushitza, Museum of the Jewish Diaspora, Computerized summary, December 1981.

Grabowski, John, and Lucinda, Arnold. *A Guide to Jewish Historical Sources*. Cleveland: Western Reserve Historical Sources, 1983.

Harkabi, Yehoshafat. *The Bar Kochba Syndrome*. Chappaqua, N.Y.: Rossel Books, 1983.

"Hebrew Union College Confers Degree upon Monsky, Proskaur, Rabbi Wohl, and Dr. Bloch." Jewish Telegraphic Agency, June 1953.

Heller, James G. *As Yesterday When It Is Past*. Cincinnati: M. Singer, 1942.

Herzl, Theodor. *Theodor Herzl: Excepts from His Diaries*. Jewish Pocket Library. New York: Scopus, 1941.

Holmes, John Haynes, *Palestine Today and Tomorrow*. New York: Macmillan, 1929.

Hort, M., R. Hort, and C. A. Burger. *Who's Who in World Jewry*. Baltimore: Who's Who in World Jewry, 1938.

Howe, Irving. *World of Our Fathers*. New York: Galahad Books, 1976.

Jewish Encyclopedia Handbook: The Jewish People, Vol. I–ID. New York: Hudson Offset Co., 1946–55.

Jewish News and Observer. Collected papers, Cleveland, April 11, 1930.

Kahn, Roger. *The Passionate People*. New York: William Morrow, 1968.

Katz, Schlomo (ed.). *The Midstream Reader*. New York: Thomas Yoseloff, 1958.

Katzman, Jacob. *Commitment*. New York: Labor Zionist Letters, 1975.

Knox, Israel. *Rabbi in America*. Edited by Oscar Handlin. Boston: Little, Brown, 1957.

Lafoon, Polk, IV. "Cincinnati's Jewish Community." *Cincinnati Magazine*, April 1977, pp. 46–57.

Landau, Eli. *Jerusalem the Eternal*, New York: Bloch Publishing Co., 1968.

Laqueur, Walter. *A History of Zionism*. New York: Schocken Books, 1976.

Leviant, Curt (ed.). *Shalom Aleichem*. New York: Paperback Library, 1947.

Levy, Richard (ed.). *Reform Judaism: Spring*. New York: Union of American Hebrew Congregations, 1999.

Lipman, Eugene J., and Albert Vorspan (eds.). *A Tale of Ten Cities: The Triple Ghetto in American Religious Life*. New York: 1962.

Marcus, Jacob R. "Rabbi Samuel Wohl." Address delivered at the Samuel Wohl 70th birthday observance. Cincinnati, 1965.

Marcus, Paul, and Alan Rosenberg. "Another Look at Jewish Self-Hatred." *Journal of Reform Judaism*, Summer 1989, pp. 37–59.

Marmer, Dov. "The Odd Couple No More." *Reform Judaism*, Spring 1997.

Michener, James A. *The Source*. New York: Random House, 1965.

National Cyclopedia of American Biography (1979), s.v. "Samuel Wohl," vol. 58. Clifton, N.J.: James T. White.

Oz, Amos. "Ben-Gurion." *Time*, April 13, 1998.

Peled, Yoav. *Class and Ethnicity in the Pale*. New York: St. Martins Press, 1989.

Philipson, David, *Centenary Papers and Others*. Cincinnati: Ark Publishing, 1919.

———— (ed.). *Reminiscences by Isaac M. Wise*. Cincinnati: Leo Wise, 1901.

Plaut, W. Gunther. *The Rise of Reform Judaism*. New York: World Union for Progressive Judaism, 1963.

————. *The Growth of Reform Judaism*. New York: World Union for Progressive Judaism, 1965.

Polish, David. *Renew Our Days*. Jerusalem: World Zionist Organization and World Union for Progressive Judaism, 1976.

Raider, Mark A., Jonathan D. Sarna, and Ronald W. Zweig (eds.). *Abba Hillel Silver and American Zionism*. Frank Cass, London, 1977.

Rakeffet-Rothkoff, Aaron. *The Silver Era*. New York: Yeshiva University Press, 1981.

Rivkin, Ellis. *The Unity Principle*. Springfield, N.J.: Behrman House, 2003.

Rosenberg, Bernard, and Gilbert Shapiro. "Marginality and Jewish Humor." In *The Mainstream Reader*, edited by Schlomo Katz. New York: Thomas Yoseloff, 1958.

Roskies, Diane, and David Roskies. *The Shtetl*. 2d ed. New York: Ktav Publishing House, 1979.

Sachar, Howard M. *A History of Jews in America*. New York: Alfred A Knopf, 1992.

Sarna, Jonathan. "Jewish Community Called a Sort of Paradise for Hebrews." *American Israelite*, Cincinnati, July 1988.

Saxon, Wolfgang. "Rabbi Eugene Lipman: A Leader in Reform Judaism." *New York Times*, 1994.

Schulzinger, Morris S. *The Tale of a Litvak*. New York: Philosophical Library, 1985.

Schartzman, Sylvan D. *Reform Judaism Then and Now*. New York: Union of American Hebrew Congregations, 1971.

Seltzer, Robert. Foreword to *The Unity Principle*, by Ellis Rivkin. Springfield, N.J.: Behrman House, 2003.

Shirer, William L. *The Rise and Fall of the Third Reich*. New York: Simon & Schuster, 1960.

Silver, Abba Hillel, *The Democratic Impulse in Jewish History*. New York: Bloch Publishing Co., 1928.

Silver, Samuel. *Portrait of a Rabbi*. Cleveland: Barnett Brickner Memorial Foundation, 1959.

Singer, Celia. "Mourning Is Remembering." *Isaac M. Wise Temple Bulletin* 5, no. 5 (January 1973).

St. John, Robert. *Ben-Gurion: Builder of Israel*. Washington, D.C.: B'nai B'rith Books, 1986.

St. John, Robert. *Shalom Means Peace*. Garden City, N.Y.: Doubleday, 1949.

Telushkin, Joseph, *Jewish Literacy*. New York: William Morrow, 1991.

Union Hymnal. Musical Services for Sabbath and Festivals. Central Conference of American Rabbis, 1942.

Universal Jewish Encyclopedia (1943), s.v. "Russia: From Earliest Times to the First Partition of Poland," vol. 9, pp. 278–286.

Vincent, Sidney. *Personal and Professional*. Cleveland: Jewish Community Federation of Cleveland, 1982.

Wise, David. *Reform Judaism and Zionism: A Non-Zionist Interpretation*. Cincinnati: Hebrew Union College Press, 1949.

Wohl, Amiel. "How to Be a Successful Rabbi." *Central Conference of American Rabbis Journal*, June 1962.

———. "Masters of Reform Judaism." *Temple Israel of New Rochelle Newsletter* (New Rochelle, N.Y., March 1993).

Wohl, Samuel. "The Trials of Youth." English theme, University of Cincinnati, 1925.

———. "An Examination in Russia (Fear)." English theme, University of Cincinnati, 1926.

———. Collected sermons. In Collected papers. Isaac M. Wise Temple Congregation, 1927–65.

———. Address to Cosmic Club, Cincinnati, May 1942.

Wyman, David. *The Abandonment of the Jews*. New York: New Press, 1984.

Zeldin, Michael. "Understanding Informal Jewish Education: Reflections on the Philosophical Foundations of NFTY." *Journal of Reform Judaism* 36, no. 4 (Fall 1989).

Index of Names

269